Applying Standards-Based Constructivism:

A Two-Step Guide for Motivating Middle and High School Students

Pat Flynn, Don Mesibov,
Paul J. Vermette, R. Michael Smith

EYE ON EDUCATION
6 DEPOT WAY WEST, SUITE 106
LARCHMONT, NY 10538
(914) 833–0551
(914) 833–0761 fax
www.eyeoneducation.com

Library of Congress Cataloging-in-Publication Data

    Applying standards-based constructivism : a two-step guide for motivating middle and high school students / Pat Flynn ... [et al.].
    Patrick Flynn ... [et al.].
       p. cm.
       Includes bibliographical references and index.
       ISBN 1-930556-68-3
       1. High school teaching--United States. 2. Middle school teaching--United States. 3. Constructivism (Education)--United States. 4. Motivation in education--United States. I. Title: Two-step guide for motivating middle and high school students. II. Flynn, Pat, 1940-

    LB1607.5.A66 2004
    373.1102--dc22

                                             2004047213

10 9 8 7 6 5 4 3 2 1

Editorial and production services provided by
Richard H. Adin Freelance Editorial Services
52 Oakwood Blvd., Poughkeepsie, NY 12603-4112
(845-471-3566)

Also Available from Eye On Education

Applying Standards-Based Constructivism:
A Two-Step Guide for Motivating Elementary Students
Flynn, Mesibov, and Smith

Differentiated Instruction:
A Guide for Middle and High School Teachers
Amy Benjamin

Constructivist Strategies:
Meeting Standards and Engaging Adolescent Minds
Foote, Vermette, and Battaglia

Writing in the Content Areas
Amy Benjamin

Student Transitions from Middle to High School:
Improving Achievement and Creating a Safer Environment
J. Allen Queen

An English Teacher's Guide to Performance Tasks and Rubrics:
High School

An English Teacher's Guide to Performance Tasks and Rubrics:
Middle School
Amy Benjamin

Social Studies: Standards, Meaning, and Understanding
Barbara Slater Stern

The Student-Centered Classroom Handbook:
A Guide to Implementation Social Studies/History
Bil Johnson

Helping Students Graduate:
A Strategic Approach to Dropout Prevention
Jay Smink and Franklin Schargel

At-Risk Students:
Reaching and Teaching Them, Second Edition
Richard Sagor and Jonas Cox

Preface

The goal of this book is to combine basic concepts of constructivist theories of learning with practical classroom applications. It is not our intent to try to convert nonbelievers. Rather, we want to provide practical application strategies for those who have already begun to explore constructivist theories of learning, but are seeking ways to improve on implementation.

This book is designed to be the place where the rhetoric hits the road. The theory is described, the research is cited, and most importantly, the discussion and examples of practical application in a school and classroom setting are here. What we're trying to demonstrate is a practical way to apply constructivist theory in a teacher's day-to-day classroom life.

The authors' viewpoints have been honed through their experiences each year, with cutting edge professional educators, students, and parents—pre-K through university—who participate in The Constructivist Design Conference at St. Lawrence University, held each summer since 1995. The conference, which invites active engagement of approximately 300 people, is a five day model of what the authors would like to see happening in schools and classrooms.

Participants come on teams that model the collaboration and group work that research demonstrates is an essential part of learning. Team participants come with a task and after five days, they leave with a product that is authentic for them.

A facilitator, assigned to each team, models the role of the teacher in the classroom.

Participants are immersed in behaviors essential to a constructivist environment: they design a rubric to define their expectations for the week; they reflect individually, in journals, and collectively as a team; conference organizers view their role as resource providers and gophers.

The opening afternoon of the conference represents the exploratory phase of the Two-Step lesson model described in this book; most teams move into discovery by the second day.

The Conference serves two interrelated purposes: through the Conference participants begin to work on their tasks, and simultaneously, they experience what it is like to work in a constructivist learning environment. Additional information is available on the website of the Institute for Learning Centered Education, www.learnercentereded.org.

This book is designed to be accessible to the reader and to serve as a ready reference. It is organized to be read straight through or to be read by skipping from section to section. The chapters are set up to accommodate either approach. There are four chapters and each is divided into sections.

The Way the Sections are Organized

Section Heading

A section heading indicates where the section is going.

Learning Objective

A learning objective states what the reader will learn from the section.

Main Points

The Main Points outline a section.

Reality Check Questions

These are questions that the reader may have while reading a section of the book. Some of the answers to these questions are written as hyperlinks designed to link one section of the book to another.

Thoughts for Reflection

These are quotes placed at the end of a section to prompt the reader to ruminate on a central point of the section.

End of the Section Assessment

These are questions posed to help readers self-assess the degree to which they have understood the last section.

Examples of the Two-Step

These are abbreviated versions of the Two-Step lessons provided to keep the reader in touch with the ultimate purpose of the book—the reader's ability to create Two-Step Model lessons. These abbreviated lessons appear in section 2, but are more fully developed in Appendix A.

Other Details Regarding this Book

- *Concept Map*: Sections of the Two-Step Concept Map appear throughout the book to assist the reader.

- *Pronoun Use* (avoiding he/she): To sustain the flow of the book, the authors have elected to use the singular pronouns *he* and *she*, alternately, in lieu of using the he/she construction.

- *Use of State/Provincial Standards*: Forty-nine out of 50 states have established state learning standards and performance indicators. Most states have also developed core curriculum to express their learning standards (Iowa is the sole exception). The examples and exemplars put forth in the book make use of New York State learning standards, performance indicators, and core curriculum. Because there is a high degree of similarity among state standards, it should be relatively easy to let New York State's standards stand in for those of other states and provinces in Canada. Other State and Provincial standards are referenced. Then again, a reader may be more comfortable replacing the book's standards' elements with those of his own state/province.

About the Authors

Pat Flynn taught on both the elementary and the secondary levels. He has been a Language Arts Coordinator, a Title I Coordinator, a Resource Room Teacher, a Labor Relations Specialist, and an Associate in Educational Services for the NYS United Teachers union. He was the co-creator of the union's School Reform Initiative. He represented teachers regarding the development of the NYS Learning Standards, student assessment, and school accountability system. He served on State councils, including those dealing with Career and Occupational Education. He has studied firsthand, innovative schools and school structures in the United States and overseas. He and his wife, Marge, reside in Albany, NY. They have three daughters and four grandchildren. pmflynn@aol.com

Don Mesibov is founder of the Institute for Learning Centered Education. He has been a weekly newspaper editor, childcare counselor at a school for the emotionally disturbed, grocery store clerk, middle school English teacher, and labor relations specialist for a teachers' union. Mesibov credits "whatever I bring to the table in the field of education" to his many years as a camper, counselor, and athletic director at eight-week overnight summer camps where "We collaborated for the welfare of every child and the organizational structure supported a team approach." He and his wife, Susan, reside in Potsdam, New York with their daughter, Raina, a middle school student. Their son Darren is a pilot and older daughter Marli is a sophomore at Brandeis University. dmesibov@twcny.rr.com

Paul Vermette received his doctorate in Learning and Instruction in 1983 from SUNY at Buffalo and has been a professor of Education at Niagara University, since 1985. He has authored "*Making Cooperative Learning Work*," from Prentice-Hall/Merrill and coauthored, with Chandra Foote and Cathy Battaglia, "*Constructivist Strategies: Engaging Adolescent Minds and Meeting Standards*" from Eye On Education. He has published over 20 articles and has given presentations at conferences of every major educational organization. He, and his wife Kathleen, live in Niagara Falls, New York. Their son, Matt, is currently completing a BA in Education from Niagara University. pjv@niagara.edu

Dr. R. Michael (Mike) Smith received his undergraduate degree from Brock University, two Masters of Science in Education from Niagara University (Foundations and Teaching and Elementary Education Pre-K to 6), and his Ph.D. in Social Foundations and Administration from the University of Buffalo. Mike is in his fourth year as an Assistant Professor of Education at Niagara University where he teaches undergraduate courses in Foundations of Education, and graduate courses in Foundations of Education, Multicultural Education, and Motivation and Classroom Management. msmith@niagara.edu

Concept Map

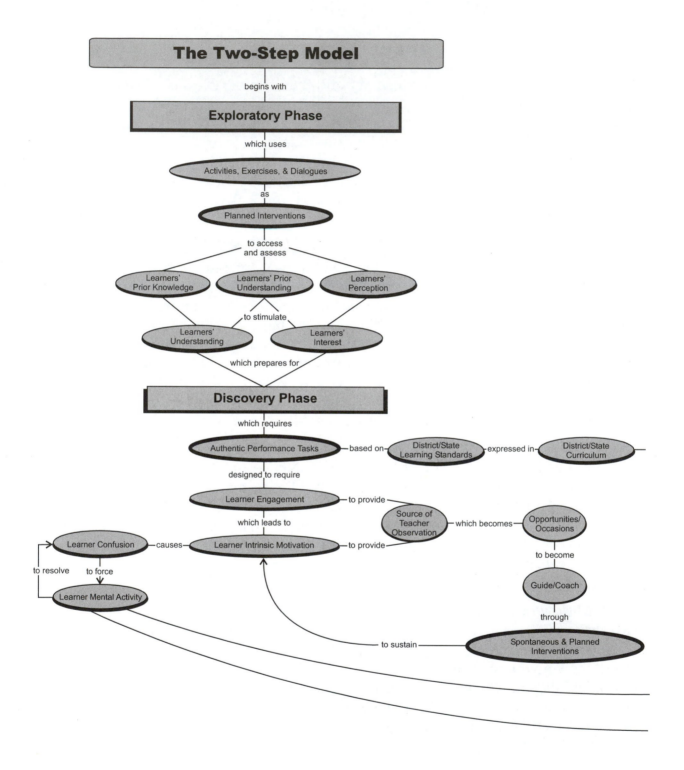

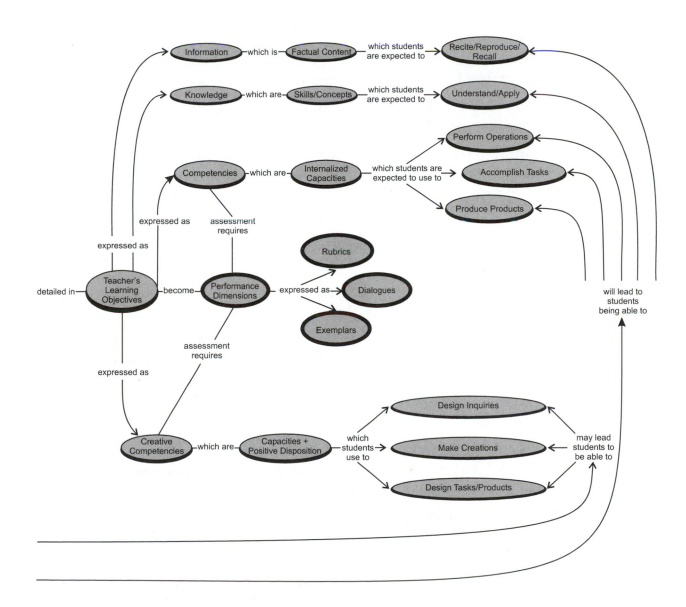

Information —which is— Factual Content —which students are expected to→ Recite/Reproduce/Recall

Knowledge —which are— Skills/Concepts —which students are expected to→ Understand/Apply

Competencies —which are— Internalized Capacities —which students are expected to use to→ Perform Operations / Accomplish Tasks / Produce Products

Teacher's Learning Objectives —detailed in—

expressed as

assessment requires

Performance Dimensions —become—

—expressed as→ Rubrics / Dialogues / Exemplars

Creative Competencies —which are— Capacities + Positive Disposition —which students use to→ Design Inquiries / Make Creations / Design Tasks/Products

assessment requires

will lead to students being able to

may lead students to be able to

Concept Map

Understanding Requires Engagement

♦ The Authentic Task Constructivist Instructional Sequence begins with the Exploration Phase that uses exercises, activities, and teacher initiated dialogues as *planned interventions* to enable the teacher to access and assess the learners' prior knowledge, the learners' prior understanding, and the learners' perceptions/paradigms. Planned interventions are instruction the teacher has anticipated will be needed. Planned interventions in the Exploratory Phase are generally provided to all the students as a class. They often involve the use of teaching techniques such as cooperative learning procedures (e.g., jigsaws, carousels, pair-shares).

♦ The Exploratory Phase is designed to introduce and foreshadow the underlying knowledge and concepts to be addressed in the Discovery Phase. Thus, the Exploratory Phase begins to broaden the learners' understanding and stimulates the learners' interest in the curriculum content/unit of study being explored.

♦ The Discovery Phase follows the Exploratory Phase. In the Discovery Phase learners are assigned an Authentic-Performance Learning Task.

  • These learning tasks are based on the district/state learning standards expressed in district/state curriculum, and detailed in the teacher's learning objectives.

  • The teacher's learning objectives may include:

    ▪ Information that is factual content; students are expected to recite, reproduce, and recall.

    ▪ Knowledge: skills/concepts students are expected to understand and apply.

    ▪ Competencies that are internalized capacities that students are expected to use to perform operations, accomplish tasks, and produce products.

    ▪ Creative competencies that are capacities plus positive student dispositions that students may use to design inquires, make creations, design tasks/products.

♦ The teacher's learning objectives become performance dimensions. Theses performance dimensions form the basis of rubrics, are illustrated in exemplars, and are expressed in dialogues with students.

♦ The Authentic-Performance tasks learners are assigned must be designed to require learner engagement leading to learners becoming intrinsically motivated. This allows their teacher to observe the learners working to accomplish the task.

♦ This observation facilitates the teacher's role as guide and coach through instructional responses to students' needs, which are defined through their actions and words as they continue to work on their task. This kind of instruction is called an intervention. There are two types of interventions: planned interventions and spontaneous interventions:

- Planned interventions are instruction the teacher has anticipated will be needed. In the Exploratory Phase, planned interventions may be provided to all the students as a class when they begin a task or when they have reached a specific point in working to accomplish the task. They often involve the use of teaching techniques such as; the development of rubrics, cooperative learning procedures (e.g., jigsaws, carousels, pair-shares), graphic organizers, journal writing, concept maps, etc

- Spontaneous interventions are teacher responses to individual or small group needs, usually provided on the spot as the opportunity presents itself.

♦ The learners' engagement in their authentic task causes learners to become confused. This learner confusion may come from one of two sources:

- The learner understands the goal of the task but he/she is at a loss regarding the steps to be taken to achieve the goal or,

- The learner's confusion may stem from the learner's growing awareness of the existence of knowledge/information/skills/concepts that conflict with his/her prior perceptions.

♦ It is this confusion that forces learners to become mentally active to find resolution to their confusion.

♦ If the teacher becomes aware that students are becoming so frustrated with their inability to overcome their confusion that they are in danger of giving up or developing negative attitudes, the teacher scaffolds their efforts with an intervention to assist them in sustaining their intrinsic motivation.

♦ It is through engaged mental activity that learners accumulate the factual content and come to understand and apply the skills and concepts involved in developing the capacity to perform operations, accomplish tasks, and produce products.

♦ If in the process of developing a capacity the learner also develops a positive disposition, then the learner may become able to operate at a higher level of performance; one typified by the designing of inquires, production of unique/original creations, and the designing their own tasks/products.

Acknowledgements

The authors want to give thanks to our families and friends for giving our lives a purpose.

Our sincere thanks to:

♦ Carol Amberg, Becky Buckingham, Peg D'Arpino, Laurie Harper, and Ted Werner for consultation, lesson design, and inspiration through excellent, caring teaching; Beth Konkoski-Bates, Geri Belt, Jan Peters, and Cathy Washabaugh for reviewing the manuscript, and guiding our work with candor and kindness. Thanks, also, to the following professional educators who reviewed our *Two-Step* exemplars, from the perspective of a classroom teacher, to assure accuracy and relevance: Joann Chambers, Meg Goddard, Ron Hockmuth, Sandy Latourelle, Brian Marsh, Kitty Mathews, Gerry Peters, Dan Tusa, April Tusa.

♦ Our students at Niagara University and St. Lawrence University, many of whom contributed time, research, and insights. Their grasp of many of the concepts in this book is responsible for our optimism for the future.

♦ Susan Herman Mesibov for scrutinizing the final draft, making important suggestions and validating, with silence, what she didn't propose to change.

♦ Larry Byrd for a lifetime of inspiration and a host of articulations, many of which are included in the text.

♦ And thank you to the many dedicated teachers who shared strategies, welcomed us into their classrooms, and participated in our workshops.

For more information about the Institute for Learning Centered Education and to contact the authors, visit www.learnercentereded.org

Table of Contents

CHAPTERS	SECTIONS

Chapter 1
Correlation between Standards and Constructivism

Constructivism & Standards → Understanding Requires Engagement

Chapter 2

The Components of the Two Step

Exploration → Discovery → Intervention

Learning Objectives → Assessment → Reflection

Chapter 3

How We Learn Guides How We Teach

Learning Grows from Confusion → Memorization and Critical Thinking

We Learn Best When We Teach Others

Chapter 4

How Constructivism Differs from Traditional Models

Interaction, Lecture, & Constructivism → Student Motivation through Authentic Tasks

The Effective Classroom Teacher → The Effective Student

1
Relationship Between Standards and Constructivism

Examples of Constructivist–Based Standards

English Language Arts: *The student is expected to demonstrate effective communication skills that reflect such demands as interviewing, reporting, requesting, and providing information.* (Texas Essential Knowledge and Skills for English Language Arts and Reading, Subchapter B. Middle School)

"Students will demonstrate an understanding of literacy and information forms such as...." (Ontario, Canada Curriculum, Specific Expectations Grades 9 & 10, English)

Science: *Students who meet the standard know and **apply concepts** that explain how living things function, adapt, and change by applying scienctific inquiries or technological design to (among other things) examine the cellular unit, explain boichemical reactions, and explain disease from organelle-to-population levels.* (Illinois Learning Standards, Science Perforamce Descriptors, Grades 6–12)

Science: *Analyze situations and solve problems that require combining and **applying concepts** from more than one area of science.* (California Learning Standards, Grades nine through twelve—Investigation and Experimentation)

Social Studies: *The student **will demonstrate** skills in historical research ad geographical analysis by..."* (Virginia Standards of Learning, History and Social Science, Grade nine)

Math: *Through problem-solving situations, all **students will construct** their own understanding, so that by the end of grade 12 they will: Demonstrate the properties and behaviors of patterns and relations.* (Rhode Island, Content Standards)

These standards (above) are representative of what states are requiring across the nation. The key word (either expressed or implied) is *demonstrate*. How can students *demonstrate* what they know and can apply competently while sitting passively in a classroom and taking an occasional short answer/essay test? State standards call for teaching practices based on constructivist theory about how people learn.

Constructivism and Standards

There is growing recognition that effective teachers are people who are becoming guides on the side rather than sages on the stage. This is much easier to say, than to do. To become a guide on the side requires expertise with group work, performance tasks, reflective activities, and a variety of teaching strategies that most of us did not observe when we were students, and most of us have not been taught to teach. For the past twenty years, we (the authors) have worked with teachers and future teachers, on a daily basis, striving to assist them on their journey toward shifting from a teacher centered to a learner centered approach. What have we learned?

When we find teachers who are comfortable with even one of the strategies required to conduct a learner centered classroom (cooperative learning, performance tasks, authentic assessment, journaling, etc.), they always have the same story to tell. They have worked at least three years to achieve a comfort level with the strategy, they had someone as a collaborator (a friend, spouse, or teacher down the hall), they gradually changed their approach to teaching, it did not happen overnight, and there was a great deal of trial and error.

It is with reverence for the many caring educators who will read this book, and a deep appreciation of the difficult journey to improve teaching by aligning classroom practices with constructivist theory of how people learn that we now share a "Two Step" model that we hope will make this journey easier. Our model is based on three simple concepts that will be explained throughout this book:

1. Student engagement with information must *precede* teacher explanations.

2. Instruction (guidance) should come in the form of interventions as students engage with information, ideas, and concepts.

3. Authentic tasks create an environment for student engagement and teacher interventions.

The approach, throughout this book is to model what we are asking teachers to do in the classroom. Since we believe that every lesson should be focused on specific learning objectives (derived from local, state, provincial, or national standards), we begin chapter 1, section 1 with a statement of our learning objectives for you as you read this section. At the end of each section you will find an assessment question that is designed to challenge you to see whether you have grasped the learning objective.

Learning Objective

The reader will understand that the authors view constructivism as a theory that can be applied to help learners address specific standards. Constructivism IS NOT a vehicle for allowing students to decide what is to be taught; rather it enables students to learn more effectively whatever is being taught.

Main Points

- ◆ State and provincial standards are effectively addressed by applying constructivist theory.

- ◆ While the *Two-Step* is consistent with other models, it has advantages: it increases understanding, motivates students to learn, and it is teacher-friendly for classroom application.

Many state and provincial standards, across the United States and Canada, cannot be addressed without using constructivist teaching strategies. This book is about authentic task constructivism in a standards-based environment. In this chapter we will: 1) begin to discuss the impact of constructivist teaching strategies on student motivation, 2) address the correlation between standards and constructivism, and 3) introduce the concept of the *Two-Step* as a teacher-friendly framework for constructivism in the classroom. In later chapters we will challenge the commonly held belief that there is no role for lectures in a constructivist environment and, similarly, we will argue that simply because an activity is interactive doesn't mean it is constructivist.

Student Motivation

In 1960, a teacher might have resorted to one of the following threats to assure attentiveness from a student: "Your grade will suffer," "I may have to call your parents." "One more word and I'll send you to the office." "Listen up, the test is tomorrow." While it is questionable whether this approach was ever the best way to teach for understanding, it did succeed in achieving a reasonable degree of classroom decorum and an acceptable number of passing students. Not anymore.

Presently, teachers are concerned about students "who just don't listen." The number of children who come to school unprepared, with little or no homework attempted, increases each year, discipline is harder to maintain, and parental support may be lacking, particularly for those students having the most difficulties.

To the rescue comes constructivism, a theory of how people learn, it traces its resurgence to Piaget (1970s) after lingering in the background since the early 1900s when Thorndyke's behaviorist ideas won out over Dewey's more constructivist approaches. Constructivism is far from a cure all, but a growing number of professional educators are recognizing that teaching strategies, grounded in constructivist theories of how people learn, may hold the potential to: reduce discipline problems; enable teachers to challenge students who have a wide range of abilities, interests, and intelligences; be a vehicle for multiple assessments of student performance; challenge students to utilize higher level thinking skills well beyond simple recall of information; promote intrinsic motivation; and become the primary vehicle for standards-based teaching practices

Constructivist Theory and Standards

Constructivism is a theory about how people learn, not what they should learn. Constructivist theory indicates we need to engage with information in order to understand it, and we need to understand in order to apply it competently. At the outset, we need to be as clear as we can that what we are espousing is constructivism in a standards-based environment as identified in states', districts', and provinces' learning standards and core curricula. The curriculum content—what is to be taught—is a given, as are the standards of performance that are to be used to judge competence.

Standards are about what students know, are able to do, and are able to create. This book is about pedagogy—teaching strategies for enabling students to *demonstrate* what they know and can do and can create.

All the contours, nooks, and crannies of our brand of constructivism will be explored in detail in the various chapters of the book. For now, let's just say that *constructivism is based on a body of research that supports the position that understanding can't be poured from one person's head to another's like water—that each of us creates our own picture of the world and how it works through our personal engagement with it.* As a teacher or parent, what we can do is provide structure and guidance for our children's journey to construct meaning from their environment and experiences.

Primarily, we will be dealing with a *Two-Step* model for developing lesson plans which enable teachers to employ constructivist teaching techniques and practices. The *Two-Step* is consistent with models that may be familiar to you such as those developed by Madeline Hunter, Robert Marzano, Jay McTighe, and Grant Wiggins, and others. However, the *Two-Step* may address aspects of understanding beyond what other models have to offer while also lending itself to easier and more practical classroom application. A comparison of the *Two-Step* with five models is in Appendix B.

The Two-Step

The authors offer this book with the expectation that effective teachers will find nuggets for integration in their practices whether they utilize the Two-Step as a framework for lesson or unit design, or whether they adapt aspects of the Two-Step: such as beginning each lesson with student engagement; ending each lesson with a closure activity that elicits comments from most if not all students; forcing student thinking through active engagement with information, or integrating reflection as an essential classroom strategy.

State, provincial, and district learning standards were created from a vision of a desirable future. This book is devoted to inventing ways of helping professional educators and parents bring that future into being.

Thoughts for Reflection

"That grinding sound you hear is a paradigm shift without the clutch." (Dilbert/Scott Adams)

End of Section Assessment

Can the reader offer a brief articulation of the distinction between constructivism and standards for student learning?

Understanding Requires Engagement

Learning Objective

The reader will come to appreciate that engagement is essential and that it creates the environment that nurtures learning; engagement affords us the opportunity to demonstrate what we have learned. Two-Step lessons generate engagement.

Main Points

- You remember things (including facts for a test) best when you are actively engaged in learning them.

- You can draw conclusions from what you have learned and can take effective actions based on what you have learned only if you are actively engaged in your learning.

"Demi," at the age of three, "learned his letters with his grandfather, who invented a new mode of teaching the alphabet by forming the letters with his arms and legs, thus uniting gymnastics for head and heels" (Alcott, 1868).

What Louisa May Alcott knew in 1868, and researchers, according to Roger Johnson, have told us for more than 200 years, professional educators are only now coming to accept: Understanding comes from active engagement.

In Chapter 2, we describe the Two-Step framework (exploration and discovery), which will enable you to teach well anywhere: at home, in school, or in the workplace. Two key words are needed to grasp the concept of constructivism: understanding and engagement.

- Learning is about *understanding*.

- Understanding occurs through active engagement with information; without *engagement*, there is no opportunity to develop or to demonstrate *understanding*.

- A good lesson (whether it is an activity, a unit, or a learning plan) includes two phases: exploration and discovery.

Good teaching occurs through interventions: The teacher provides hands-on instruction (coaching) while the student is actively engaged. For a teacher (or parent) to intervene, students must be engaged in an activity that provides the opportunity for interventions. One cannot intervene in a vacuum.

Why Is Student Engagement Important for Understanding?

Knowledge is inside individuals; information is outside. One must have several experiences (engagements) with information before understanding can begin. When students are engaged, the teacher can see that the students are thinking. *If you can't see the students doing something, you probably need to rethink what you are requiring.* We know that students are engaged if we can get them to the point of framing their own questions. Students, as prime actors, must frame their own questions to be directors of their own inquiry. When you challenge a student to ask the right questions, you are moving the student to ask, "What is this about anyway?"

How often do teachers ask students what they think are the most relevant questions about a topic under study? How often do teachers ask students to pose relevant questions both at the start *and* at the conclusion of the lesson? The contrast in student responses at the start and end of the lesson will give the teacher evidence of student learning and will give the student an opportunity for worthwhile reflection.

For example, at the start of a task to create a booklet that shows and explains cloud formations—a student might be addressing the question, "What is a cloud?" After engagement with the task, including prompts from the teacher, the student may have shifted his thinking toward, "Do clouds influence the weather or do weather patterns create clouds?"

Constructivist strategies create an environment that engages the student to develop the understanding that leads to the ability to use information to draw conclusions and take effective action.

All information is external and is just information until it is internalized (understood) by a learner; it then becomes knowledge. It will probably not take you more than a few minutes to memorize this information. However, to understand it and be able to use it effectively, you may want to read this book thoughtfully. We'll try to engage your mind in the type of inquiry required to develop an active understanding of the terms in this chapter.

Thoughts for Reflection

- ♦ "I (Grandpa) am not putting the thoughts into his head, but helping him unfold those already there" (from *Little Women*, by Louisa May Alcott, 1868).

- ♦ Reinsmith (1993) suggests that real learning is marked by several characteristics, including:
  - It only happens when a mind is engaged.
  - Real learning connotes use.
  - Students will only learn something that they have an interest in (or proclivity for).

- ♦ "I believe that children learn best when given the opportunity to taste, feel, see, hear, manipulate, discover, sing, and dance their way through learning" (Katy Goldman, teacher from Pine, Arizona, quoted in *Survival Guide for New Teachers*, 2002).

End of Section Assessment

Can the reader design an activity that would enable a teacher to assess whether information a student has memorized is truly understood?

2

The Components of the *Two-Step*

Two Steps: Exploration, Discovery

This chapter will address each of these terms in the following sequence:

EXPLORATION: Step one in a *Two-Step* lesson is the ***Exploratory Phase***. Its purpose is to prepare the student and the teacher for the ***Discovery Phase.***

DISCOVERY: Step two of a *Two-Step* lesson is the ***Discovery Phase***. It presents students with an authentic performance task. Students learn the subject matter by engaging in the task; they demonstrate their understanding of the subject matter by accomplishing the task.

Interventions: These take place while students are working on their tasks. Through interventions, a teacher guides and supports students. Hands-on teaching takes place during Interventions.

Learning Objectives: Everything starts with "the why" of a lesson. Exactly "why" are students being asked to do "this or that"? The learning objectives of a lesson answer the "why question." To provide a clear focus, learning objectives must be precisely and succinctly expressed. To relate to what students are being required to understand and be able to accomplish, a lesson's learning objectives must be connected to a state's learning standards and a district's curriculum. For these reasons, the teacher's learning objectives for students are the driving force; they drive how the Exploratory and Discovery Phases are designed.

Assessment: An effective assessment measures the degree to which a student has accomplished the lesson's learning objectives. (And since the lesson's learning objectives are tied to standards, the assessment measures the degree to which the student has reached the standards.)

Reflection: Research indicates that reflection is an integral part of the learning process. The purpose for providing opportunities for reflection is to guide students to become self-monitoring, independent learners.

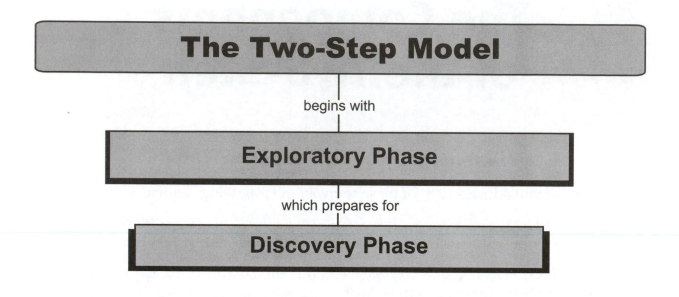

The Two-Step Model

begins with

Exploratory Phase

which prepares for

Discovery Phase

Exploration

Learning Objectives

The reader will see that lessons can be visualized in two phases: exploratory and discovery; and that exploration precedes discovery. The reader will become conversant with the six criteria for an effective exploratory phase.

Main Points

- The exploratory phase of a lesson grabs the student's attention and gets the student ready to engage in the content of the lesson.

- Teach in this order—exploratory phase, then discovery phase

- Plan in this order—discovery phase, then exploratory phase

What we are presenting on these pages is a model for a lesson plan—a formal lesson plan that a teacher might use in a classroom. This Two-Step is offered as a way of organizing your thinking, not as a rigid, inflexible doctrine.

The authors postulate that most good lessons, facilitated by the teacher in the classroom or the parent in the home, are constructivist based and consist of two phases—exploration and discovery. Instruction occurs through *interventions*, some *planned* and some *spontaneous*. These are four key terms that will recur throughout this book: *exploration, discovery, planned intervention,* and *spontaneous intervention*. A fifth term, *learning objectives*, is also important. To be effective, a teacher must design a lesson with the purpose of enabling students to learn and demonstrate their understanding of learning objectives that are taken from standards.

In any learning process there need to be the following two steps:

Step 1. Exploration

Grab the attention of the learner; in the process of grabbing the learner's attention, find out what you can about the learner—his interests, prior knowledge, strengths, and weaknesses. The more you know about the learner, the more effective you can be conveying information, generating understanding, and supporting practical application of theory to the learner's real-world environment. Also, early in the lesson, the effective teacher should put the learner in touch with her prior knowledge.

Step 2. Discovery

Once you have grabbed the learner's attention, set up situations that enable the learner to discover facts, knowledge, and concepts, and to develop skills required for competency.

The simplest way to view these two phases is to think of the discovery phase as the part of the lesson that engages the students in the creation of a product (e.g. a booklet, a map, a sketch), or, engages them in a process (e.g., an interview, a skit, an oral presentation). Exploration, which precedes discovery, prepares students for undertaking the task and prepares the teacher so that she is able to provide an appropriate structure for the discovery phase.

Here are the criteria for the exploratory phase of the Two-Step model:

♦ Create an environment conducive to learning (i.e., break the ice with something light and nonthreatening); grab the learner's attention.

♦ Access and assess the learner's prior knowledge and interests regarding the concepts and skills to be presented by the lesson.

♦ Help the learner become aware of his perceptions regarding the concepts and skills to be presented by the lesson.

♦ Begin the process of exposing the learner to information, from sources she respects, that may conflict with her perceptions.

♦ Motivate the learner to want to discover more about the knowledge, concepts, skills and/or competencies to be presented and assessed by the lesson.

♦ Begin to introduce the main purpose (content/concept) of the discovery phase that will come next or familiarize the learner with how he will engage in the discovery phase (e.g., portfolio, interview, booklet, tape, etc.).

Some of these criteria for an exploratory phase of a lesson are designed to draw attention to each other. For example, accessing prior knowledge helps the learner become aware of his perceptions and also begins to motivate the learner. Accessing the learner's prior knowledge may also help to grab the learner's attention because we are all more likely to see relevance in something that connects with what we already know. The idea is that the teacher needs to crosscheck to see if the exploratory phase he has designed is accomplishing its various purposes by addressing each of the foregoing criteria. Note, also, the difference between accessing and assessing prior knowledge: The teacher helps the learner *access* prior knowledge so that the learner can create connections with new information, and the teacher is *assessing* the learner's prior knowledge (and interests) so that the teacher can communicate new information in ways the learner is most likely to understand.

For example, the teacher uses a carousel as part of an exploratory phase of a lesson on inventors. Sheets of newsprint are taped at different stations or on the wall, and each has the name of a different inventor on top. A recorder for each group of four students is asked to write as many facts about the inventor at the top of the newsprint sheet as the group can agree on within 90 seconds. Then the groups rotate to another sheet of newsprint and add to the lists (or place an x by any facts they think are incorrect).

In addition to affording students a change of pace from seat time and, hopefully, motivation to continue the lesson, the teacher, through observation, is assessing student understandings of inventors and, perhaps, learning of student interests by overhearing student discussions (both relevant to the topic and otherwise). Also, students are accessing their own prior knowledge as they think about and discuss what they know about each inventor. This puts students in touch with their perceptions of inventors and inventions, which becomes the building block for the discovery phase. The nature of the carousel enables the accessing and assessing of student knowledge without putting any student on the spot or creating embarrassment for anyone whose prior knowledge is skimpy.

How Is the Exploratory Phase Different from an Anticipatory Set or Icebreaker?

The exploratory phase has many of the elements of what teachers have referred to as anticipatory sets, launchers, bell-ringing activities, or icebreakers. However, the exploratory phase is more encompassing. For instance, an icebreaking activity can create a positive environment yet not begin to address the main concepts to be addressed in the lesson. An anticipatory set may prepare the student for what comes next, but may do little to grab the learner's attention or create a relaxed environment conducive to learning.

An exploratory phase does what each of these activities is intended to do but more than any one of these activities will do. The exploratory phase of a lesson encourages students to play with the ideas connected to the lesson and enables them to own the concepts, skills, and competencies to be demonstrated in the discovery phase by finding links to their prior knowledge and experiences. Therefore, not only does a good exploratory phase enable the teacher to learn about each student's prior knowledge, it also helps the students make connections to their past in preparation for constructing new meanings in the future.

Grab the Learner's Attention, Then Engage the Mind

A critical criterion of the exploratory phase is the requirement that the teacher grab the learner's attention. When you wish to communicate with another person, whether a student, a friend, or someone much older, how do you proceed?

First, do you find a way to get the attention of the person with whom you wish to communicate?

Second, do you find an effective way to deliver your message? In other words, don't you help the person discover what you want him to know?

Our model is based on these two steps: *exploration*, which includes grabbing the student's attention; and *discovery*, which creates the opportunity for the student to discover what the teacher wants her to learn while simultaneously creating opportunities for teacher assessment of what the student knows and can do competently. Exploration precedes discovery.

In formal school settings, because we have a captive audience, we often assume we don't need to grab anyone's attention. Yet, even when a professional concert performer opens an act in front of an audience of people who have paid money because they want to be in attendance, the performer does something to capture their attention and stimulate interest at the very start. Have you noticed that a concert performer:

◆ Rarely begins with dialogue—usually comes on stage and begins with a bouncy number

◆ Intersperses monologues with songs only *after* the audience is warmed up and is becoming convinced it will receive what it came intent on hearing

In his autobiography, Tony Bennett states, "The best way to win over an audience is to give them something great right off the bat." If a professional performer needs to strategize how to keep the attention of an audience that has paid money to attend, is it realistic for a teacher to expect to have the undivided attention of students who would not choose to be in school and may have no interest in the topic of the lesson?

Just because a teacher can compel a student to remain in class and be quiet (and even this is not a given in every class), it does not imply that the student will be at all receptive to what the teacher wants the student to learn. Teachers themselves, for example, on a staff development day for which they are paid, are often observed reading newspapers, grading papers, or indulging in side conversations and ignoring the presenter. If educated adults (teachers) cannot be expected to listen quietly to a presentation when they are paid to attend, why do we expect students to learn in an environment they did not choose and with regard to topics they do not find relevant?

Good teaching requires that we open a child's mind before we expect it to engage with new information. As an adult, if I attend your presentation and find that it doesn't hold my interest, I can get up and leave before you finish. As teachers, we may be able to prevent children from physically leaving the classroom during a boring lesson, but can we stop them from shutting down their minds?

While grabbing the learner's attention is essential before proceeding, all the criteria for the exploratory phase should be met to pave the way for effective discovery. These two steps do not apply only to classroom teaching situations. Isn't this the way communication works in the real world?

The key word is *communication*. As educators (teachers, administrators, parents, co-workers), we must remember that to teach effectively we must be effective communicators. The central question is not: "Did I send the message?" The central question is: "Was my message received?" For a professional educator this means changing the question from "Did I teach the curriculum?" to "How much of what I taught did the student learn?" John Dewey asked, "Can there be teaching if there is no learning?"

Where Do You Start When Planning a Two-Step Lesson?

To discuss the exploratory and discovery phases, we must separate the chronological sequence (of how the lesson is taught in the classroom) from the logical sequence (of how it is planned). Chronologically, the exploratory phase comes first when the lesson is taught. During the exploratory phase, we grab the learner's attention and *explore* the concepts to be developed in the discovery phase. Then, in the discovery phase, we create a product or engage in a process that will enable us to learn one or more concepts, attain or refine skills, retain information, and demonstrate competencies.

The discovery phase includes opportunities for on-going assessments. Because the assessment opportunities are generated by student performance and usually do not require the teacher to interrupt student work in order to test, they are referred to as curriculum embedded assessments.

Chronological Sequence (for Teaching)

♦ Exploratory phase

♦ Discovery phase (includes a task)

Chronologically, a lesson begins with exploration and then moves into discovery. However, to design an effective lesson, we must *backward plan*—that is, we must plan the discovery phase first, before we can plan the exploratory phase—even though we will engage students in the exploratory phase before allowing them to proceed to discovery. To backward plan, we must know our objectives for the lesson to determine how we will teach. Once we identify our learning objectives, we must plan the nature of our discovery phase (the task that will enable students to learn and demonstrate learning) before we can effectively plan our exploratory phase. The clearer the vision the teacher has of what students will eventually do to show their understanding, the better the planning will be. This idea parallels Stephen Covey's concept, "Begin with the end in mind," the second habit from his book, *The Seven Habits of Highly Effective People* (Covey, 1990).

Logical Sequence (for Planning)

- ♦ Learning objectives identified (keeping the *end in mind*)

- ♦ Discovery phase (including authentic performance task, interventions, scoring rubrics, and/or other forms of assessment measurement).

- ♦ Exploratory phase

Let's consider this example of planning for a vacation: Can you plan a trip without knowing where you are going or what you will be doing (i.e., identifying your objectives)? What do you pack? Won't packing be different depending on whether you are going to Virginia or California? Won't it be different depending on whether you plan to ski or surf? Which motels will you stay at? What mode of transportation will you use?

Similarly, plans for the exploratory phase depend on the discovery phase. The discovery phase has to be focused on helping the learner master the learning objectives and demonstrate this mastery. What your students will produce (their "product"), or the process in which they engage will help you assess whether they have reached their destination (mastery of the learning objectives). Discovery phases could include production of a battery operated fan, design of an advertisement for a new product or a school production, artwork for showcasing on parents' night, a civil war display, a meal for a French class, a five minute skit based on a scene from a short story, or a report on the impact of eighteenth century art on twentieth century literature for presentation to a local museum. Discovery phases could also include menu planning for a class picnic, reenactment of Socrates' trial, a science inquiry, a concert, design of student-created word math problems to be solved by classmates, creating a flow chart for a science experiment, or creating a cover for a novel.

Each of these examples of a discovery phase requires a different exploratory phase to prepare students for their journey into discovery.

Reality Check Question

Do you have lesson examples of the exploratory phase?
For answers to this question, see

- ♦ The section containing a lesson on Harriet Tubman (in this chapter)

◆ The lesson on waterways and state history (in this chapter)

◆ Appendix A for additional lessons

Here are two examples. The first is a 10-minute exploratory activity as part of a 45-minute lesson on Harriet Tubman. The second example is a 45-minute exploratory phase for a two-week unit on waterways and local history.

Consider preparing a 45-minute lesson on Harriet Tubman. What are some examples of learning objectives, an exploratory phase, and a discovery phase for our lesson? Chronologically, we will begin with the exploratory phase, then engage students in the discovery phase, and conclude with our assessment (which would be embedded in the discovery phase) to determine if students have met our learning objectives. However, for planning purposes:

1. We start with identification of the teacher's learning objectives and the core curriculum. In other words, what is the purpose of our lesson? It is the identification and assessment of specific learning objectives that enables teachers to cover more curriculum with a performance task than with traditional teaching strategies. If the teacher's learning objectives reflect what is most important for students to learn, the performance task will be addressing the key aspects of the curriculum.

2. We outline our discovery phase. What will be the authentic task that will engage the students so that they master the learning objectives as a result of addressing the criteria in the rubric? How will we motivate students to reflect on their work during and after the task is completed?

3. We plan our exploratory phase. What will be the activities and dialogue that will grab the students' attention, access prior knowledge and interests, introduce the discovery phase, and motivate the students to engage in discovery?

To understand the nature of our exploratory phase for a lesson on Harriet Tubman, let's take a look at what our learning objectives and discovery phase might be (Fig. 2.1)

Figure 2.1   Learning Objectives for Harriet Tubman Lesson

Information *(facts, formulas)*	*Knowledge* *(skills, concepts)*	*Competence*
Students know about Harriet Tubman's life and her major accomplishments.	The skill of articulation (verbal, pictorially, or dramatically)	The capacity to produce a work of art or literature that depicts an aspect of Tubman's life.
	Concepts of power and authority	
	The ability to organize ideas	

Note: Figure 2.1 shows a hypothetical example of learning objectives that might be selected by a teacher for a lesson on Harriet Tubman. These objectives would be assessed with a rubric for student achievement. There are many other objectives that could be identified and assessed by the teacher using this unit. These include concepts such as *analysis, synthesis of information, ownership of property, courage, societal norms, legal responsibility, moral responsibility, civil disobedience*, and *economics of social class*. What the author refers to as the *learning objectives* for the lesson are the objectives that the teacher chooses to formally assess. Anything else learned by the students (such as analysis, synthesis of information, ownership of property, etc.), which would not be assessed in the lesson exemplified on this page, is still a valuable part of the lesson. However, the learning objectives—the information, skills, concepts, and competencies—that the teacher chooses for assessment will reflect the minimum that the teacher will expect students to demonstrate as a consequence of their engagement in the lesson (Fig. 2.2).

Figure 2.2   Learning Objectives

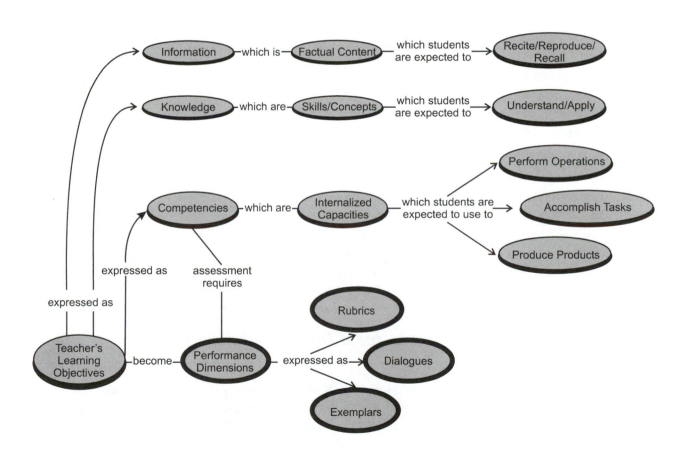

The learning objectives become the dimensions that are assessed in a rubric and are reflected in the left column of the rubric in Figure 2.3.

New York State Learning Standards & Performance Indicators

The learning objectives for the lesson on H.Tubman are based on the following learning standards.

Social Studies

Standard 1. Students will use a variety of intellectual skills to demonstrate their understanding of major ideas, eras, themes, developments, and turning points in the history of the United States and New York.

♦ Know the roots of American culture, its development from many different traditions, and the ways many people from a variety of groups and backgrounds played a role in creating it.

♦ Identify individuals who have helped to strengthen democracy in the United States and throughout the world.

♦ View historic events through the eyes of those who were there, as shown in their art, writing, music, and artifacts.

New York State Core Curriculum

The learning standards for the Harriet Tubman lesson are expressed in the following core curriculum.

♦ Organize collected information: orderly, precise, summarized notes.

♦ Use media and various visuals for communicating ideas.

♦ Write in an expository way.

♦ Recognize and use nonverbal means of communication.

♦ Key concept: Power refers to the ability of people to compel or influence the actions of others. "Legitimate power is called authority."

♦ Key concept: Human Rights are those basic political, economic, and social rights that all human beings are entitled to, such as the right to life, liberty, and the security of person, and a standard of living adequate for the health and well-being of himself and of his family.

Outline of the Discovery Phase for a Harriet Tubman Lesson

Preparing and giving a student presentation is the discovery phase of this lesson. The students are given the task of identifying one of five aspects of Harriet Tubman's life, reading a handout of less than two pages, and presenting information in the handout through written essay, artwork, or sculpture design and reenactment. As part of the presentation, students must address the concepts of power and authority—what they mean, whether Harriet Tubman had power or authority, and, if so, how she obtained and used it.

Exploratory Phase for a Harriet Tubman Lesson

Let's take an example of a good exploratory activity to begin our lesson. Then let's examine our example and see how it addresses each of the criteria for a good exploratory phase.

Examples of an Exploratory Phase

This is an exploratory phase as part of a 45-minute lesson on Harriet Tubman. This exploratory phase will take less than 10 minutes, in order to allow 35 minutes for the discovery phase. For example, the 10-minute exploratory phase as part of a 45-minute lesson on Harriet Tubman might have the following five stages:

1. The teacher asks, "Have you ever been in a situation where you have no control over your life? Want to rebel? Can't? What do you do?" (See the core curriculum box for distinction between power and authority.) The teacher accepts a few responses without commenting on them; sometimes the teacher follows up a response with a question seeking more detail or clarification. No one is told she is right or wrong.

2. The teacher asks students to "line up in the order of your birthdays; you cannot speak or write as you complete this activity."

3. The teacher creates groups of four beginning with the first four people in line; then students are asked to read any one page of a ten-page handout on Harriet Tubman and draw a picture (one picture drawn by each group of four students) that describes something they learned about Harriet Tubman. Each group is asked to agree on one person who will hold up the picture and another person who will explain what the picture is about after the class has had a chance to guess its meaning.

4. The teacher calls on each group to hold up its picture, allows others in the class to guess its meaning, and then calls on the group's reporter to respond.

5. The teacher brings the class back to the initial questions about power and seeks to have students contrast the way Harriet Tubman reacted to her circumstances with the way other people might.

The remaining 35 minutes of the lesson are devoted to the discovery phase, which centers on writing an essay, or doing artwork, sculpture design, or reenactment to demonstrate an understanding of the learning objectives of the lesson about Harriet Tubman.

In the rubric shown in Figure 2.3, the learning objectives of the Tubman lesson have been turned into the dimensions of a scoring rubric for the essay about Tubman.

Figure 2.3   Scoring Rubric for Harriet Tubman Essay

Dimensions for Harriet Tubman essay	Criteria for a score of 4	Criteria for a score of 3	Criteria for a score of 2	Criteria for a score of 1
Facts about H.T.'s life and accomplishments	Five facts	Four facts	Three facts	One fact
Concepts of power and authority	Tubman's source of power or authority and its use is fully developed.	Tubman's source of power or authority and its use is fairly well developed.	Tubman's source of power or authority and its use is somewhat developed.	Tubman's source of power or authority and its use is not developed.
Organization of ideas in the students' presentation on H.T.	The ideas are organized to support the presentation. There is a clear relationship between the what Tubman did and the presentation.	The ideas are loosely organized to support the presentation. The relationship between what Tubman did and the presentation is hard to see.	The ideas are organized to support the presentation. There is very little relationship between the what Tubman did and the presentation.	The ideas are not organized to support the presentation. There is no clear relationship between the what Tubman did and the presentation.
Artistic expression and depiction of aspects of H.T.'s life	Key elements of Tubman's life and accomplish-ments are clearly depicted.	Some of the key elements of Tubman's life and accomplish-ments are clearly depicted.	Few elements of Tubman's life and accomplishments are clearly depicted.	No elements of Tubman's life and accomplish-ments are clearly depicted.

Reality Check Question

How does this exploratory phase address the previously listed exploratory phase criteria?

♦ *Creates an environment conducive to learning (i.e., breaking the ice with something light and nonthreatening) and grabs students' attention:* The discussion of power will make a lesson about an historical figure more relevant to current times for some students. The lineup by birthdays lightens the mood; the opportunity to work in groups of four relaxes the students; the reliance on drawing enables students with artistic ability to shine, while the requirement that only one drawing can emerge from each group of four allows nonartistically inclined students to enjoy the activity; creating roles for holding up the picture and reporting on the group's intent also allows students with strong intelligences in these areas to come forth without pressuring everyone. By not grading the students, or even calling answers correct or incorrect (stage 1), the teacher creates a relaxed environment that is more likely to encourage dialogue and engagement.

How is the student's attention grabbed? For some students, the novelty of the birthday count-off (stage 2) is the attention grabber. For others, the motivating factor may be the topic (Harriet Tubman), the issue of feeling not in control of your life, something in the reading, or simply the chance to work in groups or to be the reporter. What grabs one student's attention may not have the same effect on another.

◆ *Accesses and assesses the learners' prior knowledge and interests regarding the concepts and skills to be presented by the lesson.* The responses in stage 1 begin to let the teacher see which students have prior knowledge about Harriet Tubman and to what degree. Student interests are also revealed. Perhaps a student says, "Oh, I know Harriet Tubman because my dad told me about her when we went to a museum. I remember it because we also went bowling that day, and I love to bowl." The teacher tucks away this information and may use a bowling analogy when trying to explain something to this student later in the lesson. "Did you ever have to get the bowling alley manager to clear an obstruction that was preventing the pins from setting up properly? Well, that little hallway behind the pins (that some people don't even know exists) is similar to the kinds of secret passages in old houses where people used to hide slaves who were traveling the Underground Railroad."

◆ *Helps the learners become aware of their perceptions regarding the knowledge, concepts and skills to be presented by the lesson.* Stages 1, 3, and 4 create opportunities for the students to begin exploring the knowledge, concepts, and skills that will be the focus of the discovery phase of the lesson.

◆ *Begins the process of exposing the learners to information, from a source they respect, that may conflict with their perceptions.* As soon as the students begin responding to the question in stage 1, each student hears perceptions that may differ from his own. As the students work in groups, this process of sharing perceptions continues because some students consider their peers as sources they respect. Other students may consider anything in a textbook a source due respect and, therefore, the 10-page handout may provide information that conflicts with the students' current perceptions. Spontaneous interventions by the teacher, either in front of the entire class or while observing a particular group, may provide information for students from a source (the teacher) they may respect.

◆ *Motivates the learners* to want to discover more about the knowledge, concepts, skills, and/or competencies to be presented and assessed by the lesson. Some students may be motivated to continue the work because of an interest in Harriet Tubman that is nurtured through the exploratory activity. Some students who have little interest in Harriet Tubman, or social studies, may be motivated to continue simply because they enjoy the sequence of activities or can relate to the issue of power. Students with strong bodily kinesthetic intelligences may enjoy the frequent movement in contrast to what they experience most of the school day; students with artistic talent, organizational skills, or strong interpersonal intelligences may enjoy the chance to focus in areas of their strengths. The exploratory activity has created a number of possible motivations for students to want to continue with the lesson.

♦ *Begins to introduce the main purpose* (content or concept) of the discovery phases that will come next, or familiarize the learner with how he will engage in the discovery phases (e.g., portfolio, interview, booklet, tape, etc.). This is accomplished through the gradually increased focus on Harriet Tubman, as the teacher proceeds through steps 1–5.

Now let's take a look at learning objectives and an exploratory phase for a two-week lesson (unit) on waterways and state history. The exploratory phase will take two days and will allow approximately eight more days for the discovery phase. Obviously, the length of the exploratory phase must be proportionate to the total time allotted for the entire lesson. The entire Harriet Tubman lesson was planned for 45 minutes; therefore, an exploratory activity of 10 minutes was appropriate. For a 10-day unit (on waterways and state history), it is not unreasonable to use 45 minutes (or longer) for exploration.

Once again, we must know our learning objectives and discovery phase to plan our exploration. First, let's list many possible learning objectives. Then we will create a hypothetical example of a lesson, selecting a limited number of learning objectives that will be assessed. Keep in mind that the number of learning objectives to be assessed depends on the amount of time that will be devoted to the lesson, as well as what the teacher feels is most important for the students to focus on. There is no right or wrong when selecting learning objectives as long as each identified learning objective is an important part of the curriculum, is aligned with an assessment that will provide evidence of what students understand and can achieve, and is relevant to local, district, state, or provincial standards.

For our hypothetical lesson on waterways and state history, let's assume that our learning objectives and our discovery phase are as shown in Figure 2.4:

Figure 2.4 Learning Objectives for a Unit on Waterways and State History

---

Information (facts, formulas)	*Knowledge* (skills, concepts)	*Competencies*
Students can name four types of waterways.	The concept of water and waterways as a resource that affects the economy	The ability to create product or presentation that demonstrates an understanding of the impact of one waterway on the State's history
Students can name three rivers or lakes in their home state.		

Discovery Phase for a Unit
on Waterways and State History

Discovery Phase (a Performance Task):

Students will create a video or write a report or prepare a portfolio that demonstrates an understanding of the impact of one of the state's waterways on the state's history. This product is to also include the relationship of the selected waterway to other of the state's waterways, and the economics of the waterway.

Exploratory Phase:

Here is how the teacher can prepare students for the discovery phase through exploration:

The teacher is about to begin a two-week unit on waterways and state history. Using an idea suggested by Heidi Hayes Jacobs of NCREST, six weeks prior to the start of the unit the teacher placed a bin at the front of the room and asked students to bring to class either of the following:

- Any relic or souvenir with a connection to a local waterway that they, or their parents, might be able to locate

- Newspapers, magazines, promotional brochures, internet articles, or pictures reflecting any event or information relating to a waterway in the state

The exploratory phase has begun. Each day, students drop into the bin, for example, a ship in a bottle grandpa made many years ago, a souvenir from a boat ride, and similar pieces of memorabilia related to local waterways.

The day the unit is to begin, the teacher goes to the bin and holds up one item at a time. Before allowing the student who brought the item to explain its relevance, the teacher encourages students to speculate about its significance. The student who brought in the item locates the waterway on a classroom map. After addressing the items in the bin, the teacher asks each student to take out a sheet of paper, write his/her name on top, and write a sentence "describing one thing you know about any body of water within the state." It is made clear that this will not be graded as long as the students give it their best effort. Then the teacher pairs the students and asks them to share and explain what they have written. Then the teacher combines pairs and asks each twosome to share what they have written. At this point, the teacher processes the entire class by asking each group of four to share at least one thing they are sure they know about a waterway in their state.

The teacher introduces a guest, Governor Dewitt Clinton of New York State. (A student teacher, parent, or another teacher—or even a student—is dressed as Dewitt Clinton.) The governor tells the class, "We need to do something about transportation. It takes three weeks to get things from Buffalo to Albany, in my state of New York, and it costs too much. I am proposing that we build a canal in New York. The problem is that the bodies of water that would have to be connected by a canal have different elevations above sea level." The guest asks the class to discuss, in small groups, how they would address this problem. Then he conducts a class dialogue that he inspires with a few thoughtful, probing questions.

On day two, the exploratory phase continues with students in the computer lab working with a software program that enables them to navigate through locks in a canal. After the students have experienced the canal through the computer, the teacher challenges them to think about whether a canal could be built in their state. If not, what is the closest state that might benefit from building a canal? By the conclusion of day two, the students are ready to move into engineering teams of three to work with modeling clay and design their own locks.

With a two-day exploratory activity having prepared the students and the teacher, everyone is now ready to enter a discovery phase that, in this lesson, will last almost two weeks. Working in groups of three, and working with modeling clay, milk cartons, dirt, tubs of water, toy boats, and other resources available in the classroom, students will build a working model of a lock that connects two or more bodies of water located in their state or another state.

Reality Check Question

What are the implications in the exploratory phase of the criteria that you need to grab the student's attention and access prior knowledge and interests?

Would you ask someone to walk through a doorway if the door were closed?

Of course not. You would have to open the door before you could ask someone to walk through the doorway.

Expecting students to understand (or pay attention to) a lecture without first doing something to open their minds to the information about to be imparted is like asking someone to walk through a doorway when the door is closed.

This is why we state emphatically, "*Never* begin a lesson with the teacher speaking and the students listening (passively) except to take a minute to assign a task, put students in groups, or otherwise prepare them for interaction with each other." (An exception might be when today's lesson is a continuation of a discovery phase begun on a previous day, and the students are coming to class expecting a planned intervention, ready to receive information.) Your opening activity needn't last longer than five minutes. If you have a wonderful lecture to deliver, at least get the students thinking about (and discussing) your topic before giving the lecture.

For example, If you are about to speak eloquently about the relationship between cloud formations and the following day's weather, you might ask students to write their own thoughts (in two sentences) on "The relationship of cloud formations to the weather that will follow." Allow three minutes for them to complete the task, then ask them to pair and reach consensus on one sentence to share with the class, take a few responses; collect all the papers. Instead of grading the papers, write "OK" on any papers where the effort was made to follow your directions; return the sheets of paper the next day.

What have you accomplished?

♦ You've made students think about the topic you are about to discuss, and you've forced them to articulate their perceptions. When students think about their perceptions, they are accessing their prior knowledge.

♦ You've learned what their perceptions are and which students have greater prior knowledge.

♦ You've only used 10 minutes (or less) of class time.

♦ You have not created a time-consuming grading nightmare—it should only take you a few minutes to check all the sheets of paper to see if the students followed your directions and made the effort, and to write "OK" on those that did.

♦ You've let students know they will be reinforced if they make an effort, even if their answer is inadequate. (*Note*: there will be many times when students will be required to provide "correct" information and answers. This is not to suggest anything to the contrary. However, this is one type of activity in which effort can be rewarded because you are asking for perceptions, and any perception that is truly that of the students is a correct response.) This is also higher-level thinking—evaluation.

Now if you give a lecture, it is likely that the students' retention will be higher because you have forced them to open their minds and think about the topic BEFORE you shared your information. In short, open every lesson with some kind of exploratory activity—it can be brief, it can lead into a lecture if that is your inclination. End every lesson, and most classes, with some kind of student reflection (written or verbal); it needn't require more than five minutes of class time. See Chapter 4 for more on this.

As you can see from the rain/temperatures example, an easy way to open the door to students' minds is to pair students and challenge them with a question that will focus them on the concept or topic you are about to address. To begin a lesson on math, a teacher might ask: "What is the correlation among the legs of the triangle on the piece of paper I just distributed?" Student responses would be challenged with follow-up questions. The purpose is to get students thinking about the fact that there is a correlation among legs/angles of a triangle and that there are many correct ways to respond to that question. Also, the purpose is to help students access their prior knowledge so that they can see the relevancy of what they are about to study to what they already know. This will help motivate them to engage in the task that will follow (the discovery phase) and it will begin the process of giving them hooks on which they can hang their thoughts (see Chapter 4). Before beginning a science lecture on friction, the teacher might ask students to speculate, in pairs, on "Why do we get a shock when we touch certain surfaces?"

Challenging students to *think*, then *pair*, then *share* is an effective way to get students to think about what you are about to discuss with them. The thinking you are requiring is higher level if you ask students to go beyond the recall of a fact. Asking students to speculate on the correlation among legs of a triangle is more meaningful than asking for the formula for determining the length of the third side.

A teacher will have difficulty grabbing students' attention while standing in the front of the room talking even with visuals or a PowerPoint presentation with all the bells and whistles. It is much easier to grab their attention and then to force them to think by challenging them with a question and involving them in dialogue. How do you assess students' prior knowledge and interests, and how do you help students become aware of their perceptions if you talk at them?

This need to engage students with the information you are about to share is also a strong rationale for group work. When students work in groups, there are often *at least* two people in each group thinking at the same time, and through teacher observation, you can often see or hear the evidence. When the teacher is focused on what he will say from the front of the room, he often misses evidence of student thinking even if it is available.

Reality Check Question

What is the relationship between the exploratory phase and a student's grade?

The exploratory phase of a lesson is not formally assessed (for a grade). While exploration could be unending, there comes a time when the purposes have been largely met, and the teacher's focus and emphasis need to shift to the discovery phase of the lesson.

In brief, a good exploratory phase will stir the pot, plumb the depths, grab students' attention, get students thinking at a higher level, and respect student opinions and perceptions *before* challenging them. A good exploratory phase enables the teacher to know what students think and use this information to determine how to adjust the discovery phase. It also identifies which students can be used as resources and how to effectively utilize them.

A good exploratory phase is marked by a feeling of getting kids ready. The students are led on an exploration of the lesson or unit they are about to study, and the teacher is exploring the students' prior knowledge, interests, perceptions, and ideas. The idea of grading students on their work is in conflict with the objective of engendering candor and intrinsic motivation for the discovery phase of the Two-Step.

Reality Check Question

What about misconceptions that arise during the exploratory phase? For example, you said that the teacher should not grade students during the exploratory phase.

Interestingly, this doesn't worry the author as much as it does many others. First of all, during an activity in which students work cooperatively, we see and hear students' thinking and often can help students rethink a cloudy or unclear idea. (This is called *scaffolding* and is a key concept in constructivism.) Second, we *read* their ideas and can make comments on it. Finally, because we spiral information throughout an entire unit, there are many chances for students to reconstruct their thinking. As a matter of fact, that is the point of teaching this way! First trials can be full of mistakes because these mistakes give us direction for our further study. In traditional classes, mistakes are defeats; here they are raw material and generate teachable moments!

Let's assume student misconceptions surface during the exploratory phase of the Harriet Tubman lesson as the teacher elicits feedback to the question, "What does anyone know about Harriet Tubman?" The teacher makes a mental (or written) note of these misconceptions. While we are cautioning against correcting the students at this point (unless it can be done in a completely nonthreatening way, i.e., nonthreatening to the student), the teacher will address, later in the lesson, any misconceptions that arise.

In some instances, the teacher may observe the students correcting the misconceptions themselves as they work their way through the exploratory or discovery phases. In other instances, the teacher may feel the misconceptions are limited to a few students, and she may be able to communicate most effectively with these students one-on-one or in a small group. In other instances, the teacher may sense that a misconception is widespread, and this may call for an intervention in front of the entire class. Our main point is that misconceptions expressed during the exploratory phase need to be handled delicately because one of the purposes of this phase is to access (and assess) prior knowledge, and this will not occur if students are uncomfortable being candid.

It needs to be emphasized that engaging students in dialogue with each other, or with the teacher, is not what generates misconceptions—the misconceptions exist, but many classroom environments do not allow them to surface. In many traditional classrooms, the teacher either:

◆ Does not become aware of student misconceptions because there is little opportunity to see what students are thinking when you are conducting a teacher-centered lesson from the front of the room, or

◆ Addresses any misconceptions of which he/she does become aware in front of the entire class, thereby boring the many students who may not share the misconception and, often, in an effort to teach toward the middle, still not effectively communicating with the students who have the misconception.

In summary, if student interaction reveals to the teacher that misconceptions exist, and/or are being shared by students with one another, the teacher has many options for addressing them in a learner centered environment.

Effectively identifying a student's misconceptions and addressing them compose a primary purpose of education, because misconceptions stymie the development of new knowledge. New knowledge can't be built on misconceptions.

Depending on whether the problem lies with a few or most of the class, you either provide assistance to those in need, or you reteach to the entire class. The point is that a cooperative activity shouldn't be seen as an entire lesson. It is not the beginning, middle, and end. It is a strategy to force students to think, engage in research, and articulate their thoughts through dialogue. Many students benefit from trying to articulate what they think they are learning ("I shoulda said. . . ."). John Myers, paraphrasing Vygotsky, says "We learn by talking. When we share ideas with others, totally apart from whether others learn from us, we learn by being forced to articulate what we think we know."

Often, on traditional tests, we seem satisfied with only 67% correct; this is an awfully high rate of misconception that we leave kids with *after* a course. (And, of course, students have no idea which two-thirds they know; no wonder few care if they forget it.)

Work by Sternberg (1999) and others suggest that standardized test scores *rise* when students are taught actively and conceptually (constructivistly), because students also recall more of what they have learned. In other words, the number of misconceptions that we leave students with falls when students are taught actively and conceptually.

Reality Check Question

Can you always compartmentalize the exploratory and discovery phases of a lesson so neatly?

Yes, and no. A discovery phase is easy to identify. It begins when the teacher turns the student loose to accomplish a performance task. It begins the moment the student is expected to understand the task well enough to define what must be accomplished even if she isn't yet sure how to proceed. In other words, as a student, if I understand that I must prepare a portfolio that demonstrates my understanding of the sequence of events that occurred during the Industrial Revolution, then I know what I must accomplish. I may need planned interventions to provide me with facts, methods of proceeding, or knowledge of the Industrial Revolution, but I do understand what I must do—create a portfolio about the Industrial Revolution.

If I am not clear on how to proceed, or if planned interventions still leave me uncertain, it is my responsibility to ask the teacher for guidance. The teacher will intervene spontaneously if she assesses that I am having difficulty, but ultimately, it is my responsibility as the student to conduct research, ask questions, and obtain clarification if I have any uncertainty about how to proceed. This is what is meant by teaching students to be responsible for their own learning. The teacher sets up scaffolding to guide student learning and to alert the teacher when a student is having difficulty, so the teacher can coach the student before the student gets too far off track; but the teacher's goal is to make the student responsible for his own learning.

For the discovery phase to be successful, it should be preceded by exploration, for two reasons: 1) In life, first we explore as we decide what we are interested in learning. Then we set out to learn (discover). Too often in schools, we skip the first step (exploration). Above all, we need to keep in mind that if someone hasn't decided she is ready to engage in a voyage of discovery, very little we do or say will get through to her. 2) In addition to using exploration to motivate student interest in the discovery phase task, exploration enables the teacher to understand the student better, which—in turn—equips the teacher to provide the appropriate options and structure for the discovery phase. However, this does not always mean we need to create an elaborate exploratory phase before entering our students into discovery. When a teacher works with the same students over a period of time, the teacher often has a good grasp of their prior knowledge and interests with regard to the task to be undertaken and its learning objectives. Often, previous activities have given teachers a good understanding of the prior knowledge and interests students bring to the current lesson. The teacher may be aware that the nature of the task is such that most students will be motivated to undertake it, and extra time is not needed for exploration for the purpose of building anticipation or eliciting prior knowledge. In other words, sometimes a previous lesson's exploratory and/or discovery phases have constituted exploration for a future lesson. See Figure 2.5.

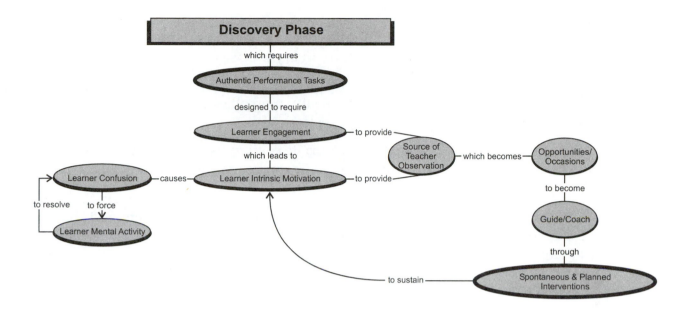

Figure 2.5   Discovery Phase

If seventh graders have been analyzing a novel and have completed a discovery phase activity of creating visual representations of various key scenes, the teacher may be able to extend it into another discovery activity by challenging them to create similes for various key characters. (For example, in the novel 1984, Winston may be seen as a bicyclist because he keeps going but does not get anywhere important very quickly.) It may not be necessary to create a separate exploratory phase because the teacher has just assessed the students' prior knowledge and activated their thinking; the students may be intrinsically motivated to carry on another discovery activity because of the success they have had with the first task. (Note: if the second task works, maybe a third is worth considering: for example, the writing of new titles for each of the chapters in the book.) In any case, once the process has begun, the discovery phase of one project can easily become the exploratory phase of the next.

When working with a group for the first time, it is beneficial to have exploration and discovery in two separate phases to achieve learning objectives, whether working with students in a class, or teachers, administrators, or parents at a workshop. However, for the reasons just cited, sometimes an entire lesson can serve as the exploration for a later discovery phase of a subsequent lesson. In this embedded (or nested) structure, we recognize that today sets up tomorrow (all the todays set up all the tomorrows), and the curriculum is coherent, structured, and spiraled into a whole, which supports the notion that constructivism is a whole-to-part approach. It also begins to address teacher concerns over the length of time it takes for a good performance task. If each of our lessons builds on previous ones, we can often limit or eliminate the need for lengthy exploration.

Here are some criteria (litmus tests) for knowing if you have successfully concluded the exploratory phase of the lesson:

♦ You have taken the temperature of the class so that you can identify the kinds of intervention you will need during the discovery phase.

♦ You have a reasonably good understanding of the prior knowledge and interests of each of your students with regard to the learning objectives they are about to address during the discovery phase of the lesson.

♦ You feel prepared to offer students appropriate options as they select the task (a process or product) that will engage their efforts during the discovery phase of the lesson.

♦ You are satisfied that you have piqued the interest of your students and that there is an emotional connection between the student and the task, as well the student and the teacher.

Thought for Reflection

"Each of us makes sense of our world by synthesizing new experiences into what we have previously come to understand" (Brooks & Brooks, 1993).

End of Section Assessment

In one sentence, can the reader explain why exploration is critical as the first step before launching into the main part of a lesson (discovery)?

Sample Summary of a Two-Step

Following is an abbreviated version of a Two-Step for 11th grade Math.
A more complete example of this same lesson appears in Appendix A.

Popular Name:	Pythagorean Theorem
Grade Level:	11th
Discipline:	Mathematics

Standards:
Students will understand mathematics and become mathematically confident, by applying mathematics to real-world settings and by solving problems through the study of trigonometry.

Learning Objectives:
Students will demonstrate an understanding of the Pythagorean Theorem by effectively teaching an alternative proof of the Pythagorean theorem to their classmates.

EXPLORATORY PHASE:
♦ Students will explore a diagram that visually demonstrates the relationships among the sides of a right angle.
♦ Students will self-discover the formula that expresses the relationships among the three sides of a right angle.

DISCOVERY PHASE:
Performance Task: Students will be assigned an alternative proof to the Pythagorean theorem, which they are to learn and teach to their classmates.

Discovery

Learning Objectives

The reader will begin to develop the understanding that the planning of an effective lesson starts with a learning task designed around learning objectives that students find engaging. The learning task is addressed by students during step 2, the discovery phase; however, it sets the tone for the entire lesson.

Main Points

♦ The heart of the discovery phase of a Two-Step lesson is an authentic task.

- The discovery phase begins when the student understands the task and is encouraged by the teacher to begin it.

- When students are engaged in an authentic task, the teacher is free to do hands-on instruction and become a coach and guide in response to students' needs.

Reality Check Question

What are examples of the discovery phase of a two-step lesson?

The discovery phase is where the student receives her authentic task. This is the phase during which the student is creating a product (e.g., a newsletter to be distributed in school, an e-mail to send to a student overseas, a wind sock, a report, a diorama, or a t-shirt) or preparing to engage in a process (e.g., an interview, a science inquiry, or a presentation). Through preparation of a product or for a process, the student is discovering that which we want the student to learn. The discovery phase also provides the teacher with an on-going assessment based on the teacher's professional observations, as well as opportunities for many other forms of assessment.

Here are some examples of discovery phases:

- Working in pairs, you are to create a set of models of elements alone and in combination. These can be three dimensional or two, but must portray the chemistry information as indicated in the textbook and on the periodic table.

- Using one of the styles of drawing we have learned, draw a picture of any object in this room and write a brief explanation regarding the way the drawing style is reflected in your drawing, for display on the classroom walls during parent night next week.

- Read the guidelines for projects for the science fair and then, working alone or with one other person, prepare a project for the fair.

- Build a scale model of the Golden Gate Bridge using the blueprints outlined on the attached page.

- Tenth graders, working in teams, will develop and deliver a lesson to some of the districts' third graders. The lesson must include the basics of their science experiment on the American Kestrel, and must include a hands-on aspect, a visual component and a way to find out what the youngsters are thinking.

- Write a poem about a relationship. Your poem will be set to music and produced on a CD *after* it has been proofed for spelling and content. This can be done at almost any grade level–the younger the students, the more prompts and coaching required of the teacher.

- Language students are asked to design a series of background displays that will be shown as they sing the song "Frere Jacques" in French to their folks on Parents' Night. Any wording on the signs MUST be in French, and must be written correctly.

♦ Design and write copy for a movie poster and YOU decide whom to advertise in the starring role.

These are brief examples of authentic tasks from discovery phases. Students would be given criteria to address and a rubric that would assess their performance meeting the teacher's learning objectives. Students would be supported by planned interventions (which can be thought of as a form of scaffolding), and the teacher would offer spontaneous interventions as needed. For additional examples, a definition of *scaffolding* appears on the next two pages and is further referenced in the glossary for this book. More information is available on the Internet at www.learnercentereded.org

The discovery phase of a lesson (activity or unit) must address the following criteria:

♦ *Learning Objectives*: In a well-designed discovery phase, the task is based on learning objectives that are rooted in state/district learning standards and curriculum.

♦ *Task Clarity:* A well-designed discovery phase enables students to understand their task, be able to articulate it, and begin to undertake it.

♦ *Teacher as Guide and Coach:* A well-designed discovery phase enables the teacher to stop formally "teaching," and slip into the background, awaiting student questions, observing to see if students need assistance, and asking questions to challenge students to self-discover whether they are proceeding in a direction that will enable them to accomplish their task.

♦ *Teaching through Planned Interventions:* In a well-designed discovery phase, instruction occurs through planned interventions, when the teacher asks for everyone's attention and provides information (lecture, reading, a guest) that the teacher feels confident most students need to complete their task. If the teacher has been effective with the exploratory phase, then students will see the need for the information provided in the planned intervention to a greater degree than if it was presented, as is often the case in a traditional classroom, with little perceived relevance.

♦ *Teaching through Spontaneous Interventions:* In a well-designed discovery phase, instruction also occurs through spontaneous interventions, when students ask questions or the teacher seizes on opportunities to provide information or ask questions based on observations of student work.

♦ *Assessment of Learning:* In a well-designed discovery phase, the learning objectives become the dimensions of the rubric used to assess the completion of the learning task.

♦ *Distinction between the Learning Objectives* of a lesson/unit and the teaching strategies used to help the learner address the objectives: A well-designed discovery phase enables the teacher to assess how well the student can address the teacher's learning objectives and does not require a method of demonstration that favors students with particular learning styles.

♦ *Task Authenticity:* A well-designed discovery phase focuses students on a task that simulates a real world context as closely as possible and has an audience beyond the teacher for a grade whenever possible.

♦ *Tasks That Require Students to Think:* A well-designed discovery phase challenges students to evaluate, synthesize, analyze, and apply a variety of thinking skills.

Extensive research supports the notion of a discovery phase that motivates students to learn through engagement in an authentic task. Modern education, and the standards, recognize that understanding, *not* memorization, is what the goals of education ought to be. Real learning is conceptual and needs engagement. Perrone (1994) suggests that these qualities help real learning take place: Students have time to wonder and to find an interesting direction for them to take; teachers encourage a variety of forms of student expression; students create original products and develop "expertness" on a topic; and students actually *do* something.

In summary, the teacher is able to shift students from the exploratory to the discovery phase when the students are able to articulate the task and begin work, while enabling the teacher to move from the front of the room into a more facilitative role. The teacher does make interventions while facilitating dialogue and activities during the exploratory phase; however, there is less teacher direction and more teacher response during the discovery phase (see Fig. 2.7)

Figure 2.7   The Exploratory and Discovery Phases

Exploratory Phase	*Discovery Phase*
♦ Highly interactive; interaction is teacher directed	♦ Highly interactive, primarily student directed
♦ Characterized by sequence of planned interventions	♦ Planned interventions only if and when necessary
♦ Some spontaneous interventions, not many	♦ Characterized by frequent spontaneous interventions

Scaffolding

When a teacher uses the Two-Step, there is a mindset that changes from a traditional approach as the discovery phase is designed. Instead of planning every step the student will take to address a task, the teacher focuses on creation and definition of the task. In other words, ask yourself, "How do I help the student to understand the task well enough so that she can determine how to accomplish it without the need for me to lead her step by step?" As a teacher, you want to guide, not lead.

However, the fear of every teacher (and parent) when we turn children loose on a task is, "What if they fail? What if they become frustrated and give up?" This is where scaffolding and prompts play a role.

Scaffolding is a teacher-designed structure to prevent a student from getting too far off-track before the teacher is alerted and can coach the student back in the direction of the task requirements. "Scaffolding essentially means doing some of the work for the student who isn't quite ready to accomplish a task independently. Like the supports that construction workers use on buildings, scaffolding is intended to be temporary. It is there to aid the completion of the task and it is eventually removed." (Bernie Dodge, http://edweb.sdsu.edu/people/bdodge/scaffolding.html)

The teacher scaffolds by providing the students with support. This can be in any of the following forms:

♦ A handout of the inverted pyramid style of writing for an assignment.

♦ A graphic organizer to help students with curriculum content.

♦ A sheet containing a resource list of math formulas for students to apply to problems.

The teacher gives the students the instructions and guidelines by:

♦ Announcing the deadline for work: Two weeks before the final project is due, students are expected to submit a detailed outline.

♦ Initially limiting the number of concepts students will be dealing with in a lesson.

♦ Stimulating student thinking through prompts:

  • "Have you done an Internet search of that term?"

  • "Have you asked Mrs. Sidney, the science teacher, whether she thinks that is a possibility?"

  • "Did you try it with cardboard?"

  • "Ask three more people and if they are unable to offer a productive suggestion, come back and see me."

In "Beyond Technology, Questioning, Research, and the Information Literate School Community," James McKenzie cites eight characteristics of effective scaffolding: 1) provides clear directions; 2) clarifies purpose; 3) keeps students on task; 4) offers assessment to clarify expectations; 5) points students to worthy sources; 6) reduces uncertainty, surprise and disappointment; 7) delivers efficiency; 8) creates momentum.

Reality Check/Reflective Question

How do the criteria for a discovery phase play out with regard to the Tubman example mentioned previously?

In our Harriet Tubman lesson, the discovery phase might require each of five groups of four students to either write a page, create and enact a sculpture, or draw a picture (or sequence of pictures) that depict an aspect of Tubman's life. Each group picks a different aspect of her life from these topics:

- ◆ Her childhood
- ◆ Her attitude toward slavery
- ◆ Her role in the underground railroad
- ◆ Her personal life and relationships
- ◆ Her hobbies and interests

Each group receives a small packet of information about Harriet Tubman (less than two pages of reading) and has 20 minutes to plan its two-minute presentation. Presentations occur during the last 15 minutes of class.

The following day, the teacher devotes at least a few minutes, possibly an entire period, for some processing out of the lesson with the students (i.e., bringing closure). The teacher addresses misconceptions that might persist and leads the class through a reflection on what they learned about Harriet Tubman and how they learned it. Also, while each student is responsible for demonstrating an understanding of the concepts included in the rubric, the teacher is also attempting to discover what else students learned, because the value of a good lesson extends to what students learn beyond what the teacher established as objectives.

During the exploratory phase, the students were asked whether they had ever felt that they had no control of their lives and whether Harriet Tubman had had control of her life. Therefore, the teacher might revisit these questions and try to generate dialogue on how Harriet Tubman gained control and whether the means she used to exercise control are available to most people or were unique to her situation. How does this discovery phase for the Harriet Tubman lesson address the criteria?

- ◆ *Learning Objectives:* The learning objectives of the task are based on the elementary-level social studies standard 1 and related core curriculum.

- ◆ *Task Clarity:* The students are focused on the task of identifying one of five aspects of Harriet Tubman's life, reading a handout of less than two pages, and presenting the information in the handout through a written essay, artwork, sculpture design, or reenactment.

- ◆ *Teacher as Guide and Coach:* As soon as the directions are given, the students begin group discussions, and the teacher, through observation and spontaneous interventions, becomes the facilitator. The teacher's first task is to quickly visit each group and, through observation from the background, determine if the students clearly understand the directions and are proceeding along the right track. This is a critical stage. The teacher must limit the time she is giving instruction to the entire class from the front of the room and must resist the temptation to over-explain the directions or respond to too many clarifying questions. Often one or two students will keep the entire class at bay with questions about the intent of the assignment, and much of everyone's time is wasted listening to (or ignoring) the teacher's clarifying responses. Once the teacher has given the directions in front of the entire class and done one or two checks for understanding, the students should immediately be allowed to proceed with group work. The teacher can, more effectively, clarify the directions on an as-needed basis with each group. Often, other students in the group will clarify the directions for the student who has all the questions.

♦ *Teaching through Planned Interventions:* The only planned intervention in this brief activity consists of some closing observations the teacher plans to make during the reflection that will occur following the group presentations.

♦ *Teaching through Spontaneous Interventions:* The group work and presentations will afford the teacher myriad opportunities for spontaneous interventions. If facts are misstated during a presentation, the teacher may intervene and ask, "Are you certain the Underground Railroad ended at Grand Island? Isn't that in the United States? Would slaves be safe while still in the States? Would the Underground Railroad have existed in our city or town? Did it? Could it have? Why? Why not?"

♦ *Assessment of Learning:* The learning objectives of the lesson have been translated into the dimensions of the assessment rubric used to make judgments regarding the completion of the task.

♦ *Distinction between the Learning Objectives* of a lesson/unit and the teaching strategies used to help the learner address the objectives: The teacher's learning objectives are clearly stated, and the options for demonstration include draw, write, create, or enact. Also, because students are in groups of four, some can contribute to the planning verbally, using organizing skills or keeping the group focused on its task and functioning smoothly. In other words, it isn't necessary for each of the four students in the group to draw, create, write, and/or enact. The teacher can use an individual assessment after the student demonstrations, if the teacher has difficulty assessing which students understood what as she worked the room and observed the evidence of the student learning.

♦ *Task Authenticity:* The connection made in the exploratory phase between students' feelings of lack of control of their lives and the status of slaves was designed to give the lesson a degree of real-world context. The students' performances before their classmates provide an audience beyond the teacher.

♦ *Tasks That Require Students to Think:* The task requires the students to make connections between the information contained on the two-page reading and their presentation, as well as translate the information into a new means of expression.

Reality Check Question

Do you have examples of entire two-step lessons?

In Appendix A, you will find in-depth plans for teaching each of the following using the Two-Step (exploration/discovery) format:

Math:	Pythagorean Theorem
English Language Arts:	Music Box Personal Profile
Social Studies:	Explorers' Resume
Science:	Seed Inquiry

Additional exemplars in secondary and elementary English, math, science, and social studies are available on the web site of the Institute for Learning Centered Education, www.learnercentereded.org

Reality Check Question

How do you make sure students will address your learning objectives during the discovery phase of the lesson/unit?

According to Grant Wiggins (from an interview in Scholastic):

> Teachers need to design assessments backward from the task, asking at each step of the way, "What's the evidence I need of children's understanding? Will this assessment get at it?" For example, if you're considering using a diorama of the Civil War as an assessment, ask, "Could students do a diorama but not understand the Civil War? Could students not do a diorama well, but understand the Civil War?" The answer to both is yes, so it's a good idea to either rethink using the diorama as assessment or use other types of assessment, such as oral presentations, in conjunction with it.

A Thought for Reflection

> Students learn best when new ideas are connected to what they already know and have experienced; when they use real-world problems to apply and test their knowledge; when they are given clear, high goals with much practice in reaching them; when they can build on what they have learned; and when their own interests and strengths are a springboard for learning. (Sugrue, 1995)

End of Section Assessment:

Can the reader think of a performance task she has experienced in a classroom setting, then apply the criteria for the discovery phase and assess how many were successfully addressed by the performance task?

Sample Summary of a Two-Step

Following is an abbreviated example of a Two-Step for tenth grade science. A more complete example of this same lesson appears in Appendix A.

Popular Name:	Seed Inquiry
Grade Level:	10th
Discipline:	Science

Standards: Students will:
♦ Construct explanations of natural phenomena
♦ Prepare and conduct research, record observations, and measurements
♦ Interpret organized data.

Learning Objectives:
Students will increase their capacity to understand the nature of science by conducting an inquiry into how seed-characteristics affect the distance traveled by wind-dispersed seeds.

EXPLORATORY PHASE:
Through handling and observing local naturally-occurring, wind-dispersed seeds, students create a listing of the seeds descriptive characteristics.

DISCOVERY PHASE:
Performance Task:
Students will design and conduct a scientific inquiry into how seed-characteristics affect the distance traveled by wind-dispersed seeds.

Interventions

Learning Objective

The reader will gain an appreciation for the fact that instruction is most effective when accomplished through interventions. This means that effective instruction requires students to be engaged in a task that provides the teacher with opportunities for hands-on instruction. See Figure 2.8.

Figure 2.8   Exploratory and Discovery Phases

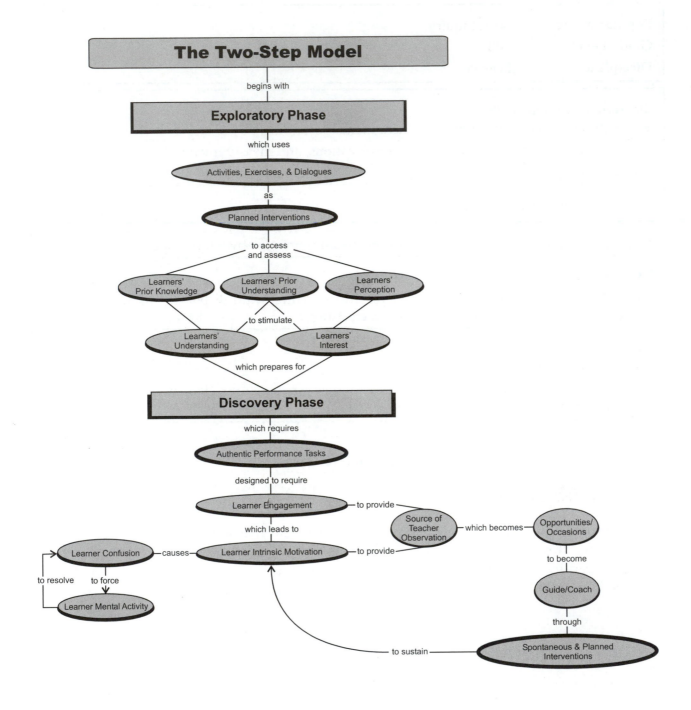

Main Points

- The *Two-Step* model provides abundant opportunities for teacher interventions at *teachable moments*.

- When a teacher assists students while they are engaged in a performance task, this is called an *intervention*.

- When this teacher assistance is designed in advance to take place at a specific time, it is called a *planned intervention*.

- When this teacher assistance is not planned in advance and is prompted by either student questions or by teacher observation of student performance, it is called a *spontaneous intervention*.

- Interventions comprise hands-on instruction.

- Engagement should precede theoretical discussion; theory should be introduced through interventions in student performance (engagement).

Effective teaching occurs through interventions. Instinctively, we know this is true. That's why the term *teachable moment* was coined. It refers to that point in time when the student is asking for the information, knowledge, or understanding that teachers are constantly trying to impart to him. A teachable moment occurs when the student sees the need to learn what the teacher is ready to teach. The role of the teacher is to make the student want to learn what the teacher wants the student to learn. If this doesn't happen, the teacher will teach, but the student will not learn.

How many teachable moments occur while the teacher is in front of the room directing a lesson to students who are sitting passively, taking notes, trying (or not trying) to pay attention, or focusing their thoughts who knows where?

Teachable moments are often signaled by a question a student may ask or a perplexed look a teacher may notice on a student's face. Teachers take advantage of a teachable moment by intervening, either at the request of the student or when something the student says or does indicates the student may be receptive to support (coaching) from the teacher.

Unfortunately, a classroom environment often restricts rather than creates opportunities for interventions and thus limits opportunities for learning.

What are examples of learning through interventions?

- The batting coach stands by the batting cage and asks the hitter, "Do you think the bat might feel lighter if you choked up a little?"

- The director halts rehearsal and demonstrates the tone of voice she wants from the actor.

- The art teacher coaches the student on how to hold the brush as the student paints a portrait.

- The kindergarten teacher repositions a left-handed student's writing paper.

- ◆ The science teacher asks a pair of students about the data their inquiry is generating.

- ◆ The social studies teacher glances at a student's report outline and suggests additional sources.

One difference among the interventions in these examples is that some are questions and some are commands.

What do these examples have in common?

In each situation, the learner is engaged in performance. The performance allows the teacher:

- ◆ To observe a student demonstrate his ability to address the standards

- ◆ To see/hear student thinking

- ◆ To offer suggestions in a context that has meaning for the learner.

You cannot intervene if nothing is happening except the sound of your own voice resonating off the four walls of a classroom.

The word *intervention* implies that there is an action or performance that can serve as the basis for the intervention. To create a student performance, the teacher must engage the student in a task (through assignment or negotiations) that will result in a product, a process, or both (see Fig. 2.9).

Figure 2.9   Intervention: Product and Process

Product	*Process*
An exhibit	An interview with a parent, the principal, another student, or someone playing the role of an historical figure.
A flier to be sent home to parents	
A letter to the editor	
A radio drama	A student describing why a word is either a simile or a metaphor.
An architectural model	Apply mathematical procedures to solve real problems such as those involved in automotive mechanics, agriculture, construction, etc.
An evaluative/analytical report	
	Design and performance of a skit or enactment.
	An experiment.

By now you have probably picked up on the keyword in creating opportunities for interventions—*performance*. Performance generates engagement. Certain disciplines lend themselves more easily to student engagement in performance. Music, art, physical education, technology, and home and career education teachers are quick to point out that they have always taught through performance. This is partially, but not entirely, true. The author recently spoke with a technology teacher who indicated that he teaches fonts by sharing all possible fonts with his students, drilling them, and working with them until they can identify a reasonable number of fonts. This is an example of teaching traditionally in a performance-oriented discipline.

Instead, what if this technology teacher motivated the students by having them publish a booklet or brochure on a topic that interested them? What if the teacher offered topic options (such as autos, hair styles, sports, cooking, games, etc.) and required the use of a variety of fonts as a criterion for them to have their work published? In other words, engage them in an authentic task so that the learning becomes essential to working on the task. What a terrific opportunity for an interdisciplinary activity! Let the students work with technology to learn to use fonts for the authentic purpose of fulfilling an assignment in one or more other disciplines.

Although it is true that certain performance oriented disciplines lend themselves more easily to the design of engaging activities, it is equally true that we could devise performance tasks in the areas of English Language Arts, social studies, science, foreign language, and math if we challenged ourselves to do so. It is happening. Every day more teachers, staff developers, and text book writers are designing performance tasks (with embedded assessments). That it is more difficult to design a performance activity for a student to demonstrate an understanding of a Robert Frost poem, an Ibsen play, rock formations, mathematical formulas, the jury system, the constitution, or the difference between capitalism and socialism than it is to assess a football player's grasp of his role in a game or a technology education student's ability to trouble shoot a heating system makes it no less essential.

In the real world we judge people on the basis of performance. If school is to be preparation for the real world, we must go beyond assessing a student's ability to memorize facts and formulas, and we must find ways to assess application. We can only assess the ability to apply by creating realistic performance tasks.

Harvard University's medical school and Clarkson University's business administration school have recognized the value of an authentic task approach to learning. For its medical students, Harvard has inaugurated the New Pathways curriculum, a problem-solving, case-method approach to learning, which offers the opportunity for students to come in contact with patients' cases early in their studies.

Here are excerpts from a press release issued by Clarkson's public relations department in fall 2000 about a restructured approach in its business education program:

> Many students complain that the first two years of their college education are spent in theoretical courses, the relevancy of which is often difficult to appreciate—but not Clarkson University's business students.

> The Clarkson University School of Business has initiated an innovative first-year program for business students that requires them to create, plan, and manage an actual business their very first semester at college.

> The students are not given any prior training on how to run a business and are only provided with a course manual and a professor.

"Needless to say, as in any business, the students experience both successes and failures. And it's actually the failures that pave the greater way for learning," according to Dr. Larry Compeau, director of Undergraduate Business Programs.

Students are expected to develop their own resources to accomplish the various tasks with support and guidance from the professor, but the professor is not there to do it for them.

It is the engagement of students in the authentic task that allows the professor to become a guide on the side. This same principle applies at every level of education including prekindergarten. The difference between the role of the guide on the side for a pre-k class or for a university business course is the degree of coaching and scaffolding that may be required. Obviously, for the less advanced student, more support and monitoring may be required. But that doesn't alter the essential principle that the student must be allowed to explore and then, through addressing an authentic task, must be allowed to discover (i.e., construct her own meaning).

The article continues:

The follow-up course, taken the second semester, is designed to merge a basic understanding of theory with the students' experiences in the first semester. The course is also designed to help student s ... understand the theory behind their prior business successes and failures.

"It's the 'nitty-gritty' course," says student Charis A. Spies of Redwood. "The theories that are presented, and class discussions, help us evaluate our (previous) business experiences. This course allows us to understand why certain things did or did not work last semester."

"It's hard to appreciate the years of research, work experience and thinking that lie behind a managerial theory when it's presented abstractly in a sterile environment," Compeau noted.

"In all my years of teaching, I have never had a student come to me and seriously question the applicability of theory—until now," Compeau said.

"This first-year experience is an attention-getter. Students now know first-hand how important studies will be to their ultimate success as managers. You just can't get that point across in a lecture."

For a teacher (or parent) to intervene, students must be engaged in an activity that provides the opportunity for interventions. One cannot intervene in a vacuum. The Harvard and Clarkson programs are examples of the design of an activity to provide a vehicle for teacher interventions. Note the emphasis on experience before theory.

It may be more difficult to create performance activities in math, science, English language arts, foreign language, and social studies (simply because of our unfamiliarity with strategies for accomplishing this), but is it any less necessary? We can't learn effectively without engagement, and we cannot be fairly assessed on what we've learned without being allowed to perform.

Reality Check Question

Is a science lab, as required by many high schools in the country, an example of authentic task work (and part of a discovery phase of the Two-Step)?

There is a distinct difference between traditional science labs and teaching science through an inquiry approach. In the traditional lab approach, the student is asked to follow a process by completing a series of steps to get a predetermined result. In the inquiry approach the student is given a problem and is asked to figure out how to solve the problem by conducting a student-initiated inquiry. The lab approach doesn't require the student to demonstrate understanding, whereas the inquiry-based approach does. The inquiry approach increases the likelihood for meaningful spontaneous interventions.

Reality Check Question

If the exploratory and discovery phases (including the performance task) interact to lead to student learning through discovery, is there a role for teaching other than in the lesson design?

Yes. There are two primary vehicles (types of interventions) for teacher facilitation and guidance–the planned intervention and the spontaneous intervention.

Planned Interventions

Planned interventions are designed to accomplish two things:

1. Provide *information* (the minimum amount of information) that the teacher is certain every student will need at a particular time during accomplishment of the task

2. Provide a *structure* that fosters and promotes thinking

A teacher-planned lecture; worksheet; activity; discussion; or any other method of conveying information, skills, or concepts to students that they will need to successfully complete their work are planned interventions. A guest, an assigned reading, or a brief commentary can also be planned interventions. This is where constructivist teaching techniques come in—when students have reached a specific point in working to accomplish a task. Planned interventions often involve the use of cognitive-based teaching techniques such as the development of rubrics, cooperative learning procedures (jigsaws, carousels, pair-shares), graphic organizers, journal writing, and so forth. Planned interventions can come in the exploratory or discovery phase of a lesson; however, they should be infrequent during the discovery phase because they interrupt student work on a task and they limit the opportunities to communitcate the same information through spontaneous interventions that are often more effective.

The exploratory phase of a lesson consists almost entirely of a sequence of planned interventions (activities, exercises, and dialogues designed to reveal students' prior knowledge or interests, motivate students for the discovery phase to follow, or begin to address the learning objectives that will be pursued during the discovery phase). The few spontaneous interventions, during the exploratory phase, come when student responses indicate a need for the teacher to adjust his original plan, or when the teacher identifies a teachable moment, usually because of a question posed by a student or a student response that indicates the student has an erroneous perception or misinformation.

A planned intervention is timed for when most students will need the same information and will perceive a need for the intervention. The teacher's role is to make the student want the information. The teacher accomplishes this by engaging the student in a task that cannot be completed without the information, knowledge, and competence the teacher wants the student to demonstrate.

For example, for the discovery phase of the lesson or unit, a teacher might assign students to design a project—either individually or in pairs—for display in a mall or local museum, at a fair, in the classroom, or in the school lobby. As part of an exploratory phase to help students understand their options for a performance task they will undertake during discovery, the teacher distributes a list of five possible projects (information) and adds the option that students can choose an alternative task provided the teacher approves it. The criteria for approval are that it must have similar value, involve a similar degree of complexity to the five options offered (structure), and require students to satisfactorily address the teacher's learning objectives for the lesson.

1. The teacher's first planned intervention is an activity that allows students to brainstorm ideas and narrow their choice to two of the options (structure). After encouraging students in pairs to brainstorm ideas for a display, the teacher rotates students into groups of three, several times, to share their ideas and see what others are developing (structure). The reason for this planned intervention is to allow students to benefit from each others' ideas, generate reactions to their own, and motivate students to engage in a task that will address the teacher's learning objectives through options that enable the student to choose the best method for demonstrating competence.

2. The second planned intervention comes at the start of the discovery phase, after students have made a final determination of the project they will create, and after the teacher has allowed them a few minutes to begin to draft a plan and timeline for their project (structure). The teacher now distributes the official guidelines (information), allows a few minutes for students to study the guidelines, then puts the students in groups of three, and asks them to agree on three questions they have about the guidelines (structure).

Planned Interventions Anticipate Student Needs

Why did the teacher design these two planned interventions—interventions the teacher knew she would make even before the lesson began?

In each case, the teacher felt that almost everyone in the class would benefit from the interventions *and* would see the need. (Of course, the teacher could have changed her mind if the observations of student work indicated revisions were needed.) The teacher's assessment was that most students would be reluctant to lock in on a project and might be unclear what was intended by each of the listed options. That is why the teacher created, as a planned intervention, (1) an activity that would require students to think about, and articulate, possible options. The dialogue with each other would mandate student thinking about their projects and generate an exchange of thoughts prior to final selection.

The planned intervention (2) to discuss guidelines was designed because it was apparent to the teacher that each student would need to understand the guidelines for the projects before getting too far along in the planning process. The teacher wanted all the students to be hooked on their selection of a process *before* discussing the guidelines, because the guidelines would have less perceived relevance for the students prior to their selection of a project.

Planned interventions are built into a lesson (or unit) design based on:

◆ The teacher's assessment of students' prior knowledge and interests

◆ The likelihood that most students will perceive the need for the information to be imparted during the planned intervention

◆ The teacher's knowledge of what teaching techniques foster and promote thinking

The teacher uses *cognitive-based teaching techniques*, such as various cooperative learning procedures, to stimulate thinking and motivation. The teacher needs to determine the approximate point at which most students can be expected to understand their task (although not necessarily how to go about it) and will be motivated to want to complete the task. This is the point at which the teacher should provide information in the form of a planned intervention.

If the teacher is to err, she should err on the side of a too brief, rather than too lengthy, planned intervention. Turn the students loose too soon, rather than after boring them with information they either don't need or won't grasp.

If you provide too little guidance on how to accomplish the task, you can compensate through spontaneous interventions with individuals or small groups, provided you work the room and accurately assess student progress on the task. You don't want to allow students to continue too long if they need more support than you have provided to sustain the intrinsic motivation. If you provide too little guidance, and it becomes clear as you work the room that few if any of the students understand how to go about their task, you can always improvise a spontaneous intervention for the entire class.

A second example: In a mathematics class, the teacher, Mrs. Mooney, suspects that the students are readily using the quantity pi, but don't really have a meaning for it in their minds. She sets understanding pi as the learning objective and explaining its use in several formulas as the assessment. Each group will be required to make a presentation of how they determined what pi was and what it means and, after exploring what they already know and/or can verbalize, they will work on developing their presentations.

About fifteen minutes into their work, Mrs. Mooney takes an idea drawn from an overheard comment and combines it with a question that she had planned to ask the groups. She has them stop their work and conduct a brief investigation. The inquiry takes this form:

each group randomly cuts various lengths of string, measures them with a ruler, and then creates a circle from each piece of the string. The students will then know the perimeter. They can then also measure the radius and compute the mathematical relationship between the two. In a few minutes, the groups have compiled a list of twenty different numbers, ranging from 2.96 to 3.23. When one of the students asks about the average of the numbers, they figure it out as 3.148, or almost the value of pi in the book. Suddenly, the students want to get back in their groups to work on their presentations a little more.

The calculation investigation was a planned intervention here—a task or comment aimed at provoking student thought in a directed way. It worked like a charm; it gave the confused but engaged students direction and a powerful experience to help them make sense of the work they were doing.

As they finished their preparations and during the actual presentations, further comments by the teacher would be spontaneous interventions.

A third example: The students' task is to prepare a demonstration of their understanding of the significance of major events during the industrial revolution. The teacher speaks for fifteen minutes on the significance of six major events during the industrial revolution in Britain (this is a planned intervention for the purpose of providing information). The students take notes. Then students begin work in their groups, or individually, depending on the option they have selected for demonstrating their understanding of the industrial revolution. The reason for this "planned intervention"—speaking on the significance of six major events that occurred during the industrial revolution—was the teacher's judgment that the students would need some guidance to determine what types of events could be considered significant during the industrial revolution. The teacher wanted to leave plenty of room for student initiative and discovery, therefore, the teacher did not go into great detail, but he did highlight six major events and suggest why they were considered significant.

Was fifteen minutes sufficient time to enable every student to fully grasp how to go about the task? No. However, it was sufficient for many students to get a handle on the assignment. By limiting the "planned intervention" to 15 minutes the teacher was avoiding the risk of redundancy for those students who wouldn't need more guidance. By working the room as the students began their efforts, the teacher would be able to identify those students who needed more guidance and could provide it to them individually or in small groups.

As soon as the teacher completes his lecture, he turns the students loose to continue their work. Now is the critical moment to "work the room." The teacher walks from group to group overhearing discussions. The teacher looks over the shoulders of students working alone. As the teacher is satisfied that a student, or group, is on task and understanding its next steps, the teacher continues to another group or individual. If it becomes clear that a student or group is off track, the teacher makes a spontaneous intervention: "If you have several options for demonstrating your understanding of the industrial revolution, what questions must you address and in what order?" the teacher might ask. The teacher stays with this group of students until they have a plan for their work over the next few minutes, or the entire period, or longer. If the teacher is unsure whether a group or individual is working effectively, he may ask, "What are you working on? What do you plan to do next?"

Sometimes, as the teacher works the room, students, upon seeing the teacher nearby, will ask a question—"Ms. Johnson, is this what we should be doing?" The student question creates an opportunity for a spontaneous intervention (a teachable moment).

If the teacher notices that most groups are encountering a similar obstacle, or misconception, the teacher may make a *spontaneous intervention* by making an observation (or giving a mini lecture) to the entire class. However, having seen that the spontaneous intervention (the lecture) was needed, the next time the teacher uses the same activity, he may build in the same lecture as a planned intervention.

Spontaneous Interventions

A teacher response to a student question is a spontaneous intervention. A teacher intervention with an individual or small group of students based on the teacher's assessment that the information is needed and will be well received is also a spontaneous intervention. Spontaneous interventions are teacher responses, usually to individual or small group needs, provided as the opportunities present themselves. Spontaneous interventions are the times the teacher seizes a "teachable moment," intervening when a student is seen wrestling with an obstacle while working on a task, or by responding to a question posed by a student who recognizes the need for help with her task.

During the *discovery* phase, the teacher observation and monitoring must be on-going. The teacher must constantly assess student work as students address the learning objectives/core curriculum that are the focus of the task. It is this on-going teacher assessment that enables the teacher to know when spontaneous interventions are required.

Example: The teacher overhears a student, working in a group of three, express frustration that the textbook has so little information about Dr. Charles Drew. As a spontaneous intervention, the teacher might intervene by asking, "What other resources could you explore for information on Dr. Drew? If the student is unable to respond, the teacher might prompt by inquiring if the student has checked the biographical dictionary in the library, or the encyclopedia, or if the student has done an Internet search? When to intervene and whether to ask open ended questions or offer prompts are decisions the teacher makes as she "works the room."

Doesn't most learning in sports come through spontaneous interventions during practices and games? In fact, we call the person who often makes suggestions, through spontaneous interventions, the "coach." Players learn some things through experience and others when the coach intervenes. This is why the teacher needs to view herself as a coach. However, to set the stage for spontaneous interventions, the coach needs to engage players (students) in a game or rehearsal (practice) which educators refer to as an "authentic task." The differences between a planned and a spontaneous intervention are:

♦ A planned intervention usually involves the entire class. It is designed to address a need that the teacher anticipates will be perceived by most or all of the class. If the teacher anticipates that a few students will need information, suggestions, or micromanaging, then these prompts are offered through spontaneous interventions limited to the students, or groups, in need.

♦ A planned intervention is part of the teacher's lesson plan, is planned before the lesson begins, and is altered or eliminated only if teacher observation indicates it is not needed.

♦ A spontaneous intervention is offered when a teacher, through observation of group or individual work, or in reaction to student responses during class dialogue, identifies a need that

  • wasn't anticipated when the lesson was designed.

  • or, was anticipated but wouldn't have been understood or accepted by students unless the teacher waited until the student, while engaging in a task, came to the self realization that the information or assistance was needed.

  • or, was anticipated by the teacher, but with the recognition that not every student in the class would need the assistance offered through a planned intervention. In other words, the teacher knew that some students would require an intervention so rather than force the information on all students, the teacher waited until the class was engaged in group and/or individual work and then offered spontaneous interventions to those in need.

Reading this section may remind some of you of your days as a football player, soccer player, or basketball player, or perhaps you've seen one of the many movies depicting a coach's *chalk talk*, where the coach pulls all the players together to discuss the big picture and how everything fits together and the role of each member in pulling off the play. These chalk talks are planned interventions, in particular, when a new play is introduced and when a team's execution of a previously attempted play is analyzed.

In the latter case, the planned intervention of the chalk talk may be the result of many observations of the performance of the team in practice or from analyzing game films. It may have been preceded by several spontaneous interventions by the coach with individual players with regard to the play in question. At some point, the coach makes the decision that there is information that needs to be shared with the entire team to help the team accomplish its authentic task (preparing for the next game). Furthermore, by introducing the information (the big picture and how everything fits together) to the entire team at the same time, through a planned intervention (chalk talk), the coach is deciding it will be more effective to share the information with everyone, at once, rather than as spontaneous interventions with individuals or small groups at times deemed appropriate by the coaching staff.

Teacher Observation Is Valid Assessment

Too often, teachers overlook *teacher observation* and *judgment* as a legitimate form of assessment, yet they are the critical components for effective use of spontaneous interventions. Teachers are trained professionals. Their observations should play a major role in assessment during hands-on instruction. Would you trust your care to a doctor who refused to let her professional judgment play a role in diagnosis and treatment? Is there a doctor worth two bits who would rely solely on machine-furnished test results, blood work, and other scientific methods available to medical practitioners, and not include professional observation and probing as part of the process by which she makes a professional judgment?

Technology and cognitive-based teaching techniques that foster and promote student thinking, such as rubrics, portfolios, group work, reflective activities and the like, give teachers a much greater arsenal for teaching and assessing. These cognitive-based teaching techniques provide teachers with increased opportunities for student observation—opportunities to use what they know about how students learn to gather evidence of how well students are achieving learning objectives/core curriculum.

Often the teacher cannot prepare for a spontaneous intervention—you simply know that the opportunities will arise because students have been turned loose on a task, and you know they don't have enough information to successfully complete the task. However, as a teacher or parent, you can ask yourself, "What questions might someone have about how to complete the task?" Then you can plan to have probing responses to these questions when they come up—responses that keep the learner in the driver's seat, still driving in a searching way. "Certainty ends inquiry," (according to Martin Buber). If the role of the teacher is to promote inquiry, then providing the answer is not the route. Challenging the student with a motivating question is preferred.

For example, two fourth grade teachers combined their classes into one large group of 40 students, distributed the recipe for blueberry pudding from *Farmer Boy*, put students in groups of eight, and asked them to figure out how much each ingredient of the recipe would have to be increased to make pudding for the entire class. The recipe was for eight people. In one instance the recipe called for three-fourths of a cup. Each group of students approached this problem differently, and one student asked the teacher for a measuring cup. This allowed the teacher to make a spontaneous intervention. He could have simply said, "We don't have one," or "I want you to do the figuring on paper." Instead, he located a measuring cup, handed it to the student, and watched as the students poured a liquid into three-fourths of the cup, emptied it into another container and kept track of the total as they completed the function five times. As the teacher observed, she found opportunities to ask questions to guide the students toward correlating the data they were gathering with multiplication of fractions that might save them time in the future.

Spontaneous Interventions are spontaneous in that they come up at different times for different students; they may not come up at all for certain students. For example, in an authentic task involving the use of a PowerPoint presentation, some students may already have proficiency with PowerPoint presentations and access to the technology, some students may obtain what they need to know about PowerPoint from other members of the group, and some students may come to the teacher to request information about PowerPoint, thus giving the teacher the opportunity for spontaneous interventions. If the teacher is effectively assessing student performance, then even when students who need information about PowerPoint (or access to the technology) do not take the initiative to ask, they may be receptive to a spontaneous intervention such as, "Bill, does your group need help figuring out how to prepare a PowerPoint presentation?"

Individualize Instruction with Spontaneous Interventions

Think about this: In a traditional classroom, we would require the entire class to sit passively, listening to our dissertation on how to do a PowerPoint presentation and how to access the technology. In reality, maybe two-thirds of the class already have this information or are capable of and willing to seek it out for themselves. In a constructivist classroom, not only does the teacher avoid boring two-thirds of the class with PowerPoint information, but the teacher can more effectively communicate the information to Bill's group when she is able to sit down with just the four of them, observe their body language, and personalize her responses.

What is the connection between spontaneous interventions and the exploratory and discovery phases of a lesson? If the teacher is conducting a teacher-centered lesson and is doing most of the talking, there are infrequent opportunities for teachable moments to arise. We all know a teachable moment when it appears, but it appears all too infrequently. Why? Because the student (in the class) or the child (at home) must be motivated to want information. The teachable moment usually occurs when a child is seeking to discover or create and is confronted with an obstacle. This is when the learner is receptive to information—when it will help the learner overcome an obstacle the learner feels a need to overcome.

If the learner is listening passively to an adult speak, or is engaged in activity only to the extent of reacting to commands and following directions, it is less likely that the learner will seek out the teacher for much information other than, "What do I need to do to get the grade I want on this assignment?" Sure, there are teachable moments in any class. An inquisitive student can approach a teacher after a teacher-directed lesson and ask, "Can a virus get a virus?" or "Why does sugar dissolve in water, but oil does not?" These are teachable moments, but how often do they occur when students are not challenged to think?

Think about the concept of interventions logically. When we teach a child to ride a bike, don't we put the child on the bike and run alongside? Doesn't our teaching occur through interventions as we note what the child is doing well and what needs to be improved? When we teach a child to swim, how long do we lecture before we actually allow the child to get in the water?

Once we have engaged the biker or swimmer in performance, we often make spontaneous interventions, but our interventions are informed by our observations of the learner's performance. In schools, we lecture everyone with information only a few may need and in a context that few if any of our students can relate to. Isn't it easier to show the swimmer how to use her arms, and then observe how she uses her arms in the water, than to explain it to a potential swimmer who has never been in the water and cannot visualize what you mean by "strokes" and "head movement" and "kicking"?

If it is information we are offering the swimmer (e.g., "Lift your arms out of the water as you stroke"), won't this information be more readily received and applied if it is offered while the swimmer is in the water struggling, or after the swimmer has struggled and is reflecting on her performance, rather than if it is offered beforehand when the swimmer has no point of reference in her experience?

Yes, the English teacher makes interventions when grading an essay, and the social studies teacher makes interventions through comments on an historical report. However, if the student is not motivated to care about the assignment (other than for a grade), then the student learning from the intervention will not be the same as the swimmer or biker who is motivated by the desire to swim or ride. In other words, we must use authentic tasks to motivate students to engage in performance so that we create opportunities for interventions that will be meaningful.

A teacher, parent, or staff developer should not be too self-critical the first time using a particular Two-Step lesson or unit. Your ability to know what planned interventions to use, and when, will improve once you have seen student (child) reactions to the lesson the first time you use it.

Also, the first time you implement a lesson or unit, you may be frequently surprised at the kinds of spontaneous interventions you feel compelled to offer. However, as you gain experience with the Two-Step process, and as you gain experience with a particular lesson or unit, patterns will emerge that will make the kinds of spontaneous interventions that are necessary more predictable.

Sometimes, the only difference between a planned intervention and a spontaneous intervention is timing. Perhaps you did not build in a mini-lecture or reading because you weren't sure most of your students would need it. However, as you work the room, you notice that most students are missing (and having difficulty locating) the same information, or are running amok with the same obstacle, or are asking the same question. You may insert, as a spontaneous intervention for the entire class, an activity that you, in the future, will design for another situation as a planned intervention.

The key to knowing when to use a planned intervention is in accurately assessing your students' prior knowledge and interests. The key to knowing when to use spontaneous interventions—and whether to use them with individuals, groups, or the entire class—is your ability to work the room and accurately assess how well or poorly each student is proceeding with the authentic task (in the discovery phase of the lesson).

Spontaneous interventions need to motivate and support students. They should not provide students with answers, but they may provide information that a student needs to continue his journey toward an answer. For example, if a student is writing a story for publication, he may ask the teacher, "Do I use *to* or *two* in the sentence, 'Jack has 2 uncles?'" The teacher needs to determine whether a major goal is usage of the correct spelling of the number 2, in which case the response may be, "What is the rule for usage of *to, too,* and *two*?"

Or, the teacher may decide there is sufficient value in having the student recognize the need to pose the question and that it is better to provide the correct answer, expecting that the student will now remember it because of the authentic context and thus allowing the student to proceed with the journey toward completion of the task, writing the story.

While planned interventions are often specifically designed to provide information when students perceive a need for it, spontaneous interventions often serve one of three purposes:

1. Keeping the thinking task going (cognitive-based)

2. Establishing a comfort level

3. Providing information

♦ **Cognitive-based spontaneous interventions** are designed to keep the thinking processes going rather than structure the task. Peruse this set of questions that were asked as a business teacher "worked the room" while students were creating a set of advertisements for an invention they had designed:

- "Wouldn't that make the tool itself obsolete? Nobody would ever have to buy a second one; people could borrow other people's; what would happen to sales then?

- "Is this the kind of thing that would motivate people to buy it all over the country? Would this ad only appeal to people from our geographic region?

- "I think that Proctor & Gamble has something like that: what if your creation was just like that of another company?

- "Do you think that this ad would catch the eyes of both men and women? Who do you want to see this and think "I gotta have it!"?

In each case, the point of the question is to redirect student thinking and try to encourage students to reexamine their ideas and their work.

♦ **Comfort-level based spontaneous interventions** are designed to reassure students that their uncertainty about an answer is not an indication of their wrong-headedness. Here are three examples of comfort-level based spontaneous interventions:

- "Your confusion about how to proceed with this task is understandable. In previous years, those students who did figure out how to remove the tree limb without having it fall on the house took at least a few hours to develop their hypothesis, and then it required quite a bit more time to document their responses and prepare them in the format I have requested. If you give it your best effort, I will provide hints along the way, if necessary. But, first, I want you to come up with a hypothesis."

- Or, students working on a task involving the flooding of the Nile speculate it could lead to a food scarcity, but they're not sure how that would affect people. The teacher intervenes to suggest other sources of information that will confirm their conclusions and assumptions.

- Or students engaged in a task, ask the teacher if they are on the right track and are given reassurance that they are.

♦ **Information-based spontaneous interventions** are designed to provide information at the time the student perceives the need for it, rather than at the beginning of the lesson when it might unnecessarily slow the student's journey toward accomplishing an authentic task and might decrease student motivation to continue the journey. For example, if students are about to engage in the authentic task of scripting and performing a mock discussion between Booker T. Washington and W.E.B. Dubois for a school assembly, it might detract from their interest if the teacher began with a lengthy lecture on the format to be followed in writing the script. Also, the level of student experience with script writing may vary greatly among the students in the class, and a lecture aimed at every student could bore some while still being too advanced for others.

Instead, the teacher might encourage the students to outline their ideas and allow their enthusiasm to grow over the plot outlines they are developing. As the teacher works the room and perhaps reviews a draft outline that students are required to submit, he will get a clearer idea of whether most students need coaching on the appropriate format for a script and to what degree the need exists. Possibly, only a few students will need such coaching, and it may be offered by their peers as they work on the task. Or, it may become obvious to the teacher that there is little script writing expertise in the class, in which case a somewhat prolonged intervention, possibly in the form of a lecture, may be appropriate.

One of the teacher's ultimate objectives is to move the student to create internal dialogues, a protocol of self-interventions or, if you will, ongoing reflections. A good teacher must continually address the following questions:

♦ Am I requiring my students to think? If so, how deeply? How insightfully?

♦ How do I know they are thinking?

♦ What is the evidence that my students are thinking?

♦ Are just a few students giving evidence of thinking, or am I really challenging every student to think?

Hooks for Our Thoughts:

Constructivist approaches, using teacher interventions, offer opportunities for teachers to help students create hooks for their thoughts.

We all need hooks to hang our thoughts on, for example:

♦ I remember an Orson Welles movie, whose title I often forget, by reminding myself that "I will raise cane with myself if I can't remember it. That's right—*Citizen Kane.*

♦ "i before e except after c" gives me a hook to hang my thoughts on when I am trying to spell certain words.

The hooks can be words (raise cane), experiences, mnemonic devices, or cute expressions (i before e except after c).

Unfortunately, most of the time we teach, whether in school or at home, we try to teach (preach) before giving learners hooks to hang their thoughts on. I, as the lecturer, have hooks for the thoughts I express, but I fail to recognize that the learners need to create (or we need to help provide) their own hooks for the thoughts I will express. Often, the hooks we hang our thoughts on are activities in which we once engaged. When a lecture can connect content to an experience or to our prior knowledge, this can create the hook for our remembrance.

"Drink fluids," I tell my daughter, "or you won't get well quickly." This gives my child no hooks on which to hang her thoughts.

Instead, if I tell the story of the time her older brother had to go to the hospital and have a needle placed in his arm for intravenous feeding because he didn't drink a sufficient amount of fluids when he was sick with the flu," now I am providing some hooks. This is a concrete example we can discuss while analyzing the consequences of not drinking enough fluids. At a future time, all I need to say is, "Remember your brother and the intravenous fluids," and it will conjure up an image in my child's mind.

In a video of a 30-year veteran award-winning teacher, Miss Toliver leads her middle school math class through New York City streets and asks them to identify math symbols, count the steps in front of a building, and create maps to places in the city near the school that require the use of math or integrate math into their physical structure. One of her students identifies a right angle in the formation of two branches in a tree. The author carries that image of the two branches coming together into a 90-degree angle as a hook to hang his thoughts on whenever he thinks of that video. For many of Miss Toliver's students, the image of those two branches coming together is the hook for remembering a right angle.

We seem to have a natural inclination to explain what someone must do before letting them do it. "You are about to ride a bike. Here is what you have to know about riding a bike." While we are saying this, the child is getting antsy in anticipation of riding the bike, absorbs little if anything of what we say, and keeps interrupting with "I know, I know, just let me ride."

Well, the child doesn't know, and we all know the child doesn't know, but the child won't listen. We are not suggesting that you let the child ride alone to experience the frustration of falling down and possibly getting hurt. But when you finish your lecture, you are going to put the child on the bike anyway, and you will run alongside the bike and hang onto the back of the seat, ready to control the bike if the child should falter. Why not start with this experience? When the child inevitably can't keep the bike going, now you can take a moment to preach. However, now the child will have hooks on which to hang his thoughts.

"When the bike started to waiver, that was when you needed to speed up the pedaling. Instead, understandably, you got a little scared and stopped pedaling, and that's why the bike started to fall. Next time, speed up your pedaling if you feel the bike waivering. I'll be right next to you and will catch you if you start to fall."

Reality Check Question

How does the concept of "hooks to hang our thoughts on" relate to interventions and constructivism?

Think of the bicycle example we just discussed. By putting the child on the bike first, the parent creates the opportunity for a spontaneous intervention when the child has difficulty keeping his balance and recognizes the need for coaching. The sermonette—"When the bike started to waiver, that was when you needed to speed up the pedaling"—was a spontaneous intervention. The opportunity arose only because the child was given the opportunity to experience the bicycle. The hook for remembering to speed up the pedaling the next time the bike begins to falter will be the recollection of the feeling of falling before mom grabbed the bike and helped to steady it.

Constructivist theory indicates we need to construct our own meaning and that we do this by building on our prior knowledge. Letting the child ride the bicycle does the following:

♦ Creates an opportunity for the child's prior knowledge to come to the fore

♦ Begins the process of adding new information

♦ Enables mom to become a coach through interventions as the need arises

♦ Increases the likelihood that mom's coaching will be well received and remembered because the experience (beginning to fall) becomes the hook for recall

Think of the lacrosse coach who is able to get so much across by referring to what he observed during the last practice or by referencing what happened in the last game. Think of the play director who teaches by explaining what could have been done to improve the last scene that was rehearsed: "Jack, you turned left and then crossed the stage with your back to us. Instead, you need to turn right so that we can see you."

A teacher lectured for 20 minutes on how liquids become solids and how solids become liquids. Some of the students were able to remember enough to pass the test; none really understood much of what had been said. Perhaps she could have brought something frozen into class, let it thaw, and then begun the lesson by asking, "What happened to the block of ice, and why?" Later, the teacher could have given the same 20-minute lecture, but we suspect that the retention rate and the level of understanding of most students would have been significantly higher. The visual demonstration would have given the students hooks to hang their thoughts on, and it would have created a common reference point for the teacher's lecture. This is also another example of putting engagement before discussion of theory.

The high school science teacher who has students taste the water to see if the experiment removed the salt (it didn't) is giving her students hooks for their thoughts. The social studies teacher who dramatizes Abraham Lincoln's use of an envelope on the train to explain how the Gettysburg Address was written is creating hooks for his students. Once again, in each example, students are being actively engaged before explanation and amplification. Most of us are able to understand theory *after* we have built hooks on which to hang our thoughts. As Dewey said, "Experience precedes understanding."

Thoughts for Reflection

Coach Spence taught in the upbeat, vibrant manner of a coach and was energetic in a way that made you pay attention. He also related moments in history to quotes from movies like *The Blues Brothers*. Classic! (Jeremy Hogerson, Mamaroneck High School, 1990, 2002)

End of Session Assessment

Can you think of one planned and one spontaneous intervention you have used or seen in a classroom?

Sample Summary of a Two-Step

The following is an abbreviated version of a Two-Step for seventh and eleventh grade social studies. A more complete example of this same lesson appears in Appendix A.

Popular Name:	Explorer's Resume
Grade Level:	7th and 11th
Discipline:	Social Studies

Standards:

♦ ELA: Students will make effective use of details, evidence, and arguments and presentation strategies to influence an audience to adopt their position.

♦ SS: Students will investigate the role of individuals and groups in relation to key social, political, and cultural, and religious practices throughout world history.

Learning Objectives: Students will:

♦ Engage in historical research

♦ Make a persuasive presentation based on historical research.

EXPLORATORY PHASE:

♦ As a class, students will select three popular figures.

♦ As groups, students will develop a job resume for one the three popular figures they selected. (The resumes are to be for jobs they might apply for.)

DISCOVERY PHASE:

Performance Task:

Students will assume the identity of an explorer from the Age of Exploration and will create a resume and cover letter, and will interview before a panel attempting to secure a new exploration assignment.

Learning Objectives for a Lesson

Learning Objective

The reader will come to understand that a lesson's primary learning objectives must be assessed, and the method of assessment should be made available in advance, preferably through the use of a rubric. In the Two-Step model the taxonomy of learning objectives includes information, knowledge, and competence. A fourth learning objective, creative competence, should not be assessed; however, a good lesson should inspire it. See Figure 2.10.

Figure 2.10   Discovery Phase

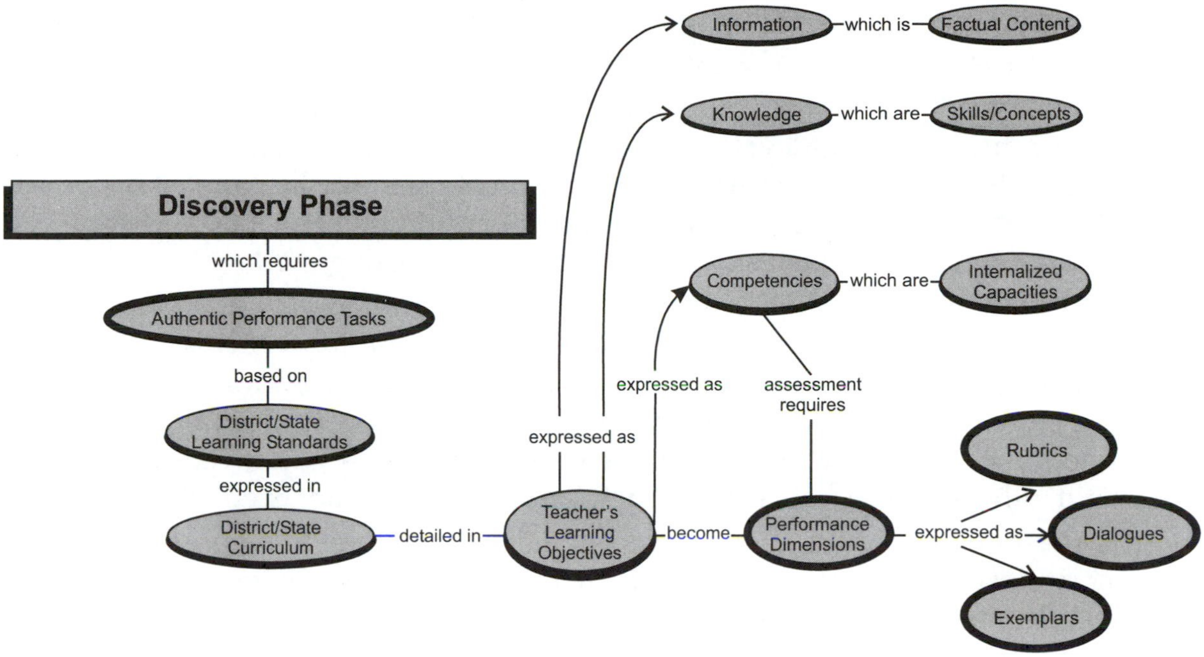

Main Points

♦ Effective lessons focus on specific learning objectives.

♦ Teachers need to distinguish between the learning objectives they have for all students and additional secondary learning objectives students may achieve as the result of a well-designed lesson.

♦ The learning objectives all students are to achieve are the primary learning objectives of the lesson.

♦ The primary learning objectives are tied directly to a state (or province's) learning standards and indicators, which are more specifically expressed in the core curriculum.

♦ Primary learning objectives are the ones to be assessed.

♦ The criteria used to assess these primary objectives should be spelled out in a scoring device called a *rubric*, which should be available in advance of the lesson to students, parents, and other teachers.

The components of the *two-step* model are exploration and discovery. A lesson becomes standards-based when the exploratory and discovery phases are designed to focus students on a limited number of learning objectives and when student performance, during the discovery phase, is assessed with regard to their performance with these objectives.

Suppose a lesson challenges students to read (or listen to) "The Lady and the Tiger," the classic story in which a woman is left with the choice of sending the man she loves to be united with another woman (one he loves) or eaten by a tiger. Then the lesson requires them to name two main characters and three characteristics of each, and to identify two sentences that give important information about the setting. Now, ask the teacher, "What were your learning objectives? What did you want students to learn from this lesson?"

After a thoughtful pause of anywhere from 20 seconds to two minutes, the responses will flow. Depending on the age level of the students, any or all of the following may be cited as learning objectives by the teacher: reading comprehension (or listening skills); understanding that plot, character, conflict, and setting are important elements of a story; a few vocabulary words, character analysis; comparing and contrasting; writing techniques; and techniques for describing the environment.

Most of these are what the author refers to as *secondary learning objectives*, which comprise information, skills, or concepts that students may (or may not) address and learn as a consequence of the lesson. A good performance task/assessment exposes students to a variety of secondary learning objectives. With regard to a particular objective, some students may master it, others may learn a little about it, and others may not even address it.

A *primary learning objective* is an objective that the teacher requires every student to master. A primary objective is assessed by the teacher for the purpose of determining whether students met the minimum standards for that objective. A *secondary* learning objective can be *primary* if the teacher assesses for it and requires that every student will master it at least at a specified minimum level.

In the Lady and the Tiger example, perhaps the primary learning objectives are student mastery of three vocabulary words and the critical thinking skills reflected in students' abilities to complete the ending of the story. Or, perhaps the primary learning objectives are student mastery of six vocabulary words and the ability to identify characteristics that define a character in a story.

There is no magical formula that says what a teacher's primary learning objectives for a lesson should be. The primary learning objectives are the objectives the teacher sets as the minimum requirement for all students participating in the lesson; the primary learning objectives are assessed so that the teacher knows which students have met the minimum standards for those objectives. What we are suggesting is that a teacher should have primary learning objectives and should identify them for herself and her students in advance, often through use of a rubric. Clearly, the identification of primary learningobjectives is a way to be sure during the course of a lesson that local, state (provincial), or national standards are being addressed.

Despite the popularity of Stephen Covey's book, *Seven Habits of Highly Effective People*, which includes constant admonitions to focus on goals, few good teachers have goals that are specific enough for assessment of student performance.

In 1998, an author met with 18 teachers who had worked on a river project the previous year with outstanding results. Students had been motivated to engage in a variety of disciplines by the enticement of at least one trip to a local waterway for the purposes of scientific inquiry, mathematical calculations, writing, and/or artistic expression. Each teacher was given a water-testing kit, a camera, and film and was asked to create some kind of project that involved an excursion to a local waterway. The reaction of the students to the river project, and the gut level assessment of student learning by teachers, made it clear the project was successful. One inner-city teacher observed, "I've been teaching for 25 years, and I realize now that I have to change. My students were so eager to complete their project in time for the public display at the mall that I was able to teach more in a few weeks than I usually cover in a year. If I hadn't seen it with my own students, I wouldn't have believed it."

Yet, when these teachers were asked to reflect specifically on what students had learned through their participation, there was a minute, at least, of dramatic silence. Finally, a laundry list of student learning objectives that were achieved began to flow from the mouths of the 18 teachers. They began responding, out loud:

- Analyzing

- Hypothesizing

- Water quality conditions

- Creative writing

- Layout

- Estimation

- Laws of gravity

- Facts about trees

- Facts about evolution

- Information about bodies of water

- Knowledge of and competence with photography

- Artistic design

Since this experience, the authors have questioned teachers more frequently about their learning objectives. Invariably, they cannot identify a limited number of learning objectives that were the focus of the lesson. After reflecting for a minute or two, as with the river project teachers, most teachers can reel off a host of facts, concepts, and skills addressed by students, but rarely can they list a limited number of objectives they had identified for student work prior to the lesson and a method of assessment that would let the teacher know which students satisfactorily addressed the primary objectives of the lesson.

In effect, most good teachers are satisfied with the awareness that they exposed all their students to a variety of learning objectives required by the curriculum, and the assumption is that some of what the students were exposed to will stick in varying degrees with most students. This is not the same as saying, "I expect every student to demonstrate this minimum understanding or these applications of knowledge; and beyond that I am confident that learning will occur in varying degrees depending on the student."

This may explain why so many teachers are ignoring, or paying limited lip service to, state standards, even though 49 of the 50 states have standards and the 50th state, Iowa, requires every district to have its own standards. Teachers are generally satisfied with knowing, in their gut, that they are teaching what students need to learn, but they seldom focus in on narrower, assessable objectives for each lesson. Most teachers are content to let the teacher-made short-answer/essay tests and the standardized tests (whether reliable or not) assess student performance. However, neither the teacher-made short-answer/essay tests nor the standardized assessments tell a teacher what the student is learning in his class. They are not an effective guide for indicating a student's day-to-day progress. A recent conversation with an award-winning teacher contained the following dialogue:

Teacher: I think the design of assessments for an aligned curriculum should be a relatively low priority.

Author: Isn't it critical that each teacher, and the administrators and parents, know exactly how student mastery of learning objectives will be assessed so that teacher expectations at each grade level are clear to everyone else in the system, including students?

Teacher: That can be accomplished by simply listing the learning objectives.

Author: But how will you know if a student is meeting your objectives?

Teacher: It's usually obvious.

Author: I know you are an outstanding teacher. You have been using group work and portfolios and reflective activities long before other teachers have been urged to utilize these strategies. How do you know whether your students are meeting your objectives?

Teacher: By walking around during group work and reviewing their work.

Author: What do you look for? How do you assess? How do you know if they are meeting your objectives?

Teacher: Ultimately, I know what my students are learning when I see the end-of-the-year test scores.

In actuality, the end-of-the-year tests do not tell the teacher what the student learned during 10 months in his class. End-of-the-year tests, if they are valid and reliable, reflect what a student knows, cumulatively—including, but not limited to, what the student has learned in class. What is needed is ongoing feedback to pinpoint what the teacher needs to do to ensure all students are learning—feedback that lets the teacher know what needs to be scaffolded with additional learning experiences and interventions. To do this a teacher needs to have specific learning objectives and the opportunity to observe student performance. While gut level assessments of student understanding and application are reasonably accurate in a good teacher (because they do have expertise in exercising professional judgment), the accuracy is not what it should be, considering the potential that now exists for assessing student learning through multiple forms of assessment that take into account the differing learning styles and multiple intelligences of all human beings.

Before the discovery of the x-ray, doctors were reasonably accurate with medical diagnoses, but they would be fools to ignore the increased precision possible with technology that now exists. Teachers cannot really know if their students are meeting their learning objectives unless they use a scoring mechanism, such as a rubric, that focuses on identified learning objectives for a lesson.

Learning objectives must be aligned with the assessment, and that is what creates a focus for the teacher, student, parent, and others. What you absolutely insist your students learn are your primary learning objectives, and they should be assessed. Additional learning objectives addressed by students (but not part of your limited set of primary objectives and not assessed) are a bonus of a good lesson. We are calling them secondary learning objectives. The primary learning objectives should be aligned with the dimensions (left column) of your rubric. (For examples, see Appendix A and note the correlation between the learning objectives and the dimensions in the rubrics.)

Most teachers end their planning process with the step that should be the beginning. They think of all the objectives that can be achieved by a student undertaking a task. For example, they may be assessing for student work with multiplication and comparison/contrast, but they realize that the lesson will encourage students to analyze, synthesize, add, subtract, and study a number of facts. This is what we refer to as the laundry list—the list of all possible objectives that can be achieved by students engaged in the lesson (or task).

This is a very difficult concept for many to grasp, perhaps because it calls for a different way of thinking. A dialogue with an excellent secondary school teacher will serve as an illustration:

Author: You said that you were teaching "Tom Sawyer": What are your learning objectives?

Teacher: Students will demonstrate their ability to work in groups.

Author: But your Tom Sawyer activity offers a rubric that assesses students' mastery of concepts related to history.

Teacher: That is because they will learn a lot about history in the activity as well.

Author: Then why not list your learning objectives in terms of the history related concepts you expect students to learn, and not the group work?

Teacher: Because group work is also important…every survey of the private sector says so!

Author: Then why not design a rubric for the group work rather than the history?

Teacher: Because the history is also important.

Author: I am suggesting you do one of three things:

◆ If history is going to be your focus, then list the concepts relating to history as your learning objectives, assess student performance with a rubric that sets quality standards for what you expect students to understand about history, and consider the group work as a valuable part of the lesson, which will not be assessed, but which will provide worthwhile practice for the students.

♦ Or, If the group work is going to be your focus, then list the group work concepts as your learning objectives, assess student performance with a rubric that sets quality standards for group work and consider the history as a valuable part of the lesson that will not be assessed, but that will provide worthwhile practice for the students.

♦ Or, list both group work and history as learning objectives and design a rubric to assess student performance with regard to group work and another rubric to assess student understanding of the history related concepts you expect them to grasp.

Here is a brief example of a teacher seeing the light bulb go on with regard to differentiating between primary and secondary learning objectives. A veteran teacher in Delaware, obviously skilled and effective, participated in a one-year training sequence to design constructivist units for use on a statewide web site. Halfway through the year, during a work session, she called over a consultant and exclaimed, "I think I finally have it. If I understand what you have been saying, I don't need a rubric for everything the students can possibly learn by engaging in my unit. I am so relieved. I have been thinking that I had to assess everything the students learn, and I couldn't figure out where I could get the time to do that."

This teacher had finally grasped the difference between primary learning objectives (referred to in this book simply as learning objectives) and secondary learning objectives.

Although all students are accountable for mastering a lesson's primary objectives, students may address different secondary learning objectives depending on the options offered by the teacher. For example, one student, Samantha, met her requirements for accomplishing a task that engaged her in addressing primary learning objectives for technology (PowerPoint skill) and critical thinking (analysis) by researching and writing a report on how horses give birth and what happens in the early years of development of the foal.

Although knowledge and understandings about horses were not part of the teacher's primary learning objectives for the class (only PowerPoint proficiency and analytical ability were assessed), what Samantha learned about horses constituted secondary learning objectives, which were a consequence of the discovery phase of the lesson. In fact, you could even label her mastery of knowledge of horses as unintended learning objectives, which we will address briefly at the end of this section. Other students, depending on options they elected, would certainly have achieved learning objectives that Samantha would not have addressed, but they might not have learned anything about horses.

Often, as in the case with Samantha, the teacher who designed the lesson did not intend some of the secondary learning objectives that were achieved by some or all of the students. Although the kinds of secondary objectives that some students will achieve are not always predictable, what is predictable is that in a good lesson the door is open to students' accomplishing a variety of unintended, but extremely worthwhile, learning objectives. The author's references to learning objectives relate to those objectives the teacher intends for all students (when designing the lesson) and those objectives for student learning that are assessed on the basis of student performance and/or products.

Many experts have defined and classified learning objectives in different ways. The authors find that anything that a student might learn, or a teacher might want to teach, can be classified in one of three categories: information, knowledge (skills and concepts), or competencies.

Information

Information comprises facts, formulas, and data that can be memorized without necessarily being understood. Examples of information include causes of a particular war, inventors, the Pythagorean Theorem, Darwin's theory of evolution, the names of the characters in "The Charge of the Light Brigade," i before e except after c, three songs by the Beatles, the names of two famous painters, how Supreme Court justices are appointed, and why the social security system was created. Information is vital to effective use of skills, conceptualization, and competent performance.

However, information by itself has limitations. Dr. John Hall, recently retired as a professor at St. Lawrence University, often quoted one of his instructors as saying, "We fail students in June for forgetting what the students who pass will forget by September."

Information is most valuable when it is used to understand concepts and when applied skillfully in a competent performance. Much of what we do in school, however, is wasted time. Mastery for the test—information that is kept for a short time for test purposes only and requires no personal engagement is de facto a waste of time.

The author's wife, a resource room teacher working with special education students, relishes those days when school is closed due to weather as much as the students do. Yet, on a Thursday, she will express fear of a possible school closing the next day, because "I drilled the kids for their test today, and they'll never remember the information through the weekend." She says this, recognizing that there is little value to the student in studying material that will be lost to them forever within 48 hours. This is why special education teachers often value the Two-Step model. When students are engaged in a performance task, it is easier for a teacher to guide them to a meaningful level of performance that suits their abilities and accommodates their disabilities.

Knowledge

Skills and concepts are mental constructs that students are expected to understand and apply. Knowledge can include concepts such as poverty, social contracts, the distribution of wealth, and the relationship between economic stability and democratic institutions; scientific concepts such as liquid purification, pollination, freezing, and boiling; mathematical concepts such as multiplication, angles, and probability; English language arts concepts such as the purposes for rules of grammar, analysis of writing, and comparing and contrasting; musical and artistic concepts such as what constitutes beauty to the ear, the eyes, and the other senses.

Knowledge can include skills such as articulation, organization, evaluation, synthesis, estimation, leadership, and teamwork. Knowledge, too, is valuable in and of itself but is most valued when skills and concepts are put to use in the service of competent performance. I can have the skill to use all kinds of tools, and I may understand conceptually how the different parts of a house can be choreographed into a well-designed structure, but the real value is when I use my skills and conceptual understanding to design or build a house.

Competencies

Competencies are internalized capacities that students use to perform operations, accomplish tasks, and produce products. The keyword is *create*. When students can apply knowledge, skills, and concepts to create products and perform operations, they are demonstrating competence. Or seen from another perspective, student competency comes from acquiring skills, knowledge, and a working understanding of concepts through the accomplishment of tasks.

It is often said that learning standards are meant to spell out what students should know and be able to do. However, if you think about it, they should spell out what students should understand and be able to create. It is interesting to note that most state/province learning standards do just that, but this message has been largely disregarded during their implementation.

A competency that the waterways and state history lesson could include is the capacity to create a replication of an authentic design (a lock) in the context of its actual environment.

The competencies of the Tubman lesson could include the capacity to produce a work of art or literature that depicts an aspect of Tubman's life. Students have the opportunity to demonstrate competence when they are asked to create a PowerPoint presentation, create a skit or play, design a functional engine, write for publication, design and build a structure (or vehicle) that requires use of mathematical knowledge, analyze music or art for an audience, or teach a lesson.

Reality Check Question

Can we review the meaning of primary and secondary learning objectives? And, are there any other kinds?

Learning objectives can be classified as information, knowledge (skills and concepts), and competencies. Primary learning objectives are those that the teacher expects of every student, and they are the objectives that are formally assessed. Secondary objectives are those that may be addressed and mastered by some or all students but that are not formally assessed. The teacher is pleased when a student does demonstrate proficiency with a secondary objective, but the teacher does not consider the lesson flawed if some or all students do not.

There is a third way to view learning objectives (in addition to primary and secondary). When students demonstrate proficiency with an objective that was not formally assessed, or even anticipated by the teacher (such as a secondary objective), then we have what some professional educators refer to as an *unintended* objective. However, the teacher deserves credit for designing a task that encourages students to pursue their own objectives in addition to those required by the teacher.

Samantha, the student who gave a PowerPoint presentation on foals becoming horses, exemplifies how a teacher can create a task/assessment that enables students to address specific district or state standards without being straitjacketed into an approach that limits the opportunity for the student to add her own objectives to those required by the teacher. This is also an example of a task/assessment that creates opportunities for students to address the standards in a variety of ways, without requiring any two students to take exactly the same approach.

Constructivism allows for different students, or different groups of students, to be working on different things at the same time. As a matter of fact, it calls for just that! Although teachers often say that they fear parental reaction if all kids don't do the same thing, parents know that kids are different, and each can be handled as an individual. Teachers tend to not like differentiation for other reasons and like the idea that one size fits all. However, "the notion of equity as sameness only makes sense when all students are exactly the same" (Ladson-Billings, 1994). Her call for culturally relevant teaching to reach African-American children is a call for constructivism: It starts with where each child is.

How do you allow students plenty of options yet focus on standards? You do it by identifying and assessing your primary learning objectives and allowing flexibility in how students demonstrate their achievement.

Reality Check Questions

What is the correlation between learning objectives, standards, and assessments? And please address the issue of alignment of standards and assessments.

Standards, in most states, are broadly stated requirements for student learning. Learning objectives are specific objectives that are part of the core curriculum intended to address a broader standard. For instance, a standard might read, "Students will listen, speak, read, and write for critical analysis and evaluation."

A learning objective/core curriculum for a particular lesson might be limited to the statement, "Students will demonstrate an understanding of how to compare and contrast and will apply this knowledge to solve a problem."

There is no conflict between a standard and a learning objective. Students who successfully address learning objectives are demonstrating their ability to meet part of a standard. The author usually focuses teachers on learning objectives because this creates a focus for lesson design.

There is a definite correlation between learning objectives and assessments. The learning objectives are the dimensions (left column) of rubrics because they are what should be defined and assessed.

Reality Check Question

You have defined three categories of learning objectives—information, knowledge (skills and concepts), and competence. Is there a category to distinguish the competent person who goes above and beyond what could reasonably be expected and the student who does what is asked, but stops at the point of assuring himself of the grade he desires?

The difference between a competent person and a creatively competent person is disposition. A creatively competent person is highly motivated to undertake the task. She wants to do it—that is, she is disposed toward undertaking the task. An architect who hates his work may still perform competently and earn his salary, but you will not get the extra effort that comes from someone who is intrinsically motivated. Creative competencies are capacities plus a positive disposition that students use to design inquiries, make creations, and design tasks or products.

If a student performs competently, that is as much as can be expected. Therefore, we are not suggesting that students be assessed on a rubric for the quality of being creatively competent. If the teacher has a rubric for his own performance (either on paper or in his head), it should provide a place for whether his lesson design allows students to demonstrate creative competence. Does the lesson simply require that students prepare for a traditional test? A traditional test places a lid on how much a student with ability and disposition can demonstrate his mettle. Not even all performance assessments allow for creative competency to assert itself. If students were asked to draw a lock on paper and label its component parts, this would require performance, but there would be limited potential for a student to go above and beyond.

However, by giving students access to modeling clay, cardboard, and a variety of other resources and asking them to construct a lock in the environment of a community or city, the teacher is opening the door to an unlimited display of student creativity.

Teachers usually recognize creative competence when they express amazement at how much more a student accomplished than was required to get a good grade on a task. The value of a good authentic task is that it creates opportunities for students to demonstrate competence, and creative competence, even when the teacher may only be after a demonstration of skills and understanding of concepts. The possibilities for demonstrating creative competencies through the Tubman lesson include the following:

♦ A student-designed inquiry into the relationship between Tubman and her former master.

♦ A student-designed inquiry into the relationship between Tubman and leading political figures of the time.

♦ A student-created H. Tubman web site.

♦ A student-produced video tape about Tubman.

♦ A student-designed task regarding Tubman that is appropriate for independent study at the high school level.

♦ A student-designed contest suitable for a general audience, including guidelines and scoring rubric that calls for the participants to draw parallels between current events and the Tubman experience (such as illegal immigration into the United States from Mexico, Cuba, Haiti, or South America; or the slave trade that is going on in various parts of Africa; or the sex trade slavery going on in Asia).

The term *creative competence* was coined by the author to describe "the folks who go way beyond the box." What distinguishes creatively competent performance from merely competent performance is the intrinsic motivation apparent in the performer.

Earlier, we stressed how important it is for the teacher to make sure that the lesson design allows for creative competence to assert itself. How do you know if you have such a design? It's easy: You know you have designed a lesson that allows for students to demonstrate creative competence when you see some students continue to work as the end of the class approaches, or even after the bell rings.

You know your lesson is a success when students or parents offer feedback indicating that the student worked on the task outside of class hours above and beyond what was required for homework. You know you have succeeded when the homeroom or study hall teacher lets you know that your student was working on your performance task or asking questions about it. See Figure 2.11.

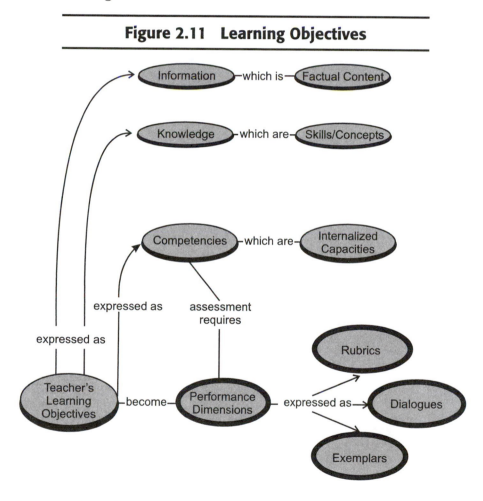

Figure 2.11 Learning Objectives

Thoughts for Reflection

"A good activity illuminates and educates, while a good assessment is designed to yield evidence of what you are trying to get students to achieve" (Wiggins, 1998)

End of Section Assessment

Can you think of a lesson you have taught or observed where you can list the primary learning objectives and cite a rubric that was used to assess them? Alternatively, can you design a lesson that would identify a primary objective and draft a rubric to assess student evidence of satisfactorily addressing that objective?

Sample Summary of a Two-Step

Following is an abbreviated versionof a Two-Step for eighth grade English Language Arts. A more complete example of this same lesson appears in Appendix A.

Popular Name:	Museum Box Personal Profile
Grade Level:	8th
Discipline:	English Language Arts

Standards:

Students will read, write, listen, and speak for information and understanding.

Learning Objectives:

Students will write a personal profile.

EXPLORATORY PHASE:

♦ Students will use a variety of resources to learn the types of museums that exist.

♦ Students will create a museum box, which represents the student; the box contains a specified collection of items.

DISCOVERY PHASE:

Performance Task:

Students will write a personal profile using their museum box as way of focusing and organizing their written expression.

Assessment

Learning Objective

The reader will come to see that task-based learning requires consistent assessment procedures; that high-stakes testing is only one kind of assessment; that teachers need to use multiple forms of assessment to know what students are learning, where they are encountering difficulties, and how the lessons can be improved.

Main Points

- The Two-Step model uses task-based learning, which requires the use of consistent assessment procedures.

- There are three general types of assessments: high-stakes assessments, instructional improvement assessment, and program assessment.

- There are a variety of ways for students to demonstrate success and a variety of ways for teachers to measure student success.

- How a teacher grades depends on how the teacher assesses student work; and how a teacher assesses student work depends on how the teacher designs his lessons.

- Assessing task-based learning requires the use of rubrics; assessment should continue, not interrupt, the learning process.

- There are quick-take techniques that can be used to take the temperature of the class and get feedback on what is going well and what needs improvement or additional emphasis.

Three Purposes for Assessment of Student Performance

Teachers need to assess student learning to adjust their lessons based on student feedback. Teachers also need to give grades. How do we use exploratory and discovery phases of a lesson to accomplish student learning objectives and, simultaneously, produce equitable grades for all students? First, let's distinguish among three types of assessment:

1. *High-Stakes Assessment:* Is all graded stuff high stakes? High stakes has a more refined meaning, which usually implies passing a course, moving to another grade level, graduation, and having heavy accountability for a school (as in state assessments). Use the term *assessment*, and most people, whether they are the person in the street or a professional educator, will immediately think of a test that will influence a student's grade on a report card. This is high-stakes testing. It is also high-stakes testing for a school or district when the student scores are used for purposes of school accountability. However, there are two additional purposes for assessment.

2. *Instructional Improvement:* Perhaps the most important reason to assess student performance is for *instructional improvement,* to enable the teacher to determine whether to adjust teaching strategies with a particular learner. A student's ability—which is the basis for many high-stakes tests—is the product of a lifetime of experiences (and genetic composition) and will not change dramatically over a short period of time. However, a student's progress (relative to his own starting point) is critical information for a teacher because it should guide instructional practice.

3. *Program Assessment:* Is a new approach, program, or strategy achieving the desired effect, or should it be scrapped or adjusted?

Strategies for Assessment of Student Performance

High-Stakes assessments may be necessary to make pass/fail decisions, to enable universities to assess the merits of applicants, and for students and parents to understand how a child performs in relation to classmates. However, we don't need to test a student regularly, throughout the school year, just to remind her that her standing relative to her peers hasn't changed that much. What we do want to influence is whether a student is giving maximum effort to grasp a particular lesson, or whether the learning objectives for the day, week, or month are being grasped. This should be assessed by an effective teacher on an ongoing basis. And if the goal is to have an accurate assessment, then we need to assess performance on actual tasks, not memorization of the steps to take while performing a task.

I can tell you how to hold a bat; how to detect whether a pitcher is about to throw a curve ball, fastball, or screwball; every rule that governs the game of baseball; and more statistics over the past half century than most of the current baseball stars. I'll bet I could score better than most major league ball players on any true–false, multiple choice, or essay question about baseball rules, statistics, and guidelines for effective performance. Yet, I have never had the capability of translating this knowledge into ball field performance that could even approach anything above average for a little leaguer. Similarly, one can know the ingredients to use for a recipe, and can have the skill of being able to follow a set of directions, and still not be competent to cook an above-average meal.

There is a distinction between knowing what to do and being able to do it. In the real world, our students will be assessed on the basis on what they can do. Therefore, to prepare them for the real world, teachers must assess students on the basis of what they can do. To assess students on the basis of what they can do, schools must afford opportunities for students to demonstrate what they can do and teachers must assess this performance.

Students learn better when they are engaged. John Holt puts it simply: "We learn to do something by doing it. There is no other way." We have stressed this point in Chapter 1 and will detail further research in Chapter 3. It is also true that teachers must observe student performance to assess whether students are able to apply what they are learning.

Some teachers think, and some parents expect, that they are getting an accurate assessment of student performance through short-answer and essay tests. The term *multiple as-*

sessments is gaining acceptance because of a growing recognition that essays and short-answer tests are a small part of the total assessment process. This total assessment must be administered by a competent teacher to find out what students are learning and whether modification of teaching strategies (with an individual student or an entire class) is warranted.

Later in this chapter, we list some of the types of assessments that should be integrated into an effective assessment process. Perhaps the most significant but underutilized method is teacher observation. We tend to discard this as an effective method of assessment because it gives the appearance of subjectivity.

Actually, there is little objectivity about what we label an "objective test." All that is objective is the scoring. The design of the questions is completely subjective. Have you ever walked out of an exam and complained, "This test was stupid. It didn't give me a chance to show what I know, and it asked questions that had nothing to do with what I thought I was supposed to be learning."

Knowing what learning is when they see it is something that teachers need to think about, especially when they are attempting to assess students to help them further. According to Grant Wiggins, "Good assessment is about expanding the assessment repertoire because no single form is sufficient. There are reliability and validity problems with each. Every method has its strengths and weaknesses, and its place."

Reality Check Question

What are some examples of student performance that can be used to demonstrate student success?

Essays and short-answer quizzes serve a purpose when retention of information is being assessed, but there are many aspects of student performance that are also important and that lend themselves to assessment by alternative means. Following are some of the many components of effective assessment that may be used at different times by a competent teacher attempting to maintain an understanding of what her students are capable of performing.

Evidence of Student Success

What can students do to demonstrate success?

- ◆ Responses—written and oral
- ◆ Presentations
- ◆ Portfolios
- ◆ Logs and journals
- ◆ Examinations
- ◆ Class tests and quizzes
- ◆ Debate
- ◆ Dialogue

- Simulations

- Role playing

- Graphic organizers

- Essays

- Designing lessons

- Teaching lessons

- Producing storybooks or series of drawings

- Videotape documentaries

How Can Teachers Measure Success?

- Observation

- Selected responses

- Contracts

- Q and A

- Conferences and interviews

- At-a-Glance

- Checklist

- Rubrics and other scoring guides

- Rating scales

- Graphic organizers, mind maps, and concept maps

Reality Check Question

How do these ways of demonstrating and measuring success relate to grading?

- How you grade depends on how you assess.

- How you assess depends on how you design your lessons.

Let's take a look at three aspects of lesson design before directly addressing the answer to the question of correlating grades to assessment: (1) What are some key questions when designing a lesson? (2) How do I generate student feedback beyond what I receive through observation, interaction, and tests? (3) What is the significance of the rubric as a vehicle for assessment?

Key Design Questions

Starting with the lesson, here are some key design questions to guide teachers in planning lessons:

- What are my objectives? What information, knowledge (skills and concepts), and competencies do I want my students to learn?

- Am I designing an activity whose primary purpose is student learning, or is the primary purpose to be a vehicle for assessment of student learning while furthering the learning process?

- What evidence will I look for to let me know that learning has occurred?

- What learning activities and tasks will enable me to move my students to the intended learning objectives while simultaneously creating opportunities for me to assess what they have learned?

How You Design Your Lesson

The lesson design determines how much evidence of student learning will be available to the teacher.

- When I conduct a traditional teacher-centered lesson—me talking, students listening and, maybe, taking notes—how much do I know about what students are thinking?

- When I require students to demonstrate understanding through an essay (rather than through performance or some other modality) how do I know if they really understand the content? For example, if I ask students to explain how to convert feet into meters, can any number of accurate words (verbally or in writing) give the same evidence of understanding that would come from asking students to redesign a house plan that is in inches, but do it for a prospective Canadian buyer?

The paradigm that imprisons so many of us has us convinced that when a student explains *why*, she is demonstrating understanding. This is why we think that student understanding can be assessed by an essay that challenges a student to explain why. Most of the time, explaining why doesnot necessarily demonstrate understanding. A person with a good memory can explain the theme of *Johnny Tremain* by remembering what was written in a textbook, or was taken down in her notes, without necessarily understanding what she is explaining. When a student performs, he demonstrates what he does and does not understand.

If I require students to demonstrate understanding with no options other than an essay, will I be able to assess whether the student with poor writing capability understands the content, or will I simply be learning whether this student is capable of expressing her thoughts through an essay? If the learning objective is to write a good essay, then naturally the assessment has to include writing an essay. However, if the learning objective has nothing to do with essay writing, then why limit student demonstration of learning to that which can be expressed through an essay?

If the teacher wants to assess which students can demonstrate competence in understanding different cultures, it might be a mistake to require a 200-word essay as the vehicle. An essay can be offered as an option as part of an authentic task, but perhaps the student can also be offered the chance to produce a portfolio or do an artistic representation of a different culture. If the teacher wants to give students practice with essay writing precisely because it is a weak skill for some of them, then there are other ways to do it without making it the only vehicle for the assessment of other learning objectives. For instance, while conducting a planned intervention to help students prepare for the discovery phase of a lesson on cultures, an essay can be required (it is a good way to spiral essay writing into the curriculum). But when the teacher is assessing student achievement of primary learning objectives for the lesson, and the primary learning objective is an understanding of cultural differences, then the student needs to be offered options for demonstrating knowledge and competence through vehicles with which the student has a high comfort level. This is why teacher mastery of multiple forms of assessment is so essential. In the real world we are primarily judged on whether we can accomplish the assigned task, not so much on which method or vehicle we choose for accomplishing it. A criticism of standardized math, social studies, and science tests in New York State, and some other states, is that they are as much an assessment of a student's ability to read as they are a test of the subject matter. Think of the damage to a student's motivation if he knows the content, but fails the test because he is unable to fully understand the questions. Is the purpose to assess reading levels or the understanding of content in social studies, math, or science? The authors recognize that teachers in disciplines other than English Language Arts are now inclined to see the need to teach reading across the disciplines and this is one value of requiring adequate reading skills in order to demonstrate mastery of content in other disciplines, but is this worth the distorted assessment that occurs when we are trying to assess a student's knowledge of science, math, or social studies when that student is a poor reader?

How You Assess
(What Evidence of student learning will you seek)?

To assess student performance, the teacher must focus on the purpose of the assessment:

♦ Is the assessment for the purpose of high stakes, instructional improvement, program assessment, or a combination of any two or all three?

♦ Is the assessment formative or summative?

Also, the teacher should abandon the paradigm that all assessments are in the form of short-answer or essay tests or an occasional project. Think, instead, of the multiple forms of assessment listed earlier.

When the term *multiple assessments* is used, it refers to what a teacher can learn about a student when constantly integrating a variety of methods of assessment. Seeking answers to the following questions, which inform the teacher about the effectiveness of his teaching strategies, should be among the purposes of the teacher's multiple forms of assessment:

♦ Am I requiring my students to think?

♦ If so, how deeply?

♦ How insightfully?

♦ How do I know they are thinking? What is the evidence that my students are thinking? Are just a few students giving evidence of thinking, or am I really challenging every student to think?

Think of what a teacher learns about a student by:

♦ Working the room and observing the student doing group work, working individually, or working in a pair on a task.

♦ Examining the completed project that is the outcome of an authentic task assignment, and/or viewing the process the student uses to complete the task.

♦ Reviewing written feedback elicited by a feedback form, process, or some kind of journaling.

♦ Reviewing the student's verbal response to the kinds of questions that would appear on a feedback form.

Obviously, a primary value of assessment, as noted earlier, is for instructional improvement, to guide the teacher with regard to which learning objectives are being grasped and which need renewed emphasis.

Throughout this book, we have emphasized the importance of working the room—actively observing student thinking and student production by looking over shoulders and being easily accessible while students work individually or in groups. The elementary school teacher who designed the waterways and history lesson claims, "You can tell when you are with a group of kids which ones know about locks and which don't, and you know when they've taken ownership of the task." Another teacher added, "You can tell what they are thinking; you can see the wheels turning."

Generating Student Feedback

There are quick-take techniques that a teacher can use to take the temperature of a class and to determine what is going well and what needs improvement or additional emphasis. Two strategies for generating student feedback beyond what a teacher receives through observation, interaction, and tests involve asking students what they have learned. One is the use of a student feedback sheet (Fig. 2.12) at the end of class (occasionally, frequently, or every day). Another is to ask a question of students in the last five minutes of class and request a 10-second response from every student. Alternatively, occasionally put students in groups of three or four, pose a question, allow three minutes for internal group discussion, and then ask a reporter from each group to summarize the group's response in 15 seconds or less.

Figure 2.12   Student Feedback Sheet—A Sample

Name _____ Date _____

1.   Today, the topic that we investigated _____

2.   My teacher should give me 5 4 3 2 1 0 (circle one) bonus points today because
_____

3.   One thing that I learned from my partner(s) was _____

4.   It was really interesting to learn that _____

5.   The neatest thing that I did today was _____

6.   One thing that I am still wondering about is _____

7.   A song that will remind me of today is _____ because _____

When the authors don't use the written feedback form, they close classes with a question that elicits a response, in 10 seconds or less, from every student (or they seek group responses as suggested earlier). The question may be any of the following—and the author will change the question, partly for variety and partly depending on the nature of the lesson and the kind of feedback that is desired:

♦ What is one thing you know now that you didn't know when you walked into class 43 minutes ago?

♦ What have you chosen as a topic for the paper (project) that is due next week?

♦ What is one thing you learned today?

♦ What do you feel is the most important quality for a person to possess as a member of a group?

♦ What part of this course have you found the most difficult to learn?

♦ What do we do in class that you enjoy the most?

♦ When you are studying effectively (at home or in school), what do you find helps you to learn well?

♦ Can you give one reason why it is important to learn about chemistry?

♦ What is one thing we can learn from the American Revolution that we can apply in today's society?

- What makes a "classic" a classic? We speak of certain books being classics and certain songs being classics. Name one thing that makes something a classic.

- What is a time in your life when you may need to use fractions?

- Please complete one of these three phrases in 10 seconds or less:

  - During class today, I learned …

  - During class today, I relearned …

  - During class today, I became aware of …

All of the techniques described earlier in this section provide powerful data for the teacher who is observant and who creates opportunities to observe student thinking. Every good teacher has used a variety of techniques, including observation, to determine what students are learning, which students are learning what, and whether to reteach or move on. But because these decisions are often made at the gut level, they are not always thought of as assessment. When a doctor assesses your medical condition, doesn't the assessment reflect a combination of test results, other medical findings, and observation based on the doctor's judgment from observing you and listening to your feedback?

However, the doctor's subjective judgments are based on a framework of objective criteria she brings with her through years of study and experience. A teacher is an expert in his field. When we speak of using teacher observation and other forms of subjective assessment, we are thinking of structuring these techniques to render assessments that are as objective as possible. The rubric can be of great assistance.

Reality Check Question

Before you discuss the significance of the rubric, are we speaking primarily of formative or summative assessments?

Both! Here's a unique concept: If the teacher focuses on formative assessments, the summative assessments will be accomplished without additional effort on the part of the teacher. If a formative assessment process is designed, as it should be, to provide evidence of student learning so the teacher can adjust teaching strategies appropriately, then that same evidence, on an ongoing basis, provides the data the teacher needs for a summative assessment at the end of the lesson or unit. A good culminating event, in the form of a discovery phase (authentic task) will give the teacher a final glimpse of the information, skills, concepts, and competence the student is able to demonstrate.

Stiggins quotes an English study by Paul Black and Dylan Wiliam on the impact of formative classroom assessment of learning. In a November, 2002 article in *Kappan*, he states, "These studies exhibit another feature. Many of them show that improved formative assessment helps the (so-called) low attainers more than the rest, and so reduces the spread of attainment while also raising it overall." Many of the strategies we have been discussing will aid teachers with formative as well as summative assessments.

Do formative tests have to count toward the report card grade? No, formative assessments are the process of keeping the teacher, and students, attuned to student progress. A reason for grading a formative assessment might be to reward effort to encourage the learner to study and engage in learning activities. If a formative assessment is graded, the impact doesn't have to be so great that the overall class grade will mislead an outsider as to the ability of the student, but it can count enough that the student who knows less than others doesn't give up at the outset knowing that no amount of effort will be rewarded.

Often, student learning occurs through participation in an activity (and reflection, afterwards), and teacher assessment occurs through observation of, and interaction with, the student (as opposed to seeing how well the student can do on a traditional test). In these instances—where the activity and reflection are the learning process—the only purposes served by giving a grade are 1) to motivate the student to participate in the activity and 2) to reinforce those students who do participate. Some people need visible evidence that the teacher has taken note of their efforts and/or that other students haven't gotten away with ignoring what they have worked hard to accomplish.

Formative assessments are constantly being utilized throughout the exploratory phase of the lesson as well as throughout the discovery phase. Almost every time the teacher conducts a planned or spontaneous intervention, information is provided that contributes to the formative assessment of every student. When the teacher is in front of the entire class, lecturing (even though lecture is necessary and valuable, at appropriate times), the opportunities for assessing individual student progress are extremely limited compared with times when students are engaged in group work, or working individually as the teacher works the room. The summative assessment is utilized when the teacher feels the student is ready to demonstrate competence with the knowledge, skills, and concepts that have been the learning objectives for the lesson, almost always in the discovery phase.

When teachers approach lessons with the *Two-Step* process, all summative assessments are also formative. The summative assessments enable the teacher to grade students for high stakes purposes, while simultaneously advancing the progress of the students toward the learning objectives. This is a significant departure from the traditional way of teaching. An author highlighted this departure from traditional teaching, in 1990, when he defined education reform as being reflected by a shift from using assessments solely for the purpose of assessing student knowledge, to a process whereby the assessment is part of the learning process.

> In traditional classrooms, the author explained, we teach, then we halt our teaching and we test to see what the student knows, and then we resume teaching, and then we halt. …

> However, in a constructivist classroom, the assessment furthers the learning process. As such, it is more of an on-going approach that facilitates interdisciplinary learning.

As an example of assessment furthering the learning process, think about a sporting event or a theatrical production. We learn from the practices, but don't we often learn the most from the day of the game when we have the opportunity to put all of our prior learning to the test? Doesn't our performance the night of the show, and the audience reaction, move our learning forward at least as much as any of the rehearsals? Similarly, a well designed student activity/task creates an opportunity for a summative assessment, but it also serves the formative purpose of advancing student learning toward the objectives. It is a curriculum embedded assessment.

"Assessment is the engine that drives education reform." It is happening, slowly, but inexorably.

The Significance of the Rubric

Once we accept that engagement is necessary for understanding, the following chain is set in motion: active learning begets constructivism, which leads to authentic assessment, which begets rubrics. Figure 2.13 is a template for a rubric. Notice that the teacher's learning objectives should be replicated in the dimensions column to guide the student toward understanding the teacher's expectations for the lesson.

Figure 2.13   Rubric for Assessment of the Performance Task

Dimensions	Criteria for a score of 4	Criteria for a score of 3	Criteria for a score of 2	Criteria for a score of 1
Learning objectives				
Learning objectives				
Learning objectives				
See examples in Appendix A, for an understanding of how "learning objectives" can become "Dimensions" in a rubric.				

The significance of the rubric is its function as a vehicle for assessing student performance.

Teacher understanding and utilization of rubrics is in its infancy. In the early 1990s, the authors could locate only a handful of teachers (sometimes just one or two) in any school who had even heard the term rubric and were making some kind of effort to use rubrics in classroom settings. In 1995, when the authors conducted their first week-long constructivist conference at Grand Island, New York, despite the presence of nearly 200 cutting edge professionals, less than five percent had ever even heard the word rubric and very few had ever tried to use a rubric with their students. Yet, at the 2002 summer conference, every parent and teacher from among 300 cutting edge people had seen a rubric, some had been gaining expertise and using rubrics for at least three years, and most were at least beginning their journey toward competence with rubrics.

However, even among educators experienced with rubrics, most are utilizing them as a better way to assess that which they have always assessed—student retention of information. Even as we write these words, relatively few people have made the connection that the real significance of rubrics is that they provide a vehicle for assessing student performance, much like judges in the Olympics assess ice skaters and divers with a rubric. The judges know the criteria that skaters must address, they know what a skater must do to obtain a perfect score addressing a specific criterion, and they compare scores while observing the same performances as they refine their rubrics and prepare for Olympic judging.

Educational assessments have been typified by the example of teaching public speaking through teacher lecture and then assessing on the basis of student responses to questions like, "Is it true or false that a good speaker should maintain eye contact?"

As the need to engage students in their learning takes hold, a growing number of educators might now teach public speaking by engaging students in debates; however, many would still use the short answer quiz for purposes of assessment. The rubric provides the vehicle for assessing the performance as it is occurring and it limits or, at times, eliminates the need for a short answer quiz assessment of the information retained by the learner. In baseball, my ability to get an A on a short-answer test or essay would be obscured by my performance of four strike outs in four at-bats and errors on the only three fielding chances to come my way. The baseball manager would have a rubric in his mind, if not on paper, that would clearly assess a four strikeout, three-error performance as unsatisfactory.

Because rubric assessment is a new concept to educators, experts do not always use identical terms to mean the same thing. What we are calling dimensions, Charlotte Danielson refers to as "elements" ("Embracing Professional Practice", 1996), and others label "components," "characteristics," "criteria," and so forth. What is important is that a rubric must begin the process of providing information of expectations. Dialogue and exemplars complete the process of clarifying expectations.

How You Grade

If we throw away the simple formula of teaching, applying a short answer and/or essay test, and objectively recording a grade based on student responses, how do we compile a grade for a student? How do we grade students if it isn't as simple as adding the totals on spot quizzes, mid-unit tests and end of the unit short-answer and essay questions, with, perhaps, a few points thrown in for class participation?

It can be simple: any rubric score can be converted to a grade. At the university level, where the grading system is 1, 2, 3, 4, a professor can use four point rubrics so that a student getting a "WOW" on an assignment (meeting the criteria for a 4 on the rubric) gets a 4 on the assignment. On an individual task—for example a paper—each criterion can be given weight, "You will get a 1 to 4 rating on each of the following:"

- spelling and punctuation
- attention grabbing opening paragraph
- three supportive facts, well researched, for each opinion

- good summary paragraph
- the paper is *interesting*

The rubric would define what would constitute a 4, a 3, a 2, and a 1 for spelling and grammar, for the quality of the opening paragraph, etc. Each of these criteria could be afforded 20% of the value of the student's grade, or they could be weighted differently—15% for spelling and punctuation, 40% for the opening paragraph, 20% for supportive facts, and 10% for the summary and 15% for maintaining interest.

This would enable the teacher to attach a grade point to this writing assignment. Each task or assignment during the semester can similarly be reduced to a grade point result and the grades for every task/assignment can be weighted and totaled to arrive at a grade for the semester. For a K–12 teacher, rubrics can be similarly adjusted to result in grade point results.

Wiggins tells us "There's nothing to prevent teachers from expanding their modes of assessment while still living in a letter-grade world. Assessment reform is about getting different and richer information about students' performance, all of which teachers can factor into a grade. It's a matter of expanding your pile of evidence, not necessarily changing the grading system."

Reality Check Question

Isn't this is a very, very simplistic rendition of a much more complex issue. Aren't there other issues you haven't addressed?

Yes, there are many other issues. We are not going to delve into these issues in any kind of depth because there are excellent articles and books already written. Here is a cursory listing of some of these issues:

- The problem connected with giving a student's work-product an all-over grade. Rubrics are designed to give specific feedback to students regarding the various dimensions of a task. Giving students one holistic grade can deflect the student's and teacher's attention from pinpointing what the student needs to work on to become more competent

- The whole idea of what to turn into grades—the formative vs. summative issue; at what point is a product or process ready to be judged regarding a grade?

- The disciplinary aspects of grades with regard to homework, completing foundational assignments etc.

- The problems inherent in rubric design.

Thoughts for Reflection

Sugrue's message is that those who elect to use performances to assess students' understanding should attempt to develop a clear idea of what they are after and what is involved in gathering relevant data (Sugrue, 1995).

End of Section Assessment:

Think of a task that engaged students in a class. Identify one primary learning objective that could have been the focus of that task How many kinds of evidence can you cite that would indicate whether students had achieved mastery of the learning objective?

Sample Summary of a Two-Step

Following is an abbreviated version of a Two-Step for eleventh and twelfth grade Social Studies and English Language Arts. A more complete example of this same lesson appears on the web site of the Institute for Learning Centered Education, www.learner centereded.org

Popular Name:	World War II Newspaper
Grade Level:	11th & 12th
Discipline:	Social Studies/English Language Arts

Standards:
- Students will read, write, listen, and speak for information and understanding.
- Students will use a variety of intellectual skills to demonstrate their understanding of major ideas, eras, themes, developments, and turning points in world history.

Learning Objectives

Students will:
- Write in four writing styles: journalistic/reporting, opinion/persuasive, and news summary.
- Analyze and synthesize different kinds of information from different sources.
- Develop an understanding of the way WW II was reported
- Develop a perspective regarding the major events of WW II.

EXPLORATORY PHASE:
- Students will attempt to identify projected images from the WW II era.
- Students in groups will fill in a grid revealing their general knowledge of the WW II era.

DISCOVERY PHASE:

Performance Task:
- Students will create sections of a newspaper set during WW II but written in the style of "USA Today." Each student's newspaper will cover the news from one month of one year of the WW II era.
- Students will present a brief TV news report based on their newspaper.

Reflection

Learning Objective

The reader will come to view reflection as a critical study habit that needs to be taught, rehearsed, and modeled. See Figure 2.14.

Figure 2.14 Exploratory and Discovery Phase

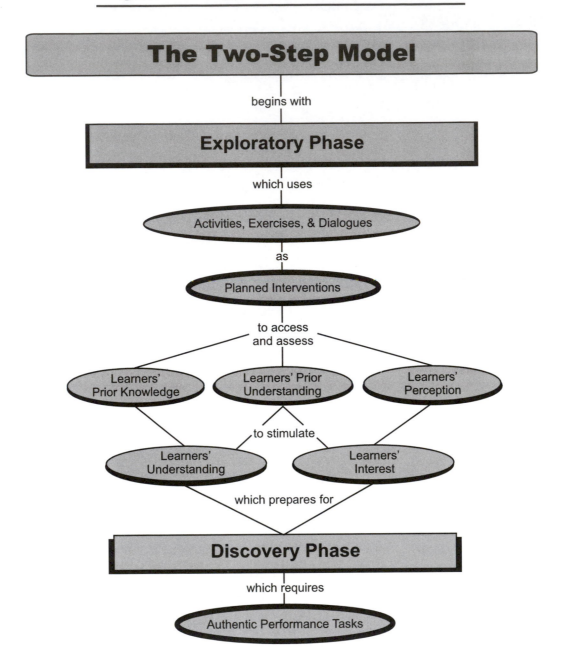

This chapter would not be complete without a section on reflection. The temptation existed to make the *two-step*, the three-step: exploration, discovery, reflection.

However, reflection needs to occur throughout exploration and discovery, as well as afterward, so the author has chosen to view reflection as an integral part of the learning process, at all stages, rather than as a separate phase.

Thoughts on Reflection

Too often, teachers regard reflective time as an expendable part of their lesson. When time is running out and they haven't "covered all the material," the reflective activity is skipped. We need to heed educational theorist James Bruner who says, "Reflection is central to all learning" (cited in Reed and Bergmann, 2001). If we recognize that reflection is critical to learning, we would no sooner skip the reflective piece of a lesson than we would omit an important content piece.

Artists utilize their writing, painting, or music to reflect on what they have learned through their engagements with people, events, the environment, and with other life circumstances. While a painting, an essay, or a musical composition can represent reflection for some, the act of performing can divert others from reflection. In fact, most of us become so engaged in what we are doing we will only reflect on our performance if someone stops the world and asks us to do so.

Following our 1995 summer constructivist conference, a building principal from Kentucky reminded 200 people who had high energy all week, and had stayed beyond the required hours to complete work on their tasks that, "We need to reflect on the fact that what motivated us to work so hard at this conference is what motivates students in a classroom—relevance, resources, opportunity and support." He was mindful that when we are actively engaged in a task, we often are so focused that we don't think about what we are doing, we just do it. In the classroom the person who needs to stop the world and cause us to reflect by asking appropriate questions is the teacher.

To paraphrase Socrates, "A life without reflection, is a life not worth living." The authors would postulate that a lesson without reflection is a lesson not worth teaching. Here's an example:

An author showed the opening two scenes from the movie "Boyz N the Hood" to thirty cutting edge teachers who were participating in a five day workshop. To the author the message of the movie is clear—there is a dramatic contrast between the two opening scenes. In the first scene the high school students are roaming the streets of Los Angeles, hearing gun shots, and viewing a dead body. Then the scene changes to a stereotypical teacher, pointer in hand, trying to teach these same students to understand and appreciate the origins of Thanksgiving in white America. As the author observed the teachers viewing these contrasting scenes, he was certain that it would be apparent to them that the lecture style of the teacher in the movie was totally irrelevant to the lives of the students. Following the brief video, and with no discussion about it, the presenter moved on to another, unrelated activity. Workshop participants found the video interesting, but it became evident from comments, and written feedback later in the day, that few saw any relevance to the purpose of the workshop. "Why did they show that clip?" was the most often heard comment.

Weeks later, the author showed the same video to an undergraduate class of college students, but followed it with some probing questions to help students process what they had seen. Journal entries submitted a few days later gave evidence that students had grasped what the teacher wanted them to learn from the video and had also been able to glean a lot more from the video, including valid concepts that the teacher had not initially appreciated.

Reflection can be an individual activity or can be done collectively. At the 1995 constructivist conference, a staff developer, Pat, was asked to lead a group reflection during the lunch hour on the third day. Valiantly, he posed one probing question after another to the 200 people gathered in the large room for lunch. Acoustics were excellent, and the large rectangular room arrangement was suitable for group discussion, but no one spoke. "What would you like to share that you have learned this week?" he asked.

No one responded. "What steps will you take to follow-through on your work, this week, when you return to your school?" Again, no response. Pat tried several more questions, and only one or two people responded (close colleagues who gamely tried to help Pat get the ball rolling). The next day, Pat made one more effort, during the lunch hour. This time his probing question picked up where the previous day's efforts had ended:

"Can anyone suggest why there was such a poor response to my questions yesterday?"

After about 30 seconds of silence, a hand went up. "I think it's because reflection is a personal thing, not something that everyone wants to share."

Then another hand went up: "I don't think you can reflect on command. Reflection has to take place when and where you want it to."

A staff member from a national organization and an associate from the State Education department weighed in with their thoughts, followed by a New York City building principal and several teachers. The dialogue continued until the lunch time had expired and participants needed to get back to their work stations. Some people agreed that collective reflection was not possible while others suggested ways to bring it about.

What may not have been apparent to everyone was that Pat had just conducted a 30 minute collective reflection. Sixteen people had spoken and more were ready when time ran out. They had reflected on why the previous day's reflective activity had failed to achieve the responses that were solicited.

Through this group reflective activity, we had all learned strategies for individual and group reflection. It is obvious that prior to the second attempt at collective reflection, Pat had reflected on what had occurred the previous day and, based on his reflections, he had adopted a strategy that worked. Pat had learned from his individual reflection after the first attempt. Instead of focusing on the term *reflection*, (which may have made some people self conscious), he simply asked effective probing questions which could not be answered without thoughtful reflection. We all learned from the group reflection the following day because good ideas were shared by a variety of people, and all of us, including those who didn't speak out loud, were forced to think.

Reed and Bergemann assert: "There is hardly a self help book on the market today that does not mention the importance of reflection. Books that claim to document the attributes of successful people always stress the reflective process that leads an individual to success. Sometimes watch the face of an accomplished athlete after he has missed the ball in the end zone or she has fallen from the balance beam; you will see in the athlete's eyes a rapid analysis of what has occurred. There may be only a few seconds to reflect on what went wrong, but reflection is necessary so that the same mistake will not occur again. This, of course, is why teams watch videos of the game and performers tape performances."

Reflection is a critical study habit that needs to be taught, rehearsed, and modeled. Reflective strategies can be learned. If reflection is a critical part of learning for successful people, then it needs to be taught (and modeled) in schools where the students' primary occupation is to learn. Here are some strategies for classroom use:

♦ The think aloud is an excellent strategy for modeling reflective practice: "Here is what was going through my mind as I tried to write a journal entry similar to the one I am asking you to write: 'What do I recall now, a day later, about the lesson we had yesterday? Is it the fact that oil and water won't mix if you pour oil in the ocean? Or, is it what I learned about the damage done to the environment when a tanker leaks oil? Or, is the fact that our climate may be getting warmer every year? Which of these will be most significant to people fifty years from now? That's easy. The implications of a climate that gets warmer every year is probably the most significant thing. I'll write about that. Now let me think about what I learned about the climate getting warmer. How rapidly is it getting warmer? At what point will we be able to feel the effects? Do tulips bloom any earlier in my town than they would have 20 years ago? Is there a change within the last five years?'"

♦ Utilize the exploratory phase of a lesson to cause students to reflect. Ask probing questions to help students access prior knowledge. "Write down three things you know about planets. Then pair and share with the person next to you."

Causing reflection with a probing question can also help grab the attention of the student audience. We all enjoy being asked our opinion; if we know we won't be graded on our response.

♦ Utilize journal entries. It can be as simple as asking students to record what they have learned since their last entry. Or, you can ask them to analyze something you've studied, or give their opinion about a hypothetical problem. Journal entries can be used for individual or collective reflection. For individual reflection, the entry can be shared only with the instructor, or, depending on the purpose, it can be kept privately by the student. For collective reflection, students can be asked to keep journal entries and can be given criteria to address, but at the designated time for group reflection, students can be asked to voluntarily share something from their entries they are willing to share.

Journal entries can be shared with other students, but students should know, before they are asked to write their entries, what the ground rules are, in other words, who may or may not read their entries.

♦ Put students in small groups and ask them to propose three questions about a passage, chapter, book, or assignment. Challenge them to develop questions that require rationale for a response. Give examples.

♦ End every class (or at least some classes) posing questions and eliciting responses from every student, either verbally, in writing, or both.

- "Complete this sentence in 10 seconds or less: "One thing I know now that I didn't know an hour ago is. …""

- "If you had to write a letter to a friend describing George Washington, what is the most important quality of his you would discuss?"

♦ Make students aware that reflection is a valuable study habit, occasionally discuss some of your strategies for your own reflection, and your strategies for generating class reflection. Ask students for examples of how and when people reflect. Point out that the lyricist, the painter, and the writer are often examples of people using their medium to reflect on past experiences. Ask students for other examples, or ask them to identify art work, music, or literature that clearly indicates reflection.

Thoughts for Reflection

♦ "Reflection is aimed at the discovery of facts that will serve a purpose" (John Dewey, 1910).

♦ "Reflective thinking is controlled doing, involving a pushing and pulling of concepts, putting them together and separating them again. Students need practice in reflective thinking just as teams need time to practice a sport" (Novak and Gowin)

End of Section Assessment:

Think of the last lesson you taught, observed, or were taught in a school setting. Can you think of a brief activity the teacher could have integrated into the lesson to have induced additional reflection by the students?

Sample Summary of a Two-Step

Following is an abbreviated version of a Two-Step for tenth grade Biology. A more complete example of this same lesson appears on the web site of the Institute for Learning Centered Education, www.learnercentereded.org

Popular Name:	Photosynthesis and Respiration
Grade Level:	10th
Discipline:	Biology

Standards:

♦ Students will use mathematical analysis, scientific inquiry, and engineering design, as appropriate, to pose questions, seek answers, and develop solutions.

♦ Students will understand that organisms maintain a dynamic equilibrium that sustains life.

Learning Objectives: Students will:

Be able to write a report based on an experiment they developed and perform.

(The experiment is to prove the scientific principle regarding carbon dioxide's contribution to both photosynthesis and respiration.)

EXPLORATORY PHASE:

♦ Students as a whole class, conduct a test involving the relationship between respiration and carbon dioxide.

♦ Students use textbook-based information to prepare to explain the relationship between respiration and photosynthesis.

DISCOVERY PHASE:

Performance Task:

♦ Students will develop and perform an experiment to prove each of the following statements:

♦ Plants carry on photosynthesis and use carbon dioxide.

♦ Plants carry on respiration and release carbon dioxide.

The task will include writing an experiment report that includes labeling diagrams. Students will present their findings to an eighth grade class and parents will be invited to be part of the audience.

3

How We Learn Guides How We Teach

- *What do we know about how people learn?*

- *How do we apply, in the classroom, what we know about how people learn?*

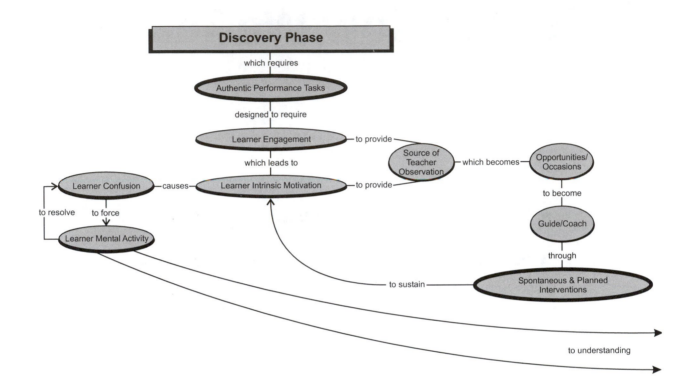

Learning Grows from Confusion

Learning Objective

The reader will become aware that we learn by fighting our way through confusion. Often, our confusion results when new information from a source we respect conflicts with our prior knowledge.

Main Points

♦ The Two-Step model capitalizes on the brain research finding that we learn in periods of confusion.

♦ Operating as a coach or guide, the teacher's role is to provide the support necessary to make students comfortable with confusion so that they will continue to fight their way through it to understanding.

The Learning Process

♦ Our current perceptions may be challenged by new information, because our current perceptions are often in conflict with this new information. We feel particularly challenged when the new information comes from a source we respect.

♦ This conflict between past perceptions and new information causes disequilibrium. (We ask ourselves, "Why does this new information not validate what I believe is true?")

♦ Learning occurs as we fight our way through the confusion toward a new understanding.

Here are two examples:

1. Most of us have been raised to believe that time is a constant. Then we hear or read that Albert Einstein has a theory of relativity. This is new information that conflicts with our prior knowledge and perceptions. The degree to which we respect Einstein (from what we know of him), or respect his opinion simply because he is labeled "scientist" will help determine how motivated we will be to try to reconcile our prior knowledge (time is a constant) with this new information (relativity). Until we are comfortable with our reconciliation of this new information with our prior knowledge, we will be confused. The battle to fight our way through the confusion to new understanding will engender our learning.

2. An adult recalled that when she was seven years old, her perception of half of eight was three. Being artistically inclined, when she looked at the number eight and someone asked her to visualize half of it, she automatically pictured the right half of the number eight and blocked out the left half in her mind. When she would hear her classmates say that half of eight was four, she thought about how much she knew that they didn't. One day, her teacher said that half of eight

was four. Because she respected her teacher as an authority on math, she began thinking about her perception (prior knowledge) that three was half of eight and began the internal process of trying to reconcile what she believed to be correct with new information from a source she respected too much to ignore. Initially, she was confused. Eventually, she learned that half of eight, numerically, is four.

The constructivist sequence of instruction recognizes that we learn by fighting our way through the confusion caused when new information conflicts with prior knowledge, and it provides the learner with opportunities to work her way through the process with skillful coaching (intervention) by the teacher.

Chaos + Process = Learning

Throughout this chapter, we shall explore, discover, discuss, and learn to apply two simply stated principles of learning. Following a discussion of these two principles, we will discuss how they can be addressed in the exploratory and discovery phases of a lesson, and through use of interventions, planned and spontaneous. These principles are simply stated: (1) Learning grows out of confusion, and (2) learning occurs as we try to reconcile our prior knowledge (or perceptions) with new information from a source we respect. This new information may conflict with our perceptions. It is this conflict between new information and our perceptions that creates confusion. These principles, however, are difficult to put into practice, whether you are a parent at home, a teacher in school, or anyone who needs to influence the thought processes of others. They are difficult to put into practice because we've had so little experience trying. Most of us have been brought up with the traditional teaching model that includes lecture, practice, and application (to the degree time allows). The teacher doesn't afford us the opportunity to access our prior knowledge so that we can wrestle with contradictions between our knowledge and new information presented either by the teacher or another source.

Here is an example of how a constructivist two-step lesson could help a student remember (memorize) and understand major events of the 1940s, as well as learning the concept of "What makes an individual or an event enduring?" As a byproduct of this lesson that is really focused on the 1940s, students will gain a much better understanding of people and events in the 1960s. As you read this example, keep in mind that even though the exploratory phase is going to focus on the 1960s, the objectives of the lesson, as will become evident during the discovery phase, relate to the 1940s and to a concept ("What makes an individual or event enduring?") that transcends the specific content of the 40s or the 60s. **During the exploratory phase,** the teacher leads students through a sequence of activities.

Exploratory Phase

1. Look at these phrases and add words to make them complete sentences:

    a. The three most significant events of the 1960s that have the most impact on our lives today are…

b. The three people whose lives in the 1960s have the most impact on our lives today are...

This activity forces the learner to activate his prior knowledge (current perceptions) of what is important about the 1960s. Notice that the teacher conducted this activity BEFORE presenting information to the students.

2. Pair off with the person next to you, share your work and see if you can agree in those instances where your responses differ.

This activity will confront the learner with new information that conflicts with his prior knowledge in each instance where his partner's responses do not agree with his own. To the degree he respects his partner for his knowledge of the 60s, in particular, or of social studies, in general, he will be more likely to try to understand why his own decisions don't always agree with his partner's.

3. Now form groups of four, by combining pairs, and share and reconcile your responses.

When you worked with one partner, you may not have respected that partner for his expertise on this subject matter. Comparing your responses with two more people increases the likelihood that you will find at least one person whom you respect for her knowledge of the 60s, or social studies, in which case, you will be more likely to feel confused over disagreements on who and what was most important about the 60s and, consequently, more likely to try to reconcile the new information (the differing opinion of one or more people in your group) with your own perceptions.

4. In your same group of four, see how many criteria you can agree upon for making decisions about the people and events that have the biggest impact on lives of people in the future. (Note: The teacher, as a planned intervention, may elicit from the entire class one or two criteria so that students understand what is meant by "criteria for making decisions about the people and events...")

5. As a class, we will now agree on the criteria for judging whether an individual or an event has had a significant impact on the lives of the people who will follow them. I will ask each group to share one criterion it identified. After each group has offered a criterion, we will continue around until each group has reported on every criterion it has listed. Then I will add any criteria I can think of, if you haven't covered them all, and we will print up one combined list for the entire class.

Steps 4 and 5 create a prompt for students to help them organize their thoughts and understand why their initial responses were either valid or incorrect.

During the discovery phase, the teacher creates a task that will require students to demonstrate their ability to apply their knowledge of what makes people and events important.

Discovery Phase

1. As a planned intervention, the teacher conducts the same activity, using the 1940s, as she just conducted for the 1960s. The purposes of the exploratory activity, using the 1960s as the focal point, were to:

    a. familiarize students with a process, and a set of criteria, for assessing the durability of the contributions of an event and/or individual to society.

    b. stimulate discussion and interest in the history of a decade as a prelude to an authentic task that will relate directly to the objectives of the lesson—an analysis of the 1940s.

    c. get students thinking about content related to the 1960s so they will have hooks on which to hang their thoughts when the 1960s are the subject for study later in the year.

2. Now the teacher helps the students understand their authentic task. The class will be divided into five groups and each group will make a 30 minute presentation analyzing a different two year period during the 1940s.

    •   Each member of the group will have a significant role in the presentation.

    •   The presentation will highlight at least two people and two events from that two year period and will make it clear why and how their legacy continues to impact our daily lives.

    •   A few parents will be invited to view the presentations and will be asked to complete a feedback sheet designed by the teacher (or jointly designed with the students).

3. Following the presentation "I will ask each student, separately, to review the criteria we developed, as a class, for judging whether an individual or an event has had a significant impact on the lives of people, and each of you will have to write a brief analysis of which criteria your group applied in your presentation, why you relied on those criteria, and how the people and events you described during your presentation met the criteria. If everyone in the group does well on this, individually, everyone in the group will have his grade raised by three points above what it would have been, based on his individual work."

4. Each student will be required to submit a journal entry that will address the following:

    a. What ideas, specifically, and time, did you contribute to preparing the presentation?

    b. What ideas did each member of your group contribute and who did what to prepare for the presentation?

c. If you were to make the same presentation again, what would you do differently, and why?

The teacher should provide a rubric, at the start of the lesson, which could address those learning objectives the teacher intended to require of every student. Among the possible learning objectives could be:

- The concept of what criteria determine the importance of an event or person to future generations?

- Facts from the 1940s that the teacher feels every student should be able to recall.

- Verbal skills and/or organizational skills that could be assessed from the preparation, group work, and actual presentation. These can include eye contact, poise, any of the skills on Bloom's Taxonomy, posture, leadership, persuasiveness, articulation, etc.

Let's continue our exploration of two of the principles of learning that are a focus of this book: (1) Learning grows out of confusion, and (2) Confusion is the inevitable consequence of having our perceptions challenged by new information from a source we respect.

The Two-Step Model and the Confusion that Leads to Understanding

The Two-Step model uses task-based learning and compatible assessment techniques to engage students in their learning and internally motivate them to reach high standards.

Most learning tasks can be framed to confront the learner with information from a source he respects that can conflict with previous perceptions. This collision between perceptions and new information is what generates confusion. If the task is well designed, it forces the student to fight his way through the confusion. The Two-Step model then calls on the teacher to assist the student by anticipating what he may need in the form of planned interventions and to observe students' needs while watching them work on their tasks and provide spontaneous interventions.

The process is outlined next:

- We help students learn when we confront their perceptions with information that may conflict, and then we guide them as they try to reconcile the new information with their perceptions.

- When our perceptions are confronted with conflicting information from a source we respect, the result is confusion. We fight our way through the confusion by trying to reconcile our prior perceptions with the new information.

- The teacher can guide students through the learning process by altering the traditional approach of content introduction followed by practice, application, and discovery by instead using a constructivist approach that begins with exploration, proceeds almost immediately to student discovery, and includes frequent teacher interventions, sometimes planned, sometimes spontaneous. Reflective activities are interspersed throughout periods of student engagement. It is during the exploratory phase of the Two-Step that opportunities abound for confronting the learner with information that may conflict with prior knowledge.

Reality Check Question

Why is it most effective when information that conflicts with a student's perceptions is from a source he will respect?

The learning only occurs if you are motivated to fight your way through the confusion created when new information and perceptions conflict. The less you respect the source of the new information, the less likely you will feel the need to try to reconcile it with prior knowledge or perceptions. It is also important to remember that no two students hold the same source in the same regard. I may consider Michael Jordan an idol, and you may have heard of him but know nothing about him. Or, I may regard Michael Jordan highly as a basketball player and a role model but not respect him as an authority on men's earrings or some other product he may be hawking in a commercial. Therefore, the issue of respect is different from whether I like you. Also, the fact that I respect you as a friend or a ballplayer doesn't necessarily mean I respect your opinions about grammatical usage.

Similarly, a student may not like a teacher but may still take as gospel anything the teacher says and therefore feel the need to reconcile new information from the teacher that conflicts with prior knowledge. Some students regard anything in a textbook as being of great value and therefore have respect for new information that is found in a textbook.

The point is that we must constantly barrage students with new information from a variety of sources with the expectation that each student will find sources she respects enough to challenge her to reconcile any perceptions that conflict. One source respected by many students is their peers. That is why group work can be so effective. Some students will not be challenged to reconcile new information from the teacher with their prior knowledge—they will choose to ignore it. However, if a student, in a small group, hears a peer say that Benjamin Franklin used a kite to discover electricity, he may be more likely to try to reconcile this new information with his perception that Franklin's contributions to history grew, solely, out of his work as a politician and diplomat. It can also work in reverse. A student may love to engage in out-of-school activities, and in-school shenanigans with a peer, but may regard that peer as the last person who would have anything intelligent to say about Benjamin Franklin.

The probability that the learner will be encouraged to take the time and effort to try to reconcile prior perceptions with new information is increased in proportion to the degree of respect the learner has for the source of the new information. If I can too easily discount new information by discrediting its source, then I will more easily cling to my prior perceptions without revisiting them.

Let's see how this can play itself out in an entire lesson: A tenth grade teacher wants to begin a lesson on the ancient Greek religious beliefs. During the exploratory phase of the lesson, the following questions get asked:

- Can anyone tell me why people would want to believe in gods or God?

- What evidence might ancient humans have had that there is a God or gods?

- How does it help understand humans today by knowing about their belief systems thousands of years ago?

The teacher poses the questions and has the students develop answers to them by working in groups. When the students share their group answers, some say they all believe, others says that their parents do but they are not sure and others just admit that they don't know: all have decent explanations for their responses to the three questions.

As students share their views, inevitably they hear ideas from classmates whom they respect (for their academic views) that they either do not agree with or are confused about; in either case, the discussion provokes deep thinking because it provides challenging ideas from respected sources. (If the teacher also shares ideas from the text, quotes recognized experts and shares anecdotes about other people's responses to the three questions, the odds are increased that every student will be confronted by at least some new information that conflicts with her prior knowledge and beliefs–even if the peer sharing does not accomplish this goal for some of them.)

How does this relate to the two principles of learning we've discussed?

As classmates share their views, other classmates are having their perceptions challenged. Johnnie had been quite content to go through life without revisiting his impression, formed as a young child, that God is an exclusively American concept and not something that had much relevance for him except on Sundays. But his best friend, Jimmie, indicates that Spanish views of religion affect their everyday lives. Johnny is traveling to Spain with his family over vacation and suddenly knowing something about how Spaniards view religion has relevance for him. Now he has to reconcile his perception that religion is a uniquely American concept with his desire to be prepared for his family trip to Spain.

Sarah shares her family's view of religion and has never been motivated to learn anything about other religions. However, she is interested in a boy in her class who is not of her religion. During the class discussion, one of her classmates tells of two friends whose relationship is rocky because of their different religious backgrounds. Now Sarah has reason to pursue the topic in greater depth.

As the teenagers reveal their perceptions, the teacher is asking others, which of the ideas they are hearing would similarly motivate them to want to learn more about different views of religion? At some point, the teacher encourages students to move from the exploration phase to discovery: "Do you think that your group of three could agree on three facts about ancient Greek perspectives on religion?

As the students work in their groups, the teacher makes interventions, either when asked a question by a group of students, or, when noticing that a group is stymied, by going over to the group and intervening. The teacher expects confusion to abound. However, if the students are motivated to engage with the question posed by the teacher, there will be frequent opportunities for the teacher to help students fight their way through the confusion.

One more example from a middle school grade (in 1968):

Teacher: We are going to study poetry. Who can tell me where we can find poems?

Student response: In poetry books, where else?

Teacher: What if I suggested that most songs are poems?

Student: Maybe the songs you like, but not our songs."

Teacher: Name me a song you like.

Student: "Michelle," by the Beatles.

Teacher: Recite the words of "Michelle" for us, please.

Obviously, the student didn't need to recite more than two lines before realizing that the song he had actually selected was written in rhyme.

Through this exploratory phase, the teacher has motivated students to learn more about poetry by confronting them with information from sources they respect (themselves and their songs), and by challenging the students to reconcile that new information (songs we like are often poems) with their prior knowledge (we don't want to have anything to do with poetry).

Paradox

Brain research indicates that we learn by fighting our way through confusion. However, sometimes when we are confused, rather than fight our way through the confusion, we simply give up in frustration.

If we need to fight our way through confusion for learning to occur, but if our reaction to confusion may be to give up rather than fight, how does a teacher reconcile these two seemingly conflicting premises? Does the teacher or parent try to prevent a child from experiencing confusion to avoid frustration? But if we need to fight our way through confusion to learn, how does learning take place if the teacher or parent reduces the amount of confusion a child experiences?

Because the thought that we learn by fighting our way through confusion is a major focus of this book, let's examine this notion more closely.

Steve Barclay of *Performance Learning Systems* tells this story of how children learn: Barclay focuses on how a three-year-old might learn what foods can be classified as dessert. Attempting to explain to her three-year-old what makes a dessert a dessert, mom explains that desserts can be apple pie, raspberry pie, or blueberry pie. However, before the child becomes confident with the knowledge of what can be called dessert, dad brings home the main course, a pizza and calls it pizza pie. This confuses the child. Then, when dessert is served, following the pizza, it is similar in size and shape to other pies, but it is called cheesecake, not cheese pie. Our three-year-old is even more confused.

The next evening, visiting the grandparents for dinner, the child is unwilling to eat even a single string bean from the plate. Grandma encourages the child by saying, "If you eat all your string beans, you can have dessert." The child eats every string bean but then is rewarded by the health-conscious grandparents with a bowl of fresh fruit and melon balls. "Yuck," the child blurts out, feeling betrayed, "That's not dessert."

A week later mom and dad have company for dinner, and what do they serve as an appetizer? You guessed it, fresh fruit cocktail—the same foods that were identified as dessert when served at grandma's house. Then, as an incentive for the child to finish the fruit cocktail, dad says, "If you finish all your fruit cocktail, you can have a hamburger." The same food that was the reward for finishing the string beans a week ago is now the requirement for getting the desired main course.

Barclay completes his presentation by pointing out that eventually the child grasps the meaning of dessert by understanding it is a combination of category (certain types of foods) and sequence (coming after the main course). To a child of three, according to Barclay, everything is confusing; the whole world is confusing. However, Barclay cites brain research that indicates that the brain is intended to make patterns out of chaos. Eventually, the child makes patterns out of what initially appeared chaotic. Hence, raspberry pie, apple pie, melon balls, cut-up fruits, and cheesecake all have two things in common: They are not meats or other items identified with the main course of meals, and they are called "dessert" when they are served *after* the main course.

When a listener reflected on Barclay's presentation, he concluded that if we learn when our brain makes patterns out of chaos, then learning cannot occur if we are not allowed to be confused. Our brain will only make patterns out of chaos when we are allowed to confront our confusion and fight our way through it.

In physics, the chaos theory recognizes that the brain brings order out of chaos and attempts to bring this same ability to understanding the physical laws of nature such as weather patterns, turbulence, the creation of snowflakes, the ebb and flow of animal populations, and the branching of dendrons. What are the organizing principles in these apparently chaotic occurrences?

In other words, learning evolves as we fight our way through the confusion caused by conflict between our prior knowledge and new information (from a source we respect).

Whoops! That's fine if we are secure enough to be willing to fight our way through our confusion. But, as we mentioned a moment ago, do all of us always accept the challenge, when confused, to fight our way through it? Obviously not. Sometimes confusion leads to frustration. Depending on the degree of frustration, we may choose to throw up our arms in despair and simply give up and move on to something else.

This recognition that we do not always fight our way through confusion leads to this reconciliation of the seemingly conflicting need to allow the learner to experience confusion so he can fight through it with the concern that the confusion will lead to damaging frustration. The role of the teacher is *not* to eliminate confusion; without confusion, the learner will not learn. In fact, the teacher has to allow confusion to occur, if there is to be meaningful learning. However, the role of the teacher is to help the learner become comfortable with the confusion so that the learner will accept the confusion as a challenge, not as an excuse for giving up in frustration.

Reality Check Question

How does a teacher make a learner comfortable with confusion?

An example is when the teacher asks for a show of hands, "How many of you can name 12 capital cities in Africa?" knowing full well that few if any students will raise their hands. The teacher is trying to let all students realize that they are not alone in not having the answers. When a teacher prefaces a question with "Here's one I can't figure out," the teacher is letting the students know that they should not feel bad if the question confuses them.

The authors frequently begin a workshop on teaching strategies with a survey of how many participants have ever used the teaching technique or planned intervention strategy known as a *jigsaw* or *carousel* in the classroom. However, before asking for a show of hands, the authors state, "Usually when we ask veteran, outstanding teachers the question we are about to ask you, less than 15 percent are able to respond affirmatively, so don't feel bad if you are unfamiliar with the strategies we are about to discuss."

In summary, when people have their interest piqued by the challenge of figuring out why new information conflicts with their prior knowledge, they will be encouraged to continue to fight through their confusion if:

♦ The teacher or facilitator helps them to feel that confusion is to be expected and is not a reflection of their own limitations.

♦ The teacher is willing to continue dialoguing with them and make suggestions (coaching) until clarity can be brought to the chaos, or at least a comfort level can be achieved with whatever confusion might continue to exist.

At the outset of this chapter, it was stated: The thought that we learn by fighting our way through confusion is one of two thoughts that will be the focus of this chapter. We also discussed the second important thought about the need to confront students with new information that conflicts with prior knowledge or perceptions. There is a direct connection between these two notions of how we learn. It is the new information that conflicts with prior knowledge or perceptions that results in confusion.

We need to state clearly that we are *not* suggesting that teachers should deliberately create confusion to allow students to learn. However, although the teacher is not intentionally trying to confuse students, she must recognize that confusion is the necessary result of creating a good lesson that motivates students by challenging them to reconcile new information with prior knowledge. An excellent strategy to make students more comfortable with their confusion is to anticipate the situation and inform them beforehand that they should expect some confusion.

We submit that in a good teaching experience (be it in the classroom, at home, in the workplace, or in a social setting), when someone is allowed to share a perception, is then confronted with information from a respected source that conflicts with that perception, he will learn by reconciling the prior perception with the new information. The support of a competent facilitator (teacher, friend, relative) increases the likelihood that reconciliation of the prior perception and the new, conflicting information will be accomplished to forge a new understanding.

This thought—elicit perceptions, offer information that conflicts with prior perceptions, and provide an environment for allowing the learner to reconcile prior perceptions with new information—creates a lens for all teaching.

Thoughts for Reflection

- Trust the process.
- Trust People.
- Trust Yourself.
- Trust Chaos. (Terry Mazany, 1994)

End of Section Assessment

- Can you describe the connection between brain research that indicates learning grows out of confusion and learning theory that suggests learning occurs when our perceptions are confronted with conflicting information?
- Why is learning enhanced if conflicting information is from a source we respect?

Memorization and Critical Thinking

Learning Objectives

The reader will come to understand why we memorize best when we are actively engaged in a learning task, not when we "drill and kill" the material.

Main Point

- Task-based learning gets better results regarding informational retention than formal memorization.

To appreciate the value of dividing lessons into two phases (exploratory and discovery), it is critical to review what research indicates about how people learn. After all, don't business people determine store layouts on the basis of what research tells them about how shoppers shop?

Did you know that most people, when they enter a store, turn to the right? Merchants build on this knowledge to guide shoppers toward what the merchant most wants them to see. Isn't it equally important that educators plan lessons based on what they know of how people learn? The purpose of what we label *constructivism* is to help the learner understand; this requires the internal processing that comes from task-based learning. We can train a horse to recall information. If we expect more of a student than we would of a horse, we need to go beyond the drill and kill we use to encourage a horse to paw the ground six times when he hears the question, "How old are you?"

Did you know that we actually retain (memorize) more information when we are actively engaged in a learning process—through a task that requires us to use new information—than when we attempt to memorize the same information in isolation? Think about this; it is significant: We actually memorize more effectively when we are actively engaged in a task than when we are required to drill and kill with words and terms that have little context or meaning for us.

Reality Check/Reflective Thought

What is so significant about the finding that we commit more information to memory when we are engaged in learning tasks than when we attempt to formally memorize that information?

Many constructivists concede that drill and kill is a superior teaching behavior for memorization. However, they argue for constructivist approaches with the claim that it is more important to teach higher-level thinking skills than to require rote memorization of discrete facts. Clearly, constructivist behaviors enable students to refine higher-level thinking skills, whereas rote memorization requires only one of the six levels of thinking on Bloom's Taxonomy: "simple recall."

The irony is that constructivists needn't concede that rote memorization is more easily accomplished through drill and kill. It's not.

David Perkins, as co-director of Project Zero at Harvard Graduate School of Education, wrote, "Research shows that the best way to remember a body of information is to organize it actively, looking for internal patterns and relating it to what you already know" (Perkins, 1999). Doesn't logic tell us the same thing? When we are actively engaged in a task, don't we often remember much of the information we use as part of the task simply as a by-product of our extended work with the information?

Reality Check/Reflective Thought

I could use additional discussion of this point: Can you amplify why it is that engagement with learning tasks is a better way to remember information than formal memorization? When I was a kid, I learned poems by repeating the lines until they were ingrained in my memory.

Think about this example, and then we'll address your poetry memorization more directly:

Each summer, Jack conducts a weeklong summer conference. For the six months prior to the conference, Jack prepares mailings for nearly 300 people he's never met, assigns them to facilitators, makes hotel reservations for them—some for nonsmoking rooms, some for single, double, or family rooms—and he puts them on sign-up lists for special events, or special meals or the like.

By the time of the conference, Jack probably has memorized most of the 300 names without a conscious effort. The hooks he hangs his thoughts on include the special requests they may have made, a strange e-mail address, an unusual street address, or anything that may distinguish a particular person in his mind. If you were to test Jack on the 300 names, without even allowing him time to review, he would probably do pretty well. Certainly, if you gave him time to review the names, he would be quite accurate in recalling them on request.

By contrast, if you had given Jack 300 unfamiliar names six months ago and told him he had to memorize them for a test, he might put in countless hours of drill and kill and still not remember nearly as many names as he would remember of conference participants as a by-product of being actively engaged with their names. Regardless of how well Jack did on the test of 300 names, if he learned them solely through drill and kill, most of the names he might remember for the test would be lost to him forever within a week or two of having taken the test.

Why would he retain so few of the 300 names if he learned them solely through drill? Because he would have no hooks for his thoughts. When Jack prepares for the conference, he doesn't have to consciously memorize names—the hooks to hang his thoughts on come as by-products of his interaction with the names as he engages in the authentic task (authentic to him) of running the conference. Bill Johnson is the guy who called to say he was allergic to salmon, Barbara Alonzo e-mailed a thank you note when Jack sent her a list of area restaurants, Tom Egan requested a double room with Tim Bowers. These are the hooks on which Jack hangs his thoughts for remembering these people.

An undergraduate student assisted Jack this year in preparing mailings for the summer conference and doing most of the preconference preparatory work. During a break she commented, "I think I know everyone's e-mail address by heart." On another occasion, Jack asked her, "Marva, can you look up Martha Jenson's zip code?"

Marva immediately responded, "It's 14610." She didn't need to look it up.

When teachers engage students in student-run activities, they frequently report that students do better on short-answer tests following the lessons than when the teacher presents the same information. Why? Because the students are actively engaged with the information they are preparing to present to their classmates, and they retain much of that information as a by-product of their work.

If you are still not convinced, try an exercise on yourself that is often used at workshops by staff developers. Think of a time in your life when you learned a great deal. It doesn't have to have been in a school setting, although it can be.

Are you thinking of a time when you learned a great deal? What were the circumstances? How much do you remember about the learning experience? How much information have you retained?

Be honest. Did you think of a time when you learned a lot while sitting passively and listening to someone? If so, you are in a small minority. Almost everyone who is asked this question thinks of an experience when he was actively engaged. If it occurred in school, it usually was part of a class project or group activity. When three or four people are asked to identify the common denominators in their best learning experiences, they usually indicate the learning involved interaction with at least one other person, required a degree of risk taking, was under circumstances that were interesting and challenging, and inspired reflection and self-assessment long after the time of the initial experience.

What about your experience as a child of learning a poem through boring recitation? Two thoughts:

♦ Had you been asked to work with two peers and design a skit that reflected the intent of the poem, you still could have resorted to repetition of the lines (drill and kill) prior to the test, but the memorization process would have been much briefer.

- How much of the poem you will understand when you simply memorize lines because you will be tested is questionable. Engagement with the poem through design of a skit or any of a variety of other performance tasks would significantly increase understanding.

Thoughts for Reflection:

"Over and over again, studies have demonstrated that we memorize best when we analyze what we are learning, find patterns in it, and relate it to knowledge we already have (Perkins, 1992)."

End of Section Assessment

Can you articulate your own beliefs of how people learn and refer to an experience you have had that demonstrates the validity of your beliefs?

We Learn Best When We Teach Others

Learning Objective

The reader will gain an understanding of why we learn best when we teach others.

Main Points

- Teachers teach most effectively when they create authentic tasks in which the student teaches others.
- Students meet higher standards when they are independent learners who take responsibility for their own and others' learning.

One of the authors, Paul Vermette, has a "Gronk" activity he uses at the start of workshops. He describes the Gronk as "A short, plump mammal with no eyebrows, a long pointed tail, and small limbs."Paul pairs the entire audience (teachers at a staff development day, university students in an education course, or any group where the goal is to focus them on how we learn most effectively). Then he asks each pair to identify one person as a teacher and one as a student. He then announces:

> Those of you who have elected to be a student for this activity can read, relax, or do anything you want for the next few minutes. I will distribute a picture of a Gronk to the person in each pair who is acting as the teacher. I want you to study the Gronk for three minutes and then I will ask you to describe it to your student. You cannot show the Gronk to your student; however, you can be looking at it as you describe it. I want you to prepare your student to be able to describe the Gronk to the rest of us. Prepare as if your job, or your merit pay, depended on it. Prepare as if the teacher whose student can do the best job of describing the Gronk will get the biggest raise.

After distributing the Gronk to the "teachers" and allowing three minutes for study, he announces: "Begin teaching. You have five minutes to prepare your student to describe the Gronk to the rest of us."

After five minutes, Paul announces that time is up, and he collects the pictures of the Gronk from each of the "teachers." "Now, which of you, as teachers, thinks you have the best student—the student who can do the best job describing the Gronk to the rest of us?"

Marianne's hand is the first one raised, followed by several more. "OK, Marianne, can you describe the Gronk to us?"

Marianne hesitates, thinking he means it is her student who should give the description. After some hesitation, Marianne realizes she has to describe the Gronk and does so. Her description is so accurate that Paul smiles and asks, "Do you have a photographic memory?" Marianne says she doesn't, and then Paul asks if any of the other teachers in the group can add any details Marianne may have missed. Some details are added, but it is obvious that Marianne provided most of the information in her initial response. Then Paul asks, "Why do you think I called on one of the teachers, rather than one of the students? Eventually, one of the group members usually figures out it was to demonstrate how much information is retained by the teacher when the teacher is trying to convey the information to the student. Paul then elaborates on this point:

> Research indicates that we often learn most when we teach others. You all witnessed how much Marianne retained, and she wasn't even aware that she would be asked to demonstrate what she had learned. In a classroom setting, you know what you will be expected to memorize, and you are able to drill and kill and use strategies to intentionally retain information. Marianne retained this information without making a conscious effort. If this were a classroom situation, then after engaging Marianne in an activity requiring her to use this information—by teaching it—we could still have told her, 'Tomorrow you will be tested on it," and she could still have had the opportunity for some drill and kill.

Paul then cites the research from Perkins to reinforce the concept that we learn most when we are actively engaged with the information we need to learn. He concludes the Gronk activity by reminding the audience that having the learner teach others that which we want the learner to know is often the most effective way to engage the learner with new information.

The Two-Step model uses task-based learning and compatible assessment techniques to engage students in their learning and to internally motivate them to reach high standards. Students learn most when they are teaching others. When the task is cast as one in which the student is to teach others, it becomes an authentic task with an audience beyond the teacher, thereby moving the student to be intrinsically motivated to hold herself to high standards because the student tends to hold herself personally responsible.

A new term, *minds-on* has been introduced: hands-on + reflection = minds-on. The Two-Step model creates an environment conducive to hands-on learning, which creates common frames of reference for individual and group reflection, which, in-turn, generates minds-on learning. The following outline summarizes *minds-on*:

- We learn best what we teach.

- Teachers teach most effectively when they create authentic tasks in which the student teaches others what we want the student to learn. This is because we learn best through engagement in a task, particularly if the task is an authentic task that motivates student engagement.

- Students meet higher standards when they are independent learners who take responsibility for their own learning.

Thoughts for Reflection

On one of her first broadcasts in 2003, Dr. Laura Schlessinger stated, "Anyone who's ever tried to teach anything to anyone knows that's when you learn the most."

End of Chapter Assessment

Can you think of three different strategies for putting students in situations where they have to teach others what we want them to learn?

4

How Constructivism Differs from Traditional Models: A Practical Application for Teachers, Administrators, and Students

If a classroom is constructivist, most students are challenged to think continuously and the teacher knows which students are being compelled to think.

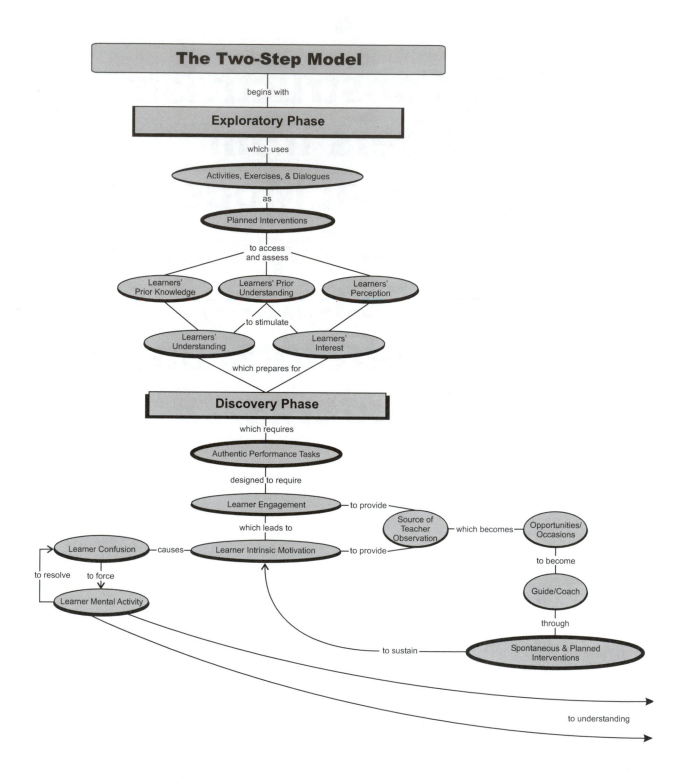

The Two-Step Model

begins with

Exploratory Phase

which uses

Activities, Exercises, & Dialogues

as

Planned Interventions

to access and assess

Learners' Prior Knowledge

Learners' Prior Understanding

Learners' Perception

to stimulate

Learners' Understanding

Learners' Interest

which prepares for

Discovery Phase

which requires

Authentic Performance Tasks

designed to require

Learner Engagement — to provide

which leads to

Learner Confusion — causes — Learner Intrinsic Motivation — to provide

Source of Teacher Observation — which becomes — Opportunities/ Occasions

to resolve   to force

Learner Mental Activity

to become

Guide/Coach

through

to sustain — Spontaneous & Planned Interventions

to understanding

Interaction, Lecture, and Constructivism

Learning Objective

The reader will focus on the following thoughts: Constructivism is not synonymous with interaction, nor does it necessarily exclude lecture. A constructivist classroom focuses on learning objectives that require higher-level thinking skills, not simple recall.

Main Points

- A constructivist lesson challenges students to think.

- Whether a classroom strategy is constructivist depends on the context in which it is applied.

- Lectures are compatible with the Two-Step model's vision of task-based learning.

- An interactive classroom is not necessarily constructivist.

- Active student engagement comes earlier, and more frequently, in a lesson when a constructivist rather than a more traditional pedagogy is applied.

Constructivism—A Definition

Constructivist theory is about facilitating the learner to go beyond simple recall (memorization) toward understanding, application, and competence. Constructivist theory indicates that understanding, application, and competence cannot be achieved without actively engaging the learner.

There can be lecture and assigned readings in a constructivist process, but they must be part of a larger picture that involves challenging the learner to apply the knowledge and to discover meanings and understandings that the learner will need to reconcile with prior knowledge and perceptions.

Although there are certain teacher behaviors that are more frequently observed in a constructivist classroom, it is not true that the simple act of demonstrating a constructivist behavior makes a person a constructivist teacher. The fact that I may allow sufficient wait time (suggested by Brooks & Brooks, 1993, as a behavior associated with constructivist teaching), while positive in and of itself, does not mean I am engaging students in a constructivist lesson.

Reality Check Question

Is defining constructivism as simple as saying it is interactive, experiential learning, or is it more complex than that?

People tend to go to two extremes in trying to understand the term constructivism: (1) complex explanations and (2) oversimplification. The overly simplistic explanation is that constructivism requires interaction, and lecture has no place in a constructivist classroom. This is not only simplistic; it is also incorrect.

However, as part of a more complex explanation, we get a picture of the threads that weave together to create a constructivist classroom. We rely on articulations by respected authors. We look at graphics that tell us in a constructivist classroom, seats are probably grouped in circles, in contrast to the rows of chairs and desks in a traditional classroom. We are also told that a constructivist classroom is student centered, not teacher centered, and a constructivist classroom encourages student activity, not the passivity that results from listening to an endless string of lectures. Although certain arrangements of chairs and desks and the use of certain teaching strategies often characterize a constructivist classroom, it is not correct that, at any given point in time, a constructivist classroom cannot have chairs in neat rows, or have the teacher in front of the room speaking.

Characterizations of what to expect in a constructivist classroom may be helpful, but they fail to enable us to classify a particular classroom as constructivist, or a particular teacher (or parent) as constructivist.

As we have indicated, constructivism requires engagement. Without engagement, there is no understanding. Without understanding, there are severe limitations on the ability to apply knowledge competently. Will Rogers used to say, "All I know is what I read in the papers." So why was what he concluded from what he read so interesting to people who read the same papers? Was it how he applied the knowledge? What is it, then, that makes a lesson constructivist? What is it that entitles a teacher to lay claim to being a constructivist teacher? Perhaps the answer lies in an analysis of critical thinking skills (sometimes referred to as higher-level thinking skills).

When you look at a lesson that is highly interactive, and yet your gut tells you it is not constructivist, the reason is usually that it is not challenging students to do much more than recall factual information. For instance, the game of telephone is interactive; each participant has to pass along a message from the previous person. But does this require much more than a good memory and an ability to hear? A constructivist lesson challenges students to address one of the higher-level thinking skills between comprehension and evaluation (in other words, to go beyond simple recall of information):

- ♦ Recall
- ♦ Comprehension
- ♦ Application
- ♦ Analysis
- ♦ Synthesis
- ♦ Evaluation

In one sense, Bloom's Taxonomy is upside down. We remember information because we have worked to use it in a meaningful way. Challenge a student to evaluate, and he will have to synthesize, analyze, apply, comprehend, and use information. Much of the information he uses he will remember because of the context in which it was used. Challenge students to evaluate why an apple falls from a tree, and they will function in all classifications of Bloom's Taxonomy.

If a lesson is constructivist, it challenges students to apply each of these components of the taxonomy.

If a lesson is constructivist, the teacher is probably employing some of the 12 constructivist behaviors suggested by Brooks and Brooks (1993) as a means toward requiring students to use higher-level thinking skills. However, it is not correct to label any strategy—whether it be interaction or a lengthy lecture—as either constructivist or not constructivist.

A lecture is a strategy; group work is a strategy; but constructivism is a theory, not a strategy (Brooks & Brooks, 1993). It is a theory about learning and knowledge.

Strategies that can be integrated into a constructivist classroom include reflection, portfolios, authentic tasks, lectures, performance assessments, assigned readings, and probing questions.

Whether a classroom is constructivist, or whether a teacher should be identified as a constructivist teacher, depends on how strategies are used, when they are used, and the purpose for which they are used. Therefore, it is not correct to say that anything interactive is constructivist, nor is it correct to say that any lecture or assigned readings are not constructivist.

If a teacher assigns students to read 10 pages and respond to the questions at the end of the chapter, this is probably not a constructivist approach. However, that same assignment could be part of a constructivist process if the assignment to read a chapter and respond to the questions is part of a student-driven process of building knowledge to develop understanding for the purpose of application. In fact, the assignment to read a chapter and respond to questions will be even more profitable as a learning activity if it is part of a task the students perceive as authentic, because this will motivate students to undertake the assignment and will create a context for understanding and applying the knowledge imparted in the chapter.

Is a constructivist lesson interactive? An example of an interactive lesson that is decidedly *not constructivist* would be as follows: Students are read a short story and then are placed in small groups and asked to agree on the names of three characters from the story. Interactive? Yes. Constructivist? No!

Wouldn't *The Wizard of Oz* have been a different story if Dorothy had never left the farm? What if Glinda had visited Dorothy in Kansas and explained why Dorothy should be grateful to be in Kansas and why she should be appreciative of all the people and surroundings that were available to her? Would Dorothy have listened for 46 minutes, nodded understandingly, and then said, "Thank you, good witch of the North, now I understand why I am so fortunate, everything I could ever want is right here in my own backyard?" Yeah, right. As Glinda says in response to a question from Scarecrow, "Dorothy had to learn it for herself."

Yet, how often do we expect students to listen to a few gems of wisdom from our lips and be able to apply the information we impart with the kind of understanding and competence that can only be gained through active engagement?

A teacher once challenged the theory that people learn to apply knowledge through social interaction by citing Thoreau and asserting that he went off into the woods by himself to learn. Wrong. Thoreau interacted with society, observed, and participated. Then he went into the woods by Walden Pond to reflect through his writings. What an artist learns is often expressed in paintings that represent the culmination of the artist's reflective process. The writer (Thoreau), the thinker (Gandhi), the painter (Van Gogh) are actively engaged in social interaction as they gather and apply information. Their writings and paintings are the culminating reflection of the meanings and understandings they have constructed. If we asked, "What was the discovery phase of Thoreau's learning (as reflected in *Walden Pond*), it would be the combination of his experiences once he decided he would write a book, as well as the reflective phase that occurred during his voluntary isolation in the woods. It was William Wordsworth who defined writing as "reflection in tranquility."

How often do we allow students to engage in social interaction focused on the information we want them to learn? How often do we allow students time to reflect on their interactions? How often do we allow students to select what they feel is the appropriate venue for expressing their understanding of the information we have shared and/or they have accumulated?

How often do we assess what students understand, rather than just what they can recall? How often do we allow students to engage in a task or dialogue with others as a vehicle for developing understandings of the information they are asked to recall?

Can there be lecture in a constructivist classroom? Absolutely. Whether a lecture is being used effectively as a strategy in a constructivist classroom depends on the context.

Reality Check Question

I need to know more about the constructivist approach that is used in the Two-Step.
OK, let's compare the traditional method of teaching with the constructivist approach.

Traditional Model

- *Teacher instructs:* teaches student the content.
- *Student learns:* studies what the teacher has taught (mostly memorization).
- *Student practices:* practices what teacher taught and practices the way teacher told him to practice.
- *Student discovers:* begins to discover, if time permits (how and when to use what teacher has taught).

Constructivist Model

- *Exploration*: The student explores the content and/or the method he will use (e.g., portfolio, essay, graphic representations) when engaged in the discovery phase. Exploration is preparation for discovery.

- *Discovery*: The student discovers how and when to use what the teacher has challenged him to learn.

  - *The teacher* intervenes sometimes with a predetermined planned intervention, providing the student with information the teacher anticipated that the student may need for discovery, sometimes with a spontaneous intervention of information or direction based on her observations of the student while he works on his task.

  - *The student* continues to discover, and the teacher and perhaps others continue to intervene.

  - *Reflection is* integrated into the process at all stages of exploration and discovery. It is through reflection on the engagement with information that learning occurs.

Let's contrast examples of teaching photography through a traditional approach versus a constructivist approach.

Photography: A Traditional Approach

- Teacher instructs: The teacher lectures on the key parts of a camera, probably with slides as graphic illustrations. These include lens, shutter, aperture setting, shutter speed setting, flash controls, and view finder.

- Student studies: The students are responsible for naming these parts, probably on a diagram. There would also be lectures regarding the qualities of good photos including, depth of field, contrast, proportion, framing, composition, point of view, and the like.

- Student Practices: Practice might consist of squeezing the button on the camera, lining up pictures with proper focus and distance, and taking some pictures of whatever is within eyesight, even if it has no practical value or relevance to the student.

- Student discovers: Taking some pictures as part of a meaningful project, if time allows and if there is enough equipment.

What is the problem with this approach? Except for those students already motivated to study photography, there is little at the start of the lesson to help students see why or how a knowledge of photography can benefit them. They are being asked to learn about photography without a context (no hooks to hang their thoughts on), and they may have little or no time to demonstrate how they can apply what they are learning in a situation where the teacher is observing and can make timely interventions.

Photography: The Constructivist Two-Step Model

Instead of following the instructional order of first explaining the principles of photography and the meaning and application of the various terms, such as f-stop, shutter speed, depth of field, contrast, composition, point of view, and the like, and only then moving into discussions and applications of this information, a constructivist teacher takes a different approach.

- *Exploration*: The teacher gives the students basic single lens reflex cameras and directs them to take a roll of 12 black-and-white slides. Each student is then asked to select a small number of slides from those he has taken, project them, and briefly talk about them with the class. This exercise, during the exploratory phase of the lesson, gives the teacher access to the students' current state of knowledge regarding photography and insight into their interests regarding photography. It also begins the intervention-discussion that over time will introduce the principles, mechanics, and aesthetics of photography.

  For example, a student might ask, "How did you get the people clear and the background blurry?" This would begin an intervention-discussion of depth of field. Or another student might comment that she liked the way the dog was jumping out of the picture; this would lead to an intervention-discussion regarding composition. Over time, the teacher will observe that the students begin to use the technical terms in their explanations and critiques. And over time, the students will begin to intentionally set f-stops and shutter speeds to obtain desired results.

- *Discovery*: At this point, the teacher is ready to enter the discovery phase by giving students their task-assignments that draw on their new understandings. Peer review is now a key component of the instructional pattern. This new order of instruction—beginning with exploration and then moving into discovery assisted by spontaneous and planned interventions—produces engaged photographers who have internalized the principles, mechanics, and aesthetics of photography rather than disengaged students with surface information and no real understanding of appreciation for the art and science of photography.

Someone hearing this example once said, "What if you can't afford to give cameras to everyone in the class? Can you still have an exploratory phase for a lesson on photography?" Of course. This is too literal an interpretation. There are many ways to explore a topic. In fact, can you think of a good example of an exploratory activity for a photography course? Here's one:

An Alternative Exploratory Phase

Encourage students to look through magazines or portfolios of photographs from a previous class. Ask them to identify the photos that they think are outstanding. Then, ask them to agree on the characteristics, in common, of the photos they identified as outstanding. This can be done as a lead-in to the design of their own photo albums.

Reality Check/Reflective Thought

I need more examples of the constructivist approach that's used in the Two-Step.

An example: 12th grade students had been studying the stock market and had done a project that required them to follow certain stocks for several months. They had developed a newspaper to show their findings and now were ready for the next unit. The teacher started the next class by posing a key question: "Is the value of a stock that is from a company that makes weather related items (such as swimming pool equipment) affected during different seasons of the year by the seasonal nature of the company's business? Students immediately had tentative answers to the query: as per usual, these varied all over the board, from yes to no to maybe. One argued that investors know about seasonal sales and factor that into the price; another argued that there should be a decline in stock price during the off-season because of lower sales. Another said that there would be fewer sales during the off season, but fluctuations in stock price would only be the same as for other stocks. Some motivated students sought access to newspapers to actually check certain stocks but were denied access by the teacher until they could make a guess and defend it with their prior knowledge about the market. After a few minutes of heated analytical discussion, the teacher generated a list of seven predictions on the board and then helped students decide how they could actually use data to test the various hypotheses. By the end of the period, students had begun to ask for library passes to go find the data, and were asking about using the next day's class to continue the investigation.

In this case, the discussion about the stock changes that flowed from the previous work acted as the exploratory phase for the discovery phase: determining seasonal market changes.

Another example: In an English 11 class, the authentic task in the discovery phase is for each student to write a poem that is creative and is clearly a poem.

A traditional teacher, Mr. Mooney, might begin the lesson by distributing a handout that contains definitions of rhyme scheme and meter and includes examples of different types of poetry. After a brief lecture in which Mr. Mooney begins by informing the class they have studied these terms in earlier grades, and after allowing for a little bit of class discussion, he describes the assignment and tells the students they will have some class time to begin their poems and then they must complete them as homework within the next two days.

A more constructivist teacher, Mrs. Lightner, distributes a handout with four writing samples, three of them are poems and the other is an essay, but they are not labeled. Mrs. Lightner asks the class to work in pairs, and to identify which are the poems and to agree on an answer to the question, "What makes a poem, a poem?" Following a sharing of responses, Mrs. Lightner then distributes the same handout used by Mr. Mooney, and gives the same lecture. However, she intersperses her lecture with references to the student responses to "What makes a poem, a poem?" and she frequently challenges the students to defend their responses when there are apparent conflicts with the information on the handout.

Beginning the lesson with engagement in order to create frames of reference for a discussion or lecture has been described by secondary teacher Cathy LaBrake as "Putting the students in the middle of the content."

Why this sequence? By beginning with the challenge to students to distinguish the three poems from the essay and then to identify the characteristics of a poem, the teacher has created a context for the handout and lecture. When Mrs. Lightner begins her lecture, the students will have hooks to hang their thoughts on. She has helped them to access their prior knowledge and to visualize the poems on the handout as they try to understand the terms in the handout and lecture. When Mr. Mooney starts the lesson with the handout and lecture, the students have nothing with which they can connect his ideas; the terms and concepts have no meaning for them. Create the context first, through student engagement with information, and then do the planned intervention—the handout and/or discussion.

By posing the exploration question, "What makes a poem, a poem?" Mrs. Lightner is beginning to frame the authentic task, which becomes a frame of reference for intervening with students much as the football practices or games and the play rehearsals or performances are for players and cast members.

Think of the sports analogy—practicing for a game or a match. This is a constructivist process. The coach may give a 30-minute (or longer) lecture as he stands at the blackboard. This is an intervention. It is successful because there is something to intervene in. The players all participated in the practice (or the previous game) and the coach makes his comments with reference to the players' authentic task engagement.

Think of a rehearsal for a school play. The director may speak at length or may offer a spontaneous intervention by approaching one performer and offering information, with reference to the rehearsal, of a particular scene that just occurred.

Student engagement in a football practice or play is a given so it is easy to offer information and suggestions as interventions. We must do the same in the "academic" subject areas. We need to create an authentic task so that a context is established for our interventions. The authentic task isn't built into the classroom automatically, as it is to the work of a football team or the cast of a school play.

When students begin work on a project, when students plan a budget for a trip to California or New York, or when students design a flier for a local tourist attraction, then a context for learning has been established. If the project or process that engages students is well planned, it will require them to use new information that they probably have not thought about in the past. This will initially confuse them. As they struggle to integrate this new information with what they already know to successfully complete the project or participate in the process, they will be learning.

Reality Check Question

What makes Glinda a constructivist?

"When," Glinda said that, "She (Dorothy) had to learn it for herself," she was telling us what we already know instinctively. That's why we all nod knowingly when someone says, "Experience is the best teacher." That's why we say, "You have to walk a mile in my moccasins" to understand me. That's why we say, "Tell me and I hear, show me and I see, let me experience it and I understand." Glinda is a constructivist because she engaged Dorothy first, then through reflection, she encouraged Dorothy to learn from her engagement in activities.

Why does the author use Glinda as an example of a constructivist when she allowed Dorothy to discover that her backyard always held the key to what she wanted out of life? It is our attempt to give the reader a hook to hang thoughts on for understanding constructivism. We are attempting to connect previous knowledge with new knowledge.

Thoughts for Reflection

"All genuine learning is active, not passive. It involves the use of the mind, not just the memory. It is a process of discovery, in which the student is the main agent, not the teacher" (Mortimer J. Adler, *The Paideia Proposal: An Educational Manifesto*, 1982).

End of Section Assessment

Can you state a learning objective and then briefly describe a traditional and a constructivist lesson that a teacher might use to help students master that objective?

Student Motivation through Authentic Tasks

Learning Objective

The reader will come to understand the relationship of performance tasks to learning objectives and the power of performance tasks to generate intrinsic motivation.

Main Points

- The Two-Step model calls for authentic tasks.

- Authentic tasks engender intrinsic motivation.

- A key to making a task authentic is to provide students with an audience to whom the students can present the process or product they have developed—someone beyond the teacher. This puts the focus on the quality of the product or process rather than on merely a grade.

- There is a continuum of performance tasks—from real-world tasks with an audience, through simulations, to tasks that are only school related.

- In task-based learning, the acceptable level of performance, the standards, are established in the task rubric and the accompanying exemplars.

- Many students are not motivated by grades and will not work unless they can be intrinsically motivated.

The discovery phase of a lesson or unit focuses students on achievement of an authentic task. Some education writers speak of the need for a culminating event to enable students to demonstrate their understanding of, and ability to, apply knowledge. The discovery phase includes the culminating event for students to demonstrate their competence at mastering the learning objective(s), however, the discovery phase also provides the process through which students acquire their understanding.

Reality Check Question

What is it about authentic tasks that engender intrinsic motivation?

If a task is authentic, it means the student perceives value (for fun or benefit) in achieving the task. It is this sense that I need, or enjoy, the task that makes it authentic for me. Also, to be authentic, the skills, knowledge, and competencies a student is applying to the task must be used in the same context that the student will use them in a real-world setting. Hence, the key phrases in defining authenticity are *perceived value* (or *enjoyment*) *to the student*, *realism of the context*, and *an audience beyond the teacher* for a grade.

To gain a better understanding of the concept of authenticity, let's first examine the issue of student motivation. Authentic tasks are designed to:

♦ Increase student motivation

♦ Create a real world context for student learning

The former Cornell University and Montreal Canadian hockey player, Ken Dryden, wrote a book based on a semester of shadowing students in Ontario. He concluded that we could make major reforms in our schools if we recognized that students learn and react the same way we all do (Dryden, 1995).

What motivates an adult to want to learn? Aren't we motivated to engage in a learning activity for any or all of these reasons:

♦ If we perceive a need for the information (or understandings) being shared

♦ If we believe the activity will be fun, even if learning is a by-product.

♦ If we feel capable of doing it

Try to engage my valuable time in an activity I do not embrace, and unless I am convinced I either need or want to learn, I wish you luck. I will become engaged in an activity if it will either serve a purpose for me or be fun, and if it is something I feel I can do reasonably well.

The keyword here is *perceive*. I must perceive the task to be one that will serve a purpose for me and/or be fun. The fact that the teacher or parent is correct in assuming that I will need a certain skill or information to succeed at what I have indicated I want to do does not matter. "Learn to type," my father frequently told me—he had first-hand knowledge of my deplorable handwriting. When I was seven years old, he would place my fingers on the typewriter keys, but I would not apply myself. At the age of 27, a job in journalism was offered if I could type. I sought out the assistance of a friend and practiced throughout a weekend, in order to type passably at a job interview the following Monday. Timing is everything. What my father was unable to motivate me to do for 20 years, I undertook immediately when I felt the need.

Do we think children are any different? Can we reasonably expect them to be motivated by our pronouncement that "someday you will need this," when we, as adults, are not motivated simply because someone else tells us to be?

I am not an opera buff (to put it mildly). If I were to agree to accompany my wife to a lecture on the opera in exchange for my wife's attendance at a football game, I suspect my retention of information from the lecture would be quite low.

However, if I am to entertain a client who I have heard is an opera buff, I might choose to attend the lecture to prepare myself. My dislike of opera has not decreased. But I now have a perceived need for the information, and I suspect my retention rate would be higher than in the initial situation. I am intrinsically motivated by my perceived need.

I will not perceive a need to attend a lecture on the opera just because you tell me, "Someday you will want this information." You might have been correct if you had said a year ago, "Someday you may have to entertain a client who loves the opera, so you'd better go to this lecture and pay attention." Sorry, no impact on me.

Yet, we expect students to pay attention just because we say, "Someday you'll need this information. Someday you'll thank me." It's not that they don't believe us. I believe you when you say that some day I may need the information about the opera. But, I think to myself, when that day comes I'll seek out the information. Then I'll be intrinsically motivated—not now. The other motivation we have for paying attention is when something is just plain fun, as in this poem found on a plaque at a ski lodge:

Learning to . . .

A child does not learn to ski to look good. He looks at it from a different angle. He likes to go over bumps and he likes speed! Chasing each other is more important than learning to turn! Make skiing a game, and the child will learn in spite of himself! (Rudi Wyrsch)

Reality Check Question

It is popular to speak of the need to intrinsically motivate students. Even when we frequently resort to external factors for motivation (reward and punishment), we bemoan the need to do so. Please further define intrinsic motivation *and explain how we engage students in ways that increase the probability that intrinsic motivation will kick in.*

One might argue that the reward of a job in journalism was an extrinsic motivating factor for the author to learn to type. Initially, it was. However, once the author began his weekend of learning to type, his pride took over, and he continued to practice long after he achieved a level of proficiency necessary to be hired for the job. We are suggesting that when a person sets out to accomplish something because he chooses to do so, intrinsic motivation (pride in accomplishment) often takes over. We know this is happening when someone continues to perfect an accomplishment even after the level of achievement required to receive the reward (perhaps an A) or to avoid a punishment has been reached.

We know we are intrinsically motivated when the journey is so enjoyable and/or challenging that arriving at the destination becomes less significant than trying to get there. It is the difference between feeling, "I want to continue working on this," and saying to yourself, "I can't wait to be done." The desire to complete the task (arrive at the destination) is a powerful intrinsic motivator. There is greater satisfaction from working on a task and knowing you achieved it, than from receiving an extrinsic reward. An extrinsic reward is nice; it's a form of validation, but it does not equal the inner gratification of knowing you have accomplished what you set out to do. To paraphrase Abraham Lincoln: *When I know I've done something poorly; 1000 angels singing my praises will not make me feel better. Conversely, nothing can detract from my satisfaction when I know I have engaged in a job well done.*

Sometimes we need external factors to initially motivate students to enter into an engagement (e.g., the implied or explicit threat of a poor grade, call home, or detention). However, if the task is perceived by the student as authentic, and if the student has the option of using some of his stronger multiple intelligences, we increase the likelihood that intrinsic motivation will take over. In other words, it may not be realistic to expect a student to undertake the replication, in miniature, of a Korean War demilitarized zone purely out of an intrinsic desire to accomplish this task. However, if the student has a chance to use supplies that she enjoys (paints, markers, tools); if the resources, peer interaction, and investment of time generate ownership of the task; and if the student anticipates a reasonable chance of success, the student may begin to enjoy the task for itself, not solely because it is required to do well in the course.

We can all think of situations where we were externally motivated (bribed) by our parents to engage in something, but once engaged, we started to like what we were doing and our intrinsic motivation kicked in. For example, my daughter went to a Broadway play with us for the first time when she was five, with a frown on her face, but knowing she could not have a friend over the next day unless she joined us. By the end of that show she was asking when we could go again, and she was fantasizing reenactments she could do with her friend the next day. Now, as a college student, she's a theater major.

Some students are intrinsically motivated to go to school (it's part of the family's culture), so the very act of going to school is an authentic task for them, and that motivates them to do their best. However, they may not be intrinsically motivated for every (or even any) of the specific assignments unless the teacher works hard at creating and negotiating tasks that will enable intrinsic motivation to kick in.

Reality Check Question

If we are motivated only when something is perceived by us to be worthwhile (needed) or fun, then what is the practical application of this awareness in the classroom?

The more authentic a task, the more likely students will see it as worthwhile and/or fun. Authenticity is an elusive concept, but one worth working toward. Performance tasks that are not completely authentic are better than the absence of a task, but authenticity really helps with motivation, and it helps the process of setting a useful and meaningful context. The key to a lesson or unit is the authentic task. The other parts of the discovery phase are in service to the authentic task. Discovery is in doing the task. It is in the process of doing the task that the student learns (discovers) what the teacher hopes to impart *and* much more.

Reality Check Question

What is it that makes a task authentic?

Fred Newmann of the University of Wisconsin has defined authenticity as a task that has personal or public value (Newmann, 1990). For instance, if a student writes a letter to the editor and mails it, there is personal value if it is on a topic that has engaged the student's interests. If the letter is published, it has public value. A more precise definition from Newmann is that there must be an audience beyond the teacher for a grade.

What motivates a student to engage in a classroom lesson? Too often the answer is simply for a grade. Instead, we can often hook students on becoming engaged in a learning activity by providing an audience beyond the teacher for a grade:

♦ Ninth grade students were motivated to do a better job on their course portfolios when they realized that they would be reviewed by their e-mail partners, college students in a teacher education program, as well as by the teachers at school.

♦ Eleventh grade students were motivated by the fact their letters of response to an article in the newspaper would be read and responded to by the author of that article who was coming as a guest speaker the following week.

♦ An 11th grade biology teacher teamed with a 4th grade teacher and offered to let the high school students skip their weekly lab if they would teach the content of the lab to the 4th graders. Each class became an audience for the other.

♦ A middle school English teacher broke his class into four sections and had each section teach the rest of the class about conflict, character, setting, and plot. Three fourths of the class was the audience for each fourth of the class.

Sometimes the building principal can be the audience beyond the teacher for a grade. Sometimes the audience can be one or two parents (you can invite all parents, but personally call one or two to be sure there will be an audience—or you can ask each parent to commit to one or two visits to the classroom per year to be the audience for a student presentation, exhibition, performance, or demonstration).

Here's one more example of an authentic task: Lake George, New York science teachers Tammy Darby and Nicole Porter regularly team with 3rd and 4th grade math/science teacher Paul Kelly to create multi-age activities that require collaboration among their students. These activities demonstrate how younger students often listen more attentively to older students, sometimes know more about certain things than older students and become more engaged, as do the older students, with the fun, challenge, and excitement of active involvement with students at other levels of the school system.

One example is a leaf sorting activity which requires students of mixed ages (and can include adults) to work in groups of six-eight around a table with a variety of leaves which they are required to categorize. Once they have sorted the leaves into several piles, they are asked to identify common characteristics of the leaves in each pile. The last step is to ask the students the names of the leaves in each pile (with the teacher ready to spontaneously intervene, when necessary). At the conclusion of this activity, the teachers inform the students that what they have just done—sorting, classifying, and then labeling—is exactly what scientists do when they begin working with raw materials (i.e., leaves) that do not yet have a name. This task is authentic because it utilizes raw, authentic, materials (leaves), and has an audience beyond the teacher for a grade—the other students. (It also lends itself to involvement of parents and/or other adults.)

This type of lesson contrasts with a more traditional approach that would begin with the teacher listing types of leaves on the board (pine, spruce, maple, elm, oak), then listing characteristics of each, and finally asking students to memorize the names and characteristics of each kind of leaf.

Do you think students are more likely to remember the names of different leaves if they are, first, actively engaged in the classification of the leaves and then given the labels, or if they are dealing with a teacher in front of the room, chalk, and memorization for the sake of memorization?

As extrinsic motivation, a grade may be enough to encourage a student to tackle an assignment, but it has two drawbacks:

1. An extrinsically motivated student will not become engrossed (emotionally involved) in a task if it doesn't become authentic or fun. A teacher observed that an honors student worked four days on a project and stopped short of completion at a point when less than an additional 20 minutes might have been needed. Why did the honors student cease working? She concluded that she had done enough to achieve her 90.

2. Not every student cares about getting a decent grade, and if a student isn't motivated by the prospect of a good grade, then there is no external motivation in using grades as an incentive. Years ago, when most students grew up in two-parent homes with one parent at home most of the time, the threat of a poor grade might motivate an overwhelming majority of students to step up their efforts. Any classroom teacher will tell you that those days are gone. Too often students are fearful, because of peer pressure, of obtaining good grades.

External motivation through grades was never the best way for students to learn. Now we can no longer delude ourselves into thinking that, for many students, it works at all.

Hence, as teachers, we need to be using authentic tasks to motivate students to engage in school lessons and units. Even for the student who is motivated because of the felt need for a good grade, and/or because he was brought up in a culture that requires it, the learning will be greater if the student at some point becomes intrinsically motivated to meet higher standards for the assignment than the teacher may require. In other words, the intrinsic motivation must take over for a lesson to have maximum value for all students. For some students, no effort will be put forth unless the authenticity of the task provides incentive for proceeding.

Newmann's definition of authenticity—having an audience beyond the teacher for a grade—is our preferred definition. For example, when second grade students begin practicing a skit that is a task. When the teacher tells them they will perform the skit on Grandparents Day, the task becomes authentic. However, there are recognized experts in the field of education who define authenticity less rigidly.

Some experts consider a task to be authentic if it is undertaken in a context that simulates the real world. For example, students may study math and social studies by planning a trip to a neighboring town. They may not actually take the trip, but the planning is done as if the trip were to be taken, and the math and social studies information used by the students is authentic because it comes from AAA tour guides and from calling establishments to request pricing information.

According to Newmann's definition, this would not qualify as authentic unless the students actually took the trip. Yet, using a definition of real-life context, this task would be authentic.

How do we reconcile these two definitions? Perhaps the answer lies in viewing authenticity on a continuum rather than thinking of it as something that either does or does not exist. A task might be said to have maximum authenticity if the student finds and works on real-life problems and does this for an audience beyond the teacher for a grade. The low end of the continuum would involve student work on isolated, discrete tasks unrelated to real life problems. See the continuum in Figure 4.1.

Figure 4.1   Authentic Task Continuum

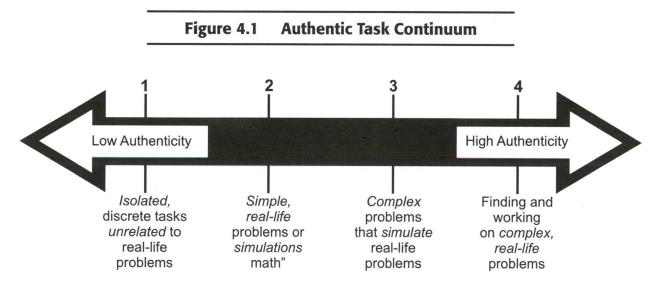

Tasks become more authentic on two dimensions: 1: their complexity, e.g., use of higher order skills, and 2: their similarity to real-life problems.

The central black area is where most teachers are as they work to make their instruction more authentic. Few classrooms use solely tasks on the far right of the continuum. Many teachers, committed to authentic instruction and assessment, try to use tasks that are to the right of the middle of the continuum, some begin more genuine and complex than others.

Jill Owen, The Regional Laboratory for School Improvement of the Northeast & Islands, May 1993.

Authenticity is relative. Some school tasks are more authentic than others. And even the same project will have greater authenticity for one student than for another. If Billy is saving money for a video game and, as part of a school task, he can figure out how much money he needs to save each month, then he will perceive the task as more authentic than Barbara who may not see any relevance in a task that involves learning to count. However, if Barbara is trying to design her own Mother's Day card and is allowed to work on that, while having to meet criteria that will also force her to address the same mathematical problems that Billy will be addressing, she may be able to find a level of authenticity in the same lesson. Jack may not be able to perceive the relevance of any task involving math, but if the task seems to be just plain fun, then Jack may be willing to engage himself along with Billy and Barbara. Authenticity is relative.

One way to increase the chances that most students will perceive a task as authentic is to negotiate the task with the students. A second method is to offer the students options. In order for the teacher to be comfortable offering options or negotiating the task, the teacher must separate, in her mind, the learning objectives from the task that will be used as the vehicle for addressing the objectives. If the teacher's learning objective is for students to understand *Taming of the Shrew*, then, obviously, the students must study that play as part of the lesson. However, if the teacher's objectives include student understanding of plot, character, setting, and conflict, why not give students options in terms of the play, or novel, they will use as the vehicle for learning these objectives? Why must they only read *Taming of the Shrew*? Too often teachers dictate the vehicles for addressing the learning objectives instead of recognizing the value of standing firm on the objectives, but increasing the latitude given students for how they learn and demonstrate their learning of the objectives.

In a journalism class, this might be analogous to assigning students to design a media campaign for the school play. In a traditional classroom, a teacher might hand out a media list and distribute a handout with an outline of a sequence of steps to be undertaken to be sure that press releases are drafted, edited, and sent to each media outlet on the list. In a constructivist classroom, the teacher might create more options, perhaps by asking the students how they think the maximum amount of effective publicity can be generated for the school play, and then letting student responses drive the decisions about which media outlets to focus on, whether to use shopping center display boards, fliers, and/or other means of filling all the seats the nights of the show.

We have stressed the need for students to be engaged in activities that will create opportunities for teacher interventions, because it is through interventions that meaningful learning, through hands-on instruction, often occurs. Therefore, when designing a discovery phase it is important to keep in mind:

- ◆ Students will become more actively engaged in those tasks they perceive to be authentic.

- ◆ People learn best when learning is related to prior knowledge and interests, and this is more easily accomplished through tasks they find to be authentic

Reality Check Question

The authors refer to their version of constructivism as authentic task constructivism. How does this differ from constructivism as described and defined by Piaget, Dewey, Vygotskii, Brooks and Brooks, and others?

The authors are suggesting that constructivist behaviors are particularly effective when utilized in the context of an authentic task. Twelve descriptors of constructivist teaching behaviors, described by Brooks and Brooks, include the strategies of allowing sufficient wait time after posing a question, allowing student responses to drive lessons, and using "raw data and primary sources, along with manipulative, interactive, and physical materials."

Although there are other ways to create an environment for using these kinds of teacher behaviors, the authors feel that teaching through use of authentic tasks (exploratory and discovery two-step) is a highly effective way of creating an environment for applying these behaviors that reflect constructivist theory (what we know about how people learn). Authentic tasks provide a plethora of opportunities for application of constructivist theory in situations where students are motivated to participate and learn.

The foregoing experts are proponents of constructivist theory, and each has recognized the value of using the context of an authentic task for implementation of constructivist behaviors, but none has emphasized the use of authentic tasks to the extent recommended by the authors. Hence, we have applied the term *Authentic Task Constructivism* to define constructivist theory when applied in an authentic task context.

Reality Check Question

How about one more example of practical application of the authentic task concept?

Two years ago, a staff developer worked with 10 teachers at monthly full-day sessions to hone their skills at unit design. At his September session with the teachers he announced that in May the superintendent and building principals would attend so that each teacher could make a 10-minute presentation explaining what had been learned and accomplished. Therefore, the teacher's work on unit design was an authentic task: authentic because it was in preparation for a presentation before a real audience (the superintendent and building principals); also authentic because the work of the teachers would directly lead to improved instruction in the classroom (a perceived need of many of the teachers).

In November, the staff developer proposed adding two days to the schedule of nine monthly sessions. The teachers objected. The staff developer dropped the request. In March, as the reality of the May presentation to the superintendent and principals sank in, two of the teachers asked the staff developer to schedule extra sessions to coach them as they prepared. The staff developer scheduled three extra sessions, on a voluntary basis, and eight of the ten teachers attended all three sessions. The motivation of the authentic task (the presentation) generated the attendance. For some of the teachers, it was the desire to do well (perceived need) that brought them to the voluntary sessions in the spring that they had rejected in the fall. For others, it was the fun, excitement, and pride, now that they were hooked on the authentic task and were enjoying it.

Reality Check Question

Because authenticity is relative, what one student finds to be highly authentic another student may perceive to be irrelevant. What is an example of how a classroom teacher can increase the chances that every student will find a degree of authenticity in the same lesson?

If the learning objectives of the teacher were to have students demonstrate analytical and articulation skills, then the teacher could allow a great deal of latitude in terms of the topics the students could choose among. The assignment might be to work alone or in groups of three. It might allow students the option to write a two-page report, draw a series of pictures, write a song, or act out a skit that clearly shows an opinion of one of the following:

- ◆ Whether the Viet Nam War was justified or not.

- ◆ How cutting down the rain forest ruins the eco system.

- ◆ What would happen if you spilled two thousand gallons of oil near the ocean shoreline?

- ◆ How would U.S. foreign policy be different since 9/11/01 if Gore had been elected President?

- ◆ Why do athletes from New York have a more difficult time adjusting to the climate when they play in Denver than when they play in Los Angeles?

- ◆ How would our lives be different if we used a base of 12 for our number system rather than the one we do use, base 10?

In this example, students can choose from among five methods to offer a demonstration of their ability to analyze and articulate and among five topics to focus their task. Because they have the option of group or individual work, the likelihood is greatly increased that each student will be able to invest sufficient time, effort, and interest to reach the point where intrinsic motivation takes over.

How important are the types of things we speak about as motivational factors? Glasser has cited fun, freedom, sense of belonging and power, or the notion that student interest must be cultivated before real understanding can begin. Okolo et al. said in 1995 (cited in Newton, 2000), "Students are more likely to engage in a task if they feel that they are in control and able to develop it in a direction which satisfies their needs for self-determination." If they have no control, they'll be defensive, avoid challenge, and stay passive!

Boy, that is no surprise to anyone who has ever seen a class of typical students. Even if one's sole motivation is for good grades (so she memorizes the dictionary), the feeling of *control* (my choice) is present. Apparently, our job is to motivate them to think and make good decisions and then *facilitate* their learning.

Reality Check Question

How does student investment of time and effort relate to the development of intrinsic motivation?

Investment of time is a key factor in determining how important something becomes to any of us. If we have just begun a task and encounter obstacles, it is easier to decide to give up than if we have worked long and hard on a project and then encountered what we perceive to be major hurdles. The more time and energy we have invested, the more likely we will switch the question, when confronted with hurdles, from "Should we continue?" to "How do we overcome?"

Also, the more time and effort we invest, the more pride we take from accomplishment of the task. Often, we cross a threshold of time and effort invested that motivates us (intrinsically) to want to continue to feel that our time was not wasted.

Here are some keys to intrinsic motivation:

♦ *Attitudes*: The teacher can successfully tap into this by truly getting to know his student.

♦ *Needs*: The student's needs (Maslow) must be met first.

♦ *Stimulation*: Accomplish stimultion by offering choices and facilitating in a positive fashion.

♦ *Reinforcement*: This should come naturally to the student but can be supplemented by praise and offering further choices.

Reality Check Question

Can you relate intrinsic motivation and Covey's habits to the discovery phase of the Two-Step, authentic task assessment, and rubrics?

♦ When students complete an exploratory phase of a lesson and begin to engage in the discovery phase, they are trying to understand the authentic task they must accomplish to be successful (because the discovery phase involves student pursuit of an authentic task). Covey's second habit, "Begin with the end in mind," comes into play as students identify the form of evaluation that will be used to assess their success on the task by studying the rubric, reviewing exemplars of quality work on similar tasks, and dialoguing with the teacher through engagement in planned and spontaneous interventions.

♦ Once students know what constitutes success (i.e., the expectations), they are starting their journey with Covey's third habit, "Put first things first," when they involve themselves with engaging, fact-finding activities that relate to their finished product.

Reality Check Question

Can you summarize what every classroom teacher should know about intrinsic motivation?

Learning for the love of learning is essentially intrinsic motivation. Therefore, intrinsic motivation must come from within (the students' responsibility) and cannot be achieved by teaching practices alone. However, a constructivist learning environment that supports students' choices and prior knowledge, in combination with a teacher's efforts to promote students' positive attitudes, needs, stimulation, affect, competence, and reinforcement, can provide the appropriate foundation for intrinsic student motivation. Many constructivist learning activities that involve exploration, information processing, manipulation, and choice usually provide satisfaction in and of themselves, and as a result, facilitate intrinsic motivation.

Classroom teachers want to know how to encourage and facilitate students to become intrinsically motivated:

- Praise them, accept them, and have high expectations.
- Build strong relationships—create a sense of trust, respect, and caring.
- Expose them to new experiences and opportunities.
- Offer them choices, and have them set their own goals.
- Accept them for who they are.
- Adapt to different learning styles.
- Celebrate diversity and promote acceptance.
- Be a positive role model and display enthusiasm.
- Encourage risk taking.

Reality Check Question

Does authentic task constructivism as reflected in the Two-Step model hold any significance for students with disabilities?

One of the motivating factors for anyone is whether we believe we can be successful. Despite the fact that many students with disabilities have above-average intelligence and ability, the perception of many of these students is that they will not do well at their studies, and this is often reinforced by poor grades. In a traditional classroom setting with assessments primarily of memorization through measurements that favor linguistic and mathematical-logical intelligences, students with disabilities often see the handwriting on the wall before they begin a lesson, and therefore, they often tune out before the teacher has asked them to tune in.

A Two-Step authentic task model increases the potential for motivating students with disabilities because:

- It offers options that enable these students to function in areas of their interests and strengths.

♦ It sometimes enables these students to achieve higher grades because they are being assessed on what they can demonstrate, not what they can memorize.

Reality Check Question

If we focus students on an outcome (or product), does this conflict with the statement that intrinsically motivated students value the journey?

Most journeys have a destination. It is learning how to enjoy the journey, rather than feeling only the successful conclusion will justify the trip, that makes the journey satisfying.

When the author designed a newsletter workshop for teacher union representatives, the authentic task that motivated participant performance was the design of a flier to be placed in teacher mailboxes the following day—perhaps advertising a contractual right or a discount insurance benefit. Some of the teacher participants would become so involved in cutting and pasting borders and art work and would take so much pride in the appearance of their fliers that they would continue working long after the session ended. It was the journey that motivated the teachers—they were having just plain fun, and taking pride, in designing their fliers. The end product, and its distribution in faculty mailboxes, afforded reinforcement and had a value, but it was the work itself that inspired additional work.

Steve Rudolph of the Jiva Institute, India, indicated that it is part of the culture in India to value the journey over arrival at the destination. Harry Chapin said the same thing in his story-song, "Greyhound":

It's got to be the goin'

Not the gettin there that's good

That's a thought for keepin'

If I could

It's got to be the goin'

Not the getting' there that's good!

Thoughts for Reflection

♦ "Most of the learning community, and most learners, now recognize, at least intuitively, that we don't learn by having someone teach us, but rather, we learn by engaging with something we want to learn. This is pretty *commonsensical*" (Giselle Martin-Kniep).

♦ "No use to shout at them to pay attention. If the situation, the materials, the problems before the child do not interest him, his attention will slip off to what does interest him, and no amount of exhortation of threats will bring it back" (John Holt, 1923–1985).

End of Section Assessment

Describe one time when your motivation to complete an assignment as a student was solely extrinsic, and one time when your intrinsic motivation drove you to achieve far more than the teacher demanded. What were the differences between the two assignments?

The Effective Classroom Teacher

Learning Objective

The reader will understand that there are practical ways to identify an effective classroom teacher.

Main Points

- There are at least seven ways to determine if a teacher is basing his classroom practice on constructivist principles.

- Clarifying teacher expectations requires a rubric, a dialogue, and an exemplar.

- Teachers need to work the room during student work on a performance task in order to assess student learning.

- The Two-Step model creates opportunities for parental involvement.

- There is value to bringing closure to the day.

- There are strong connections between brain research and the Two-Step model.

- Spiraling the curriculum allows the teacher to increase her use of the Two-Step's task-based learning.

Is the author suggesting that teachers have to use the Two-Step to be effective? No. Teachers who find the engineering design of the Two-Step practical for classroom application will be infusing their classrooms with the concepts that research indicates generate meaningful learning, but this is not the only model that creates an environment for such concepts to flourish. As indicated in Appendix B, there are good, time-tested models that employ many of these same concepts.

While the author hopes that teachers will try the Two-Step, even those teachers who have bought in completely to the viability and practicality of this model will want to introduce it slowly into their classroom practice as they adjust to its nuances and experience student reactions.

However, we *are saying* that the concepts that are the foundation of the Two-Step should be the basis for classroom instruction regardless of the lesson design process used by the teacher. These concepts should be readily apparent from the preceding chapters. This section will attempt to further define these concepts, with examples of their practical application in classroom settings.

Can an observer walk into class and expect students to explain individually what they are doing, why they are doing it, and what will be their next steps?

An author visited a unique pilot program, in which 95 students, grades 9–12, worked with five teachers, and the year was divided into 10 week interdisciplinary units. For example, some students were working on a 10-week study of the environment around the high school in preparation for a report to the board of education (an authentic task), while another group wrote articles and essays that would actually be mailed to magazines identified by the students.

A visitor to this class observed students who began their work as soon as they entered the classroom because it was a continuation of what they had been doing when the bell rang the day before. The visitor, afraid of interrupting students at work, was encouraged by the teachers to ask questions of the students as they worked individually or in groups, because the teachers realized that student learning would occur as students were forced to articulate what they were doing to a stranger. When a visitor walks into a classroom, it is worth taking the time to ask the students to brief the visitor on what they are doing, why they are doing it, and what they will do next. In fact, if chance doesn't bring a visitor to a classroom often enough, it is a good strategy to contrive a visit from someone just to create an opportunity for student sharing with an authentic audience.

A Constructivist Lesson

Throughout this book, numerous examples of the Two-Step have been discussed. Here's a simple lesson that was conducted in 45 minutes in sixth grade social studies:

The purpose was to review students on the following content (taken from questions at the end of a chapter):

♦ What was the connection between the story of Aeneas and the Trojan War?

♦ Why did the Romans overthrow rule by kings?

♦ Why wasn't the Roman Republic a government by will of the people?

♦ What can we learn from the legend of Horatius at the bridge?

♦ What was the outcome of each of the Punic Wars?

Task One (exploratory phase)—A Planned Intervention

The teacher said to the class: "For this first task (exploratory), I want you each to have a blank sheet of paper and to do your own work, but you can discuss the task within your group, and help each other.

"I want you to draw a sculpture for an award to Cincinnatus or Horatius. The sculpture should represent something he has accomplished and should include as many people as there are people in your group. You have six minutes."

The students worked diligently on this task. The teacher walked among the groups and responded to questions for clarity of the task. After six minutes, the teacher asked if anyone needed more time. Quite a few students indicated they did, and the teacher allowed another four minutes.

Task Two (continuing the exploratory phase)—Another Planned Intervention

The teacher wrote the words *Plebeian* and *Patrician* on the board, vertically:

P	P
A	L
T	E
R	B
I	I
C	A
I	N
A	
N	

He then said, "Pick one or the other of these words. Think of other words that connect with the word you've chosen and begin with one of its letters." The students went right to work, for example:

Powerful
Atop
T
Rich
In charge
Commanding
I
A
Not poor

The teacher had each group share, very briefly, some of its words.

Task Three (discovery phase)

The teacher said, "Turn to the timeline in your text book, from 753 B.C. to A.D. 476. Select three events on the time line and be ready to share what music you would select to play in the background if you were describing that event.

The students set right to work, enjoying the chance to explore their own type of music in relation to the historical events on the timeline.

Responses were then shared. Here are two:

- Punic Wars, 106—"Hit Me Baby, One More Time."
- Julius Caesar killed, 44 B.C.—"Mission Impossible."

Task Four (reflection, as part of the discovery phase)

When the students completed this third task, the teacher asked the students to share one thing they had learned since they first entered class today that they hadn't known before the class.

He repeated the question several times and explained that he would take a volunteer, and then continue around the class. He said, "If you're not ready, you can pass, and we'll get your response in a little while."

When he asked who was ready, there was a pause, and then two hands shot up. One student said, "I've learned about the Punic Wars some things I didn't know."

The student to her left said, "I've learned about Horatius." Another student said, "I know a lot more about Alexander the Great."

The teacher asked him, "What did you learn about Alexander the Great?"

He immediately responded that Alexander the Great had conquered a number of countries, and then he added two other accurate facts about Alexander.

Two students passed when it was their turn but were ready with responses when the teacher turned to them after everyone else had responded. It only took three minutes to elicit a response from all 17 students. The teacher also responded to the same question.

Then the teacher said, "I have one more question. I don't have time to take a response from each of you, but I'd like at least a few of you to tell me what you learned about working with the people in your group on the tasks we engaged in."

"I learned how to cooperate," said one student.

"I learned that if you listen, you are showing someone respect," said another.

Task Five (more reflection)

After three more students responded, the teacher concluded the lesson by asking each group to review the sculpture they had designed earlier, revisit it if they felt it could be improved, and then stand up and create an enactment of their sculpture. Five minutes later, the students all stood, created all sorts of amorphous shapes, and demonstrated physically what they had drawn on paper.

- It was obvious that this teacher had done a lot of group work (effectively) with her class. This demonstrates that when teachers feel group work can't succeed because of resistance from the students, it may just be that the students need more training, just as the teacher may. If students have not had much group work in previous years, we need to expect it to take awhile before they acclimate to a teacher who uses group work.

- By designing tasks that require (and allow for) a variety of intelligences, we increase the number of students who have the chance to succeed.

A constructivist teacher uses a variety of activities, including lecture and note taking. You cannot tell whether a teacher is constructivist by taking a snapshot of the classroom at one point in time. What makes a classroom constructivist is variety, options, forced thinking, and the chance for students to learn in different ways at different times. For example, the student with musical ability can demonstrate what he knows through song or musical instrument, while the linguistically strong student can use essays and the artistic student can reflect learning through pictures.

Yes, we all need to be required to use modes of expression where we are weak so that we can develop a minimum proficiency, but we also need to have opportunities to function in modalities where we are strong and can take pride in what we can do.

A constructivist teacher distinguishes between the learning objective and the means for demonstrating student knowledge, understanding, or application of the learning objective. In the social studies lesson just recounted, the learning objectives were clearly stated: "Review students on five areas of study." In the course of one lesson, the teacher allowed students to learn and demonstrate learning in a variety of ways, including essay, pictorial, verbal, musical, and kinesthetic, but he stayed focused on the specific learning objectives established by the teacher whose class he was teaching.

The constructivist teacher does not focus on thinking, "How do I get this information, or these understandings, across to my students?" Instead, the teacher is focused on "What kind of activity, or task, can I create that cannot be accomplished by students without satisfactorily addressing the learning objectives for the lesson or unit?"

Questions for the Constructivist Teacher to Address for Self-Assessment

These questions have been suggested twice before in this book. They bear repeating. These questions are what teaching is all about. They go to the heart of what a constructivist teacher must have in the forefront of her mind:

- Am I requiring my students to think? If so, how deeply? How insightfully?

- How do I know they are thinking—each and every one of them?

- What is the evidence that my students are thinking?

- Are just a few students giving evidence of thinking, or am I really challenging every student to think?

Being a constructivist teacher requires, more than anything, a change in mindset. To plan a traditional lesson, I think, "How do I prepare the students to address a task (apply information)?"

To plan a constructivist lesson, I think, "What kind of a task can I introduce (or negotiate) that will require students to master the learning objectives I have for the lesson to complete the task?"

It is an entirely different way of approaching lesson design. In the traditional way of teaching, if I even get to the point of creating an opportunity for application of knowledge, it will come *after* I have led students through a step by step process of learning information and processes for application. In other words, as a teacher or a parent in a traditional way of thinking, I want to do everything possible to prevent children from failing *before* I let them do something. However, in a constructivist approach, I set the task and know that if I have structured it well, the students will seek out, from me or somewhere else, the information and understandings they need to accomplish the task. In a constructivist approach, I build the field and know that if it is a good field, the students will come to play.

To determine if a teacher is constructivist, here are some questions an observer might ask:

- *Purposefulness of Instruction*: Can the teacher clearly articulate the knowledge (including skills), concepts, and competencies every student is expected to understand and demonstrate and the tasks they will be able to accomplish by the end of the lesson or unit of study? In other words, is there a narrow focus for the lesson so that one can reasonably expect most students to attain the objectives of the lesson?

- *Assessment of Student Learning*: Is there a formal assessment scoring scale—or scales—(rubric) for the information, knowledge (skills and concepts), and competencies articulated by the teacher as the goals of the lesson? The assessment can be teacher observation of a student product or performance, or it can be by a written test or any combination of assessments.

- *Lesson Construction*: Are students in either the exploratory or discovery phase of a lesson? If they are in the exploratory phase of a lesson, are they being challenged with questions, and is the teacher creating opportunities, to access and assess their prior knowledge and interests? Are students beginning to address the major concept that will be the focus of the lesson? And are students being motivated to take an interest in the discovery phase that will follow? Can students in the discovery phase of a lesson tell you, individually, what they are doing, why they are doing it, and what the next steps will be?

- *Clarity of Expectations*: Do students fully understand the teacher's expectations? Is there a rubric and dialogue about the meaning of the interpretation of the rubric? Is there an exemplar? If the teacher negotiates the rubric with the students, this takes care of the dialogue and assures similar interpretations of students and teacher. Otherwise, the teacher must share the rubric and generate discussion to be sure students are interpreting the rubric's criteria the same way the teacher is.

It is the combination of the rubric, the dialogue, and the exemplar that clarify expectations. None of these three is as effective as all three in combination.

♦ *Student Focus on Task Understanding*: If students are listening to a lecture, or involved in an assigned reading, can they articulate a task they are engaged in, what they need to do to successfully accomplish the task, and how the lecture or assigned reading will provide information they need to complete the assigned task?

♦ *Classroom Environment*: Do chair, table, and resource arrangements change frequently, sometimes even within a 40-minute (or longer) class? At times, are students seated in groups of three or four, or as pairs, and at other times are they in larger groups, possibly even in straight rows? Does the room arrangement fit the need of the activity, which may be a lecture, group activity, class discussion, or work time for individuals, pairs, and groups?

♦ *Reflection*: Are there frequent opportunities for student reflection? Are students led through reflective processes as they engage with information during the exploratory and discovery phases of a lesson?

Reality Check Question

Is the seating arrangement really that important?

Yes. When student-to-student or student-to-teacher dialogue is desired, the seating arrangement and layout of the room create an appropriate environment for discussion. The teacher must be conscious of the impact of the seating arrangement on people's sense of belonging to the group and the effect this has on people's willingness to participate in group discussion. In a whole-class discussion, seating is arranged in a circle, to the degree possible, and no one is permitted to sit on the outside of the circle. If seats are nailed to the floor, then the teacher wanders around the room so that student seating doesn't determine who is closest to, or farthest from, the teacher. As students speak, the teacher wanders to the farthest point from the speaker encouraging the speaker to speak loudly enough for the teacher and all others to hear. Students are reinforced for offering their opinions at the same time they are required to support them with rationale.

The critical importance of the seating arrangement is exemplified with two quick anecdotes, each involving adults, teachers, and administrators. A facilitator had asked two groups of participants at a workshop, seated at opposite ends of a room approximately 100-feet long, to agree on a response to a question. After allowing five minutes, the facilitator asked the groups to share their responses and try to reach consensus. A reporter from one group stood up and shouted across the room. A reporter from the other group stood up and shouted his group's response. For at least five minutes the two groups attempted to reach consensus by shouting back and forth before one person suggested, "Why don't we move our chairs together and form one group?" In the second instance, a workshop was conducted in a cafeteria with long, narrow tables attached to benches. When the facilitator asked groups of 10 to work together, discussion began, and participants stretched to observe and hear whoever was speaking. After five minutes, only the few people at the center of each long table were engaged in relevant discussion, while almost everyone else had given up the efforts to stretch their necks, and their ears, far enough to participate. They, instead, were engaged in side conversations or were making good company to themselves reading a newspaper or correcting papers.

People too often accept whatever seating arrangement exists when they enter the room. Empowerment for adults or students means being cognizant of how the seating arrangement will encourage or discourage group discussion.

Reality Check Question

What are the skills and abilities required of a teacher who wants to apply constructivist theories of how people learn to classroom lessons?

- Cooperative learning strategies
- Journals as a vehicle for teaching
- Portfolios
- Performance tasks
- Graphic organizers

The tool kit of the facilitative teacher includes the ability to:

- Teach to clearly defined standards.
- Design authentic assessments/rubrics.
- Design and teach authentic performance tasks.
- Design strategies for students to take responsibility for their learning.
- Design and use reflective activities.
- Create activities in which students are learning by teaching.
- Understand and use technology:
  - For record keeping and planning
  - As an instructional tool
  - As an end in itself (e.g., teach students to know and use technology)
- Teach to concepts instead of memorization of discrete sets of facts.
- Understand learning styles and multiple intelligences.
- Design and use probing questions.
- Link exploratory activities with concepts.
- Frame concepts into essential questions.
- Understand and implement constructivist teaching strategies.

- Access parent, community, and business involvement.

- Address the needs of all students including, but not limited to, those with disabilities.

As you peruse this list of strategies, please keep this context in mind:

- Most teachers who feel confident with any one of these strategies (cooperative learning, portfolios, reflective activities) have probably been attending conferences, trying out the strategy, dialoguing with a colleague about it, and gradually increasing usage of the strategy for at least three years. The journey toward a comfort level with even a majority of these strategies takes many years.

- We are not suggesting that every teacher should use each of these strategies in equal amounts. Depending on a teacher's own strengths and interests, and her assessment of her students, different teachers may use different strategies to accomplish the same objective. I may prefer to offer portfolio demonstrations as an instrument of assessment while another teacher may choose a different approach.

- We are suggesting that every teacher should work toward competence with these strategies. It is acceptable to know how to use a strategy but decide, for a defensible reason, that a particular lesson is not an appropriate situation to use that strategy. It is quite another thing not to consider using a particular strategy simply because you don't know how. I can accept a doctor's opinion that my injury does not require x-rays, if I feel the doctor understands when to use x-rays and, in her expert opinion, does not feel this is a situation that warrants it. However, I would switch doctors if I felt her knowledge of, and access to, x-rays was insufficient for her to consider it as an option. Wouldn't you?

Reality Check Question

Much has been written suggesting that students will rise (or sink) to the level of the teacher's expectations. Is this important?

Yes. However, equally important for a teacher as having high expectations is that the expectations be clear. Too often, when teachers don't receive what they thought they requested of students, they complain, "The students just didn't listen." Sometimes students don't listen, however, sometimes what the teacher understands himself to say is not what others hear. There are countless workshop activities that focus participants on how easy it is for people to use the same words and yet apply distinctly different meanings. Earlier we cited an example of a student who gave a logical reason for thinking that three is half of eight. Educational humorists point out that an auditory learner who is instructed to move wet clothes from the washing machine into the dryer may not actually start the dryer unless given more specific direction. The human being's propensity for giving different interpretations to the same words is unending.

Therefore, we repeat what we said earlier: "It is the combination of the rubric, the dialogue, and the exemplar that clarify expectations. None of these is as effective at expectation clarification as all three in combination." Words alone, whether written or verbal, are insufficient for clarifying student expectations for a task. No matter how specific the wording in the rubric, it can still be interpreted differently. If the rubric requires that an essay must be *interesting*, what does this mean? When we discuss it, I learn that you interpret interesting to be challenging, exciting, motivating, and provoking further reading. Then, when you share an exemplar, it gives me additional insight into what you, the teacher, mean by interesting. Through the exemplar, I can see what you think is challenging, exciting, and motivating.

Negotiating the rubric with the students is one way to generate dialogue about the rubric. The teacher can ask the students what they think should be weighed when the teacher assesses their work. Students can be shown quality work from previous classes and asked to identify what the exemplary works have in common, thus creating the criteria for their own rubric. "Look at these three pieces of writing and identify the characteristics that make them outstanding." Or, "Here are three award-winning science projects from last year's class—what have they in common that distinguishes them?" The students' responses, along with the teacher's own conclusions, become the criteria for getting the highest score on the rubric.

Reality Check Question

Does the Two-Step Create Opportunities for generating parental involvement?

Absolutely: (1) parents can be involved as the audience for authentic tasks; (2) they can provide assistance as students engage in tasks; and (3) they can be presented with open-ended questions to pose to their children whenever there is a spare moment at home or around the dinner table.

The Audience for an Authentic Task

Because a task can be defined as authentic when there is an audience beyond the teacher for a grade, why not use parents as the audience some of the time? Many parents would love to be involved more in their children's education, but they don't know how, or they feel that the opportunities offered by the school are too time-consuming. However, what if the teacher worked out an informal contract with as many of her students' parents as were willing? The nature of the implied contract is, "You will agree to visit my class twice during the year for approximately 45 minutes each time, to be part of an audience for a student display, demonstration, or presentation."

Each time the teacher anticipates the need for an audience, she would send out a general notice to all parents and would obtain commitments from at least two parents. In other words, the teacher would guarantee having an audience of at least two but could make the opportunity available to all parents of her students. If a teacher had 20 students and only five of the parents agreed to make two visits a year, that would add authenticity to five assessment tasks.

Parents as Assistants

Many elementary teachers use parents as classroom assistants. The use of the Two-Step creates more opportunities for parent volunteers to help out without the need for them to have content expertise. When students are working on tasks individually and/or in groups, the teacher benefits from the assistance of any competent adult who can observe students at work, respond to procedural questions, and call the teacher over when students are either having difficulty or posing a question that the parent volunteer can't answer.

Open-Ended Questions

When lessons are traditional, I find it difficult as a parent to help my child with his homework. Often I do not understand the teacher's expectations, or I do not know how to do the homework, or I am not home the precise time the assignment needs to be done. The Two-Step opens the door to the kind of parental involvement that those parents who are caring will appreciate and find easy to support. The nature of the Two-Step often extends a lesson over several days or longer, so once I understand my child's task, I can ask open-ended questions (I don't need to know the answer) on a regular basis.

The teacher can send home a rubric for the task and perhaps a set of four or five open-ended questions that a parent can ask her child at mealtime or at bedtime, or whenever there is a spare moment. The questions can be as simple as, "What is this river project you are working on?" Or, "Do you think Harriet Tubman would be active in politics if she were alive today?" Or, "How would you estimate the number of steps inside a building if you were looking at it from the outside?"

Reality Check Question

Do I have to grade every bit of work students do in groups and on other aspects of the Two-Step?

No. You formally assess student performance with regard only to that which you identified as your primary learning objectives. You do not need to assess every student performance, in a group or otherwise. Much of the value of group work and engagement in a task (the Two-Step) is in the process of interaction. The students are learning by doing. Your goal, as a teacher, is to get them to do. You know that once they actively engage with the task you have designed, the learning will follow. Reading and writing improve when students are immersed. One reason teachers don't assign more writing is their feeling that they have to correct every assignment students turn in, and it takes a while to correct content, punctuation, spelling, and every other aspect of a written task.

Students do need to feel that the adult has taken notice of their hard work. However, they do not need a grade and in-depth feedback for every assignment. If the value of what you have students do is in the doing, then a check on the paper or a verbal acknowledgement may suffice. After group work, simply posing a probing question and hearing one brief response from a spokesperson from each group can be sufficient reinforcement for students' hard work, while simultaneously enabling the teacher to use the student work to drive the next part of the lesson.

When students are engaged in an authentic task, and are hooked on it, they will tolerate a lot of reading and writing if they feel it is necessary for them to be successful with their task. They will read directions, articles, and resource materials that are necessary for them to prepare their work for an audience beyond the teacher for a grade. They will write outlines, drafts, journal entries, and summaries if these are required in order for them to proceed with the game they are creating, the PowerPoint presentation they are preparing, or any task they want to complete. Yes, there are times we need a summative assessment. However, much of what occurs in a classroom is designed to generate student learning and does not need to be formally assessed.

Reality Check Question

The term "working the room" has appeared throughout this text. What exactly does it mean and how does it relate to the assessment of student performance?

The term was coined by an outstanding high school English teacher, Beth Konkoski. It refers to the role of the teacher while students are engaged in individual or group work on a task. Here are some guidelines for effectively working the room:

♦ *See if the task is understood*: The most important time for the teacher to wander around the room is immediately after turning students loose on a task. The teacher is listening and observing to be sure the students have correctly understood the task and are able to launch into the first steps. If students misunderstand the task, they will be like a train that begins a journey on the wrong track—the longer it is allowed to continue, the farther from its destination it will go, and the harder it will be to redirect it. Also, if students cannot figure out how to proceed, their frustration level can lead to abandoning the task entirely. On the one hand, students need the opportunity to figure out how to begin by themselves—a certain amount of confusion is a necessary prerequisite for learning; however, a balance must be struck between allowing a "healthy" amount of confusion and being available as a scaffold to prevent the damage that can be caused by hopeless frustration.

♦ *Be available for assistance*: Throughout the allotted work time, be on the lookout for those individuals or groups who may need assistance; some students may need prodding to become more involved. Because most groups can be expected to proceed independently (if it is a well designed task) this affords the teacher excellent opportunities for tutoring individuals or small groups; not only can the teacher use this time to assist the least able students, but also to challenge the more advanced students.

♦ *Teachable moments will be frequent*: Look for opportunities for "spontaneous interventions." A "spontaneous intervention" is a teachable moment that occurs when a student raises a question based on the assigned task, or when the teacher, on observing student work, is able to intervene to make a suggestion or challenge the student with a question. (Example: "What would happen if you tried that same experiment but substitute saltwater for plain water?"

- *Model vocabulary*: The teacher "models the vocabulary" after terminology that students need to learn. Teachers then use this vocabulary in response to students' questions, thereby placing the terms into classroom conversation.

- *Be a time keeper*: Periodically, announce, "You need to be ready for your report to the entire class in five minutes." Or, "If you are not on step 4, you may want to speed up a little because you should be there by now."

- *Reinforce*: Use this as a time to let individuals, and small groups of students, know that they are doing well. Praise them for what is good in their work. We are motivated to work when we believe we can be successful.

Assess: Teacher observation can be the most significant type of assessment. This is the teacher's chance to hear students think. As students become accustomed to group work (and individual work on performance tasks) they will grow increasingly oblivious to the presence of the teacher standing a few feet away observing their interaction, discussion, and/or work on task.)

Bringing Closure to the Day

We suggest to teachers that they conclude every day (at elementary) and every period at secondary with a brief closure activity to cause students to reflect on what they have learned:

"I am going to ask you a question, give you 30 seconds to think about it, and then I'll ask each person to give a response in 15 seconds or less. The question is, 'What is one thing you have learned about the Great Lakes that you didn't know before you walked into class today?' You have 30 seconds to think about your response, then we'll start with Sarah and go around the room. If you're not ready, you can pass, and we'll call on you in a few minutes after everyone else has responded. Billy, would you please watch the clock and clap at the end of 15 seconds if someone hasn't concluded a response?"

Or: "Pair with your neighbor and agree on a song title that best describes the individual we have been discussing (e.g., Pasteur, Attila the Hun, Shakespeare, Einstein, Rembrandt, Beethoven, Michael Jordan). Then I'll ask one of you to share the title with the rest of the class." Or: "In groups of four, pretend to be in a picture someone has drawn that includes George Washington, Abraham Lincoln, George Bush, and one other president of the United States." You have five minutes to decide on how you will pose for your picture, and then I'll ask each group to stand up and pretend to be the picture."

Reality Check Question

What is the connection between brain research and what you are discussing as the role of the classroom teacher?

Staff developer Gerry Peters, a retired national award-winning math teacher from Gouverneur, New York, cites brain research in support of some of the constructivist approaches to student learning which he employs. According to Peters:

- *Only* learning that *makes sense* to the learner and has *meaning* gets stored in long-term memory during deep sleep following the learning episode. Students who leave class with the attitude, "This is stupid—where am I ever going to use this?", will most likely have their brains discard that information instead of sending it to long-term memory. (His conclusions are consistent with comments on National Public Radio early in 2003 by Mary Jo Thompson, a Minnesota art teacher and project director for a program of the U.S. Department of Education in Minneapolis and New York City. Thompson cited research demonstrating, "There has to be meaning. If it doesn't make sense to children, they're not going to remember anything. That's how the brain works. The brain only has memory when there is meaning.")

- Learning deepens when tasks are imbedded in real-life experiences. Authentic tasks enable the learner to *make more sense* and *deepen* the meaning attached to the knowledge imbedded in the task.

- New learning should be linked to prior knowledge. Using direct teaching to launch a lesson often results in some of the learners failing to activate their prior knowledge for the lesson.

- Learning is social before it is cognitive. Talking about a topic helps the learner *make sense* of the topic and greatly increases the amount of *meaning* the brain attaches to the topic.

- Reflection is a *necessary* part of learning. *Closure* should be part of *every* lesson. It is a key step (and the last chance) in the learning episode for the learner to *make sense* and *attach meaning* to what is being learned.

Reality Check Question

Am I an Authentic Task Constructivist?

The difference between using strategies in a constructivist environment and identifying yourself as a constructivist teacher can be compared with the difference between baking some excellent dishes and calling oneself a chef. In one case, we are focusing on one piece of a much larger whole; in the other we are putting many pieces together into a system.

We are about to describe the ideal constructivist classroom. Do the authors always achieve the ideal when they teach a lesson or conduct a workshop? No. We'd like to believe, as W. Edwards Deming would say, that "We are on a continuous improvement path." Sometimes we come closer than at others. This process is sometimes referred to as *polishing the stone*.

In the ideal constructivist classroom, students are constantly challenged to think, evaluate, synthesize, and analyze. There is an authentic context for the work that beckons student engagement. There is an aura of excitement and the buzz we associate with interest and inquiry. Activities can vary from minute to minute and day to day; expectations for student performance are clear, and students have options for demonstrating their achievement of the teacher's expectations; the variety of activities and options allow for all students to function at times, in areas of their strongest intelligences; and when student to student or student to teacher dialogue is desired, the seating arrangement and layout of the room create an appropriate environment for discussion.

In the ideal constructivist classroom, the teacher is a guide, but the teacher guides by example and the teacher provides structure through facilitation. The teacher *is not* the repository of all information students will need for their inquiry. The teacher *is* the person who sees that resources are available to meet the needs of student inquiry. The teacher IS the catalyst for discussion, exploration, discovery, and reflection.

In the ideal constructivist classroom, there are many leaders; everyone is a leader at one time or another depending on the tasks. The role of teacher as leader is defined as the person responsible for seeing that as many students as possible master the learning objectives for the course. When allowing others to assume a leadership role is the best way to advance students toward the goal of mastering the course learning objectives, then the teacher, as a leader, encourages others to assume leadership roles.

Reality Check Question

How do I cover the curriculum, and prepare students for standardized assessments, if I use performance tasks which take longer than traditional teaching?

While some teachers simply don't want to consider changing the way they teach, the most frustrating aspect of the change process for a staff developer is the number of teachers who will use a performance task, love the results, and then proclaim, "I can only do this once or twice a year because I have too much curriculum to cover."

The single most significant obstacle to authentic task constructivist classrooms is the perception by teachers that they can't cover as much curriculum effectively if they use more than one or two performance tasks a year.

The solution: effective teachers, over time and through trial and error, and experience, come to realize that they cannot be satisfied if a constructivist lesson only peripherally addresses the curriculum. Performance tasks (the Two-Step) must be used as the primary vehicle for *teaching what needs to be taught.* Over time, effective teachers are able to cover more material through a well designed and conducted Two-Step, than if they stood in front of the class and tried to impart the information, mouth to ear.

"How do I cover the material while using time-consuming performance tasks instead of teacher directed lessons?" The answer is twofold:

1. Let's strip ourselves of the delusion that what we teach is equivalent to what students learn. If a teacher talks faster he can cover more material, but are the students learning it just as well? The Carnegie Report and countless articles have been written about the need to reform our schools precisely because students aren't learning enough of what teachers are teaching. If I cover 100% of the material and students learn 45% of what I teach, are they better off than if I teach 75% of the material well and students master 90% of what I teach? This is the short term answer: recognize that students aren't learning 100 percent of what

we teach right now so if we cover less, but they learn more they may be better prepared for the world, as well as standardized assessments, than they are now.

2. In the long run, the effective teacher will learn to cover more material through good performance tasks than he can now cover through a teacher directed lesson. How can this be?

The answer is spiraling. When teachers learn to spiral their curriculum, they will cover more material and cover it better than is currently being done with more traditional teaching strategies. The problem is it takes time to learn to spiral a curriculum well. Therefore, in the short run there is no question that it may take a good teacher longer than she would like to prepare and conduct a good Two-Step constructivist lesson.

Spiraling comes in two basic forms: spiraling within a curriculum area and spiraling across curriculum areas. Both forms of spiraling are intended to have the same effect—to provide opportunities for students to revisit and reconnect with previously learned curriculum content often taking each new opportunity to delve a little more deeply into that content.

How do you spiral the curriculum? Teachers have always spiraled parts of their curriculum even if they haven't used the term *spiral*. Why does a first grade teacher begin with reading lessons almost the first day that students walk through the door in August or September? Teachers recognize that reading is one of the more difficult and most important parts of the curriculum for students to master. They also recognize that concepts and understandings are developed over time, through immersion. They want to begin students reading as early in the year as possible, and they spiral reading lessons into curriculum whenever possible. Therefore, at times they directly address reading strategies as the learning objectives for their lesson. However, when they teach social studies or science or math, they look for opportunities to have students read. The more they can spiral reading into other lessons, the better readers their students will become.

Teachers need to approach all important parts of the curriculum, in every discipline, as they do reading. We need to move away from compartmentalizing our curriculum. We teach the American Revolution (or the conversion of meters to feet) for a few days or weeks or even a month, then we move on and don't address it again until the end of the year exam, and we wonder why students have forgotten most of what we taught. If the American Revolution is important after we have focused on it for a few weeks, let's integrate it into lessons on other subjects. When we teach about, electricity let's remind students of what we learned from Benjamin Franklin. When we study character in stories, let's refer to some of the characters we read about while studying the eighteenth century. If our purpose in reading a story is to strengthen reading comprehension and to understand plot, setting, conflict, and character analysis, why not pick a story that takes place in the same historical time frame as the several inventors we studied the previous month? Or, why not pick a story that reinforces concepts taught in science or math

Teachers need to identify the concepts and understandings they feel will be most difficult for students to master, address them early in the year, and then spiral them into almost everything they teach for the remainder of the year. Good teachers do some of this from the gut. They must actually list the learning objectives that are most important to them and make certain they are spiraled into the curriculum throughout the year.

A typical project undertaken by a teacher might involve taking students on a field trip to a river, collecting water samples or leaves, returning to class, and making a portfolio of pressed leaves or using a kit to test water samples and reach conclusions. It was after a weeklong lesson like this that a teacher said to the author, "This was great, but now I have to get back to the curriculum that needs to be covered."

How could this teacher have spiraled more curriculum into the same amount of time so that he wouldn't have felt that this project was too time-consuming despite the obvious benefits which he acknowledged were there? What if, on the trip to the river, he had asked students to conduct experiments about gravity? What if they had discussed the trip, in advance, and every student had written an essay describing what they would do and estimating the results of their experiments with gravity? What if the class had related their pending excursion to the river to part of the Lewis and Clark expedition and were to write a journal entry after the trip using the format used by Lewis and Clark? What if the students were to estimate the number of calories they would burn on their excursion and discussed an appropriate nutritional diet the week before the trip? What if a nutritionist or someone from a local community agency (agency representatives often look for opportunities to be involved with schools) were invited on the excursion to respond to what students had said about nutrition, diet, and calorie burning?

What if students were asked to determine the physical education exercise requirements that were being met by their excursion and the types of exercises they should do the morning of the excursion? What if? What if? What if?

A small rural K–8 school in Wentworth, New Hampshire, holds May and October community garden days at their school. Many students and teachers volunteer their participation and community members pitch in, offer resources, and contribute time. Many schools would be satisfied with a successful day cultivating and planting in the spring and cleaning up in the fall. However, typical of many of her colleagues, a third grade teacher displayed a notebook that indicated all the lessons, throughout the year, that she spirals into required curriculum built on the common gardening experiences of the class. Teaching photosynthesis in January, building on references to the garden, is just one example she cited.

Thoughts for Reflection:

- ♦ For a person to learn, there must be:
  - A comfortable atmosphere
  - Purpose/intent
  - Real-life connections
  - A little mystery
  - Performance (doing something)
  - Understanding

◆ "As teachers, we must constantly try to improve schools and we must keep working at changing and experimenting and trying until we have developed ways of reaching every child" (Albert Shanker 1928–1997).

End of Section Assessment

Explain what you feel is the single most significant thing a teacher can do to make a classroom constructivist and give reasons for your response.

The Effective Student

Learning Objective

The reader will recognize that constructivist students want responsibility and are given opportunities to assume responsibility by their teacher.

Main Points

◆ Does the student know what he is doing, why he is doing it, and what the next steps will be?

◆ Can the student not only explain what she is doing, why she is doing it, and what the next steps will be, but is she uncomfortable when she does not know the purpose for her work?

◆ Is the student comfortable in an environment that challenges him to think?

◆ Rather than seek to have the teacher define every step that must be taken to achieve a task, does the student strive to understand what needs to be accomplished or created?

The late W. Edwards Deming, who revolutionized the thinking of industry leaders about leadership and organizational strategies in the second half of the twentieth century, once explained that you cannot expect a worker to achieve maximum effectiveness unless he knows why he is washing the table:

◆ Is it to prepare the table for dinner, without a tablecloth covering it?

◆ Is it to prepare the table for dinner, but with a tablecloth on top?

◆ Will the table be used by people working with crayons and paint?

◆ Will surgery be performed on the table?

According to Dr. Deming, if the worker doesn't know why she is washing the table, she has no standard for knowing when the job is well done.

Similarly, students need to know why they are engaged in a task:

◆ How will achievement of the lesson's learning objectives help me succeed in life?

◆ How will this task/activity help me achieve the learning objectives?

♦ What constitutes success on this task/activity?

As teachers change the way they teach, and as they apply strategies more consistent with constructivist theory, they must be patient with themselves and their students, and allow for the fact that it takes students time to adjust to new classroom strategies. Students rebel against being passive learners of what they perceive to be irrelevant learning objectives, yet they feel secure in a passive learning environment.

I was in a faculty room awaiting the arrival of a few more teachers for a scheduled discussion when a student teacher entered with her face down around her ankles. She had just taught her first cooperative activity, and she described her frustration at how poorly the students had responded. A veteran teacher asked which class she had taught, and when the student teacher responded, the veteran said, "Well, that explains it, those kids have never been in a classroom where they've had the opportunity to interact."

Students need to adjust to unfamiliar teaching strategies just as teachers and parents do. The district I am about to describe is exceptional because it had benefited from the same strong, progressive leadership for more than a dozen years when I had the privilege of visiting. I observed a grade 1–3 multi-aged class and saw students paired, using a rubric and assessing each other on how effectively the map on one side of a paper reflected the locations of the South American countries on the other side. One student commented, "I would give this a 3; it's pretty accurate." His partner responded, "I would only give it a 2.5 because it's kind of hard to find Argentina on the map."

When those children reached middle school, the same student teacher would have had difficulty if she *didn't* use cooperative activities.

A constructivist student willingly accepts responsibility, asks questions when he doesn't know how to proceed, and takes pride in accomplishing a worthwhile task. He must be given the opportunities by a teacher who constructs instructional practices based on what we know about how people learn.

Here's an activity that has been well received by more than 60 teachers, kindergarten through 12th grade, who have tried it in the three years since we first began suggesting it. The purpose is to have students teach each other what we want them to learn. This activity also makes students responsible for their own learning:

Conduct an entirely student-run class of at least 40 minutes. It's simpler than it sounds. Create groups of three, four, or five students. Make each group responsible for teaching a portion of a lesson to the rest of the class. Tell them what to teach, but not how to teach it, although you should be ready with suggestions (prompts). Provide students with whatever resources they will need. This can include a textbook, a handout, a resource packet, or a list of references.

When this idea was originally conceived, it was with the expectation that the teacher would use one class period to allow the students to prepare their lessons and another for them to teach. The initial period would be for teacher directed preparation. The follow-up period (the next day or the next week) would be the 40-minute period when students would run the class while the teacher remained, quietly, in the back of the room, speaking only if a prompt, or need to control class discipline were absolutely necessary. In other words, a 40-minute student run class could have each group of students preparing a five-, ten-, or fifteen-minute lesson. For a kindergarten class, each group of students might be asked to teach something for five minutes.

While we envisioned something as simple as a period for preparation and a period for students running the class, many teachers have created much more involved lessons. Joann Chambers divided her 7th grade students into five groups, gave each group a resource packet, and assigned each group to teach conflict, theme, character, setting, or plot for 25 minutes on a different day of the following week. Jennifer Daniels asked her 9th grade global studies class to teach comparative religions by allowing two weeks for each group to prepare its presentation on a different religion.

A kindergarten teacher prepared six groups of three students each to listen to a story and then teach it to the rest of the class.

Here are some reflections on the success of these activities:

> Initially I was unsure how the kids would handle it, but 90 percent of the time they were on task and working hard. And the kids were excited. They learned about conjunctions and remembered what they learned, this time, even though I had taught it three times in the past. (Marc Spicer, seventh grade English teacher)

> The kids surprised me. They knew more than I expected. The test scores for both classes went up. (Jennifer Daniels, ninth grade global studies teacher)

> The students loved the novelty of choosing their own groups and activities. They tried really hard to work well together, knowing that if this went well, they would have the opportunity to make similar choices again. (Barbara Delmonico, kindergarten teacher)

> I was really impressed with how the students created their own guided notes as part of the process while other groups were presenting. This was a ninth grade CT (consultant teacher) class, not always the easiest to teach, and yet the entire 40 minutes went by flawlessly. (Pete Atchinson, principal, on observing a student-run ninth grade class.)

When we suggested this activity, it was not with the expectation that teachers would use it regularly. Rather, it was with the thought that if teachers would try it once, they would gain an appreciation of how much responsibility students are capable of assuming.This is how an effective teacher can enable a student to be responsible for her work. Many of the teachers who have tried the student-run class report that they now integrate the concept of having students take responsibility for teaching each other (and themselves) on a daily basis.

Teachers report that student retention of content is higher and test scores go up when they teach each other. In addition, according to science teacher Becky Buckingham, "There are so many social skills that are rehearsed that they will need."

In the final analysis, a constructivist educator needs to convey three things: trust, respect, and confidence. To reach students, they must feel your trust and your respect, and they must believe in your ability to create a productive environment. They must sense that you know how to frame a learning challenge and that you will be constantly monitoring their progress to meet that challenge, so that when they need help, you will be able to tailor your support to enable them to work through their confusion. The constructivist educator is the coach who knows that the students are the players and that it is her job to set up conditions through which they learn that they have it in themselves to be winners. The constructivist educator believes that a school must be a community of learners, all of us teachers, all of us learners.

Thoughts for Reflection

"Few things help an individual more than to place responsibility on him and let him know that you trust him" (Booker T. Washington, 1856–1915).

End of Chapter Assessment

See if you can design a 45-minute student-run activity for any grade level, in any discipline, in which students are front and center the entire time.

Appendix A

Exemplars:
Table of Contents

Two-Step Template

Popular name: Grade level of lesson: Discipline:
Standards Foundation
Standards and performance indicators context:
Core curriculum outline connection:
Learning objectives (which will become the dimensions of the assessment's rubric):
EXPLORATORY PHASE (estimated time):
DISCOVERY PHASE (estimated time)   **Performance Task (including planned interventions and audience beyond the teacher):**
Task specifications for developing the student generated product/process:
Assessment of the performance task:
Resources to be made available to students:
Suggestions for the teacher:

Pythagorean Theorem

Popular name:	Pythagorean Theorem
Grade level of lesson:	11th grade (see *Suggestions to the Teacher* section for additional thoughts)
Discipline:	Mathematics

Standards and Performance Indicators Context

MST Standard 3: Mathematics

Students will understand mathematics and become mathematically confident by communicating and reasoning mathematically, by applying mathematics in real-world settings, and by solving problems through the integrated study of number systems, geometry, algebra, data analysis, probability, and trigonometry.

♦ Students manipulate symbolic representations to explore concepts at an abstract level.

Core Curriculum Outline Connection

♦ Pythagorean Theorem

Learning Objectives (which will become the dimensions of the assessment's rubric)

Students will demonstrate an understanding of the Pythagorean Theorem.

EXPLORATORY PHASE

(Estimated time: 15 to 45 minutes depending on the knowledge base of the students.)

♦ Teacher puts students into groups of three.

♦ Students are directed to create a right angle triangle with sides of three different lengths using measurements that are to the half-inch. (Protractors and rulers will be needed. Assistance from group members is encouraged when needed.)

♦ Teacher directs the students to label the longest side "c" and the other sides "a" and "b".

♦ The teacher directs the students to indicate on their drawing that "a" side is "n" inches long etc.

♦ Students, in groups of three, are directed to brainstorm what they know about right angle triangles. (3 minutes)

♦ Students share what they have concluded regarding what they know about right angle triangles. (3 minutes)

♦ The teacher records the groups' conclusions, taking one item per group until all the sharing has been exhausted.

♦ The teacher conducts a debriefing/reflection regarding what has been discussed. (Note: the teacher should ask groups if they discussed particular facts/conclusions that other groups have mentioned and tally these. The intent of this reflection piece is to focus attention on the Pythagorean theorem that is expressed in the formula $c^2 = a^2 + b^2$.)

♦ If the formula doesn't emerge from this process, the teacher introduces it and asks the groups to discuss its meaning.

- If the meaning emerges from the groups' deliberations, the teacher has those who understand how to apply it explain it to the others either in small groups or in a whole class setting.

Planned intervention

- If the meaning of the formula doesn't emerge from the groups' discussions, the teacher has the students use the measurements of their triangles to show how the formula gives you the length of the long side from the other two sides.

- The teacher asks the small groups to discuss a way to demonstrate why the formula works, i.e., demonstrate a proof of the theorem.

- If a proof emerges through this process, those who have come up with the proof demonstrate it to the others.

Planned intervention

- If none emerges, the teacher introduces the diagram that appears below and asks the groups to see if this helps them develop a proof of the theorem.

- If a proof emerges through this process, those who have come up with the proof demonstrate it to the others.

- If none emerges, the teacher directs the students to create similar squares on their original triangle and mark off their squares by the half-inch and connect the marks to create a grid. (This process could be demonstrated on an overhead projector.)

- The diagram mentioned above and pictured below, is the 3, 4, 5 triangle. This triangle doesn't require students to deal with fractional parts. However, when students develop a similar diagram using their original triangles, fractional parts may be involved. Using their "messy" data to draw conclusions is part of the inquiry process.

- The application of the $c^2 = a^2 + b^2$ formula will require a knowledge of how to calculate square root. This may require an additional intervention, either planned or spontaneous.

- The small groups are then directed to use their diagrams to devise a proof of the theorem.

- The following reflection centers on the way the diagram demonstrates a proof of the theorem.

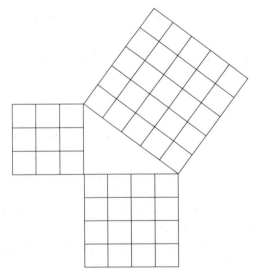

The unit of measure for this diagram is centimeters.

DISCOVERY PHASE
(Estimated time: a minimum of four, 45-minute class periods)

Performance Task (including planned interventions and audience beyond the teacher)

♦ Students are to learn an alternative proof to the Pythagorean Theorem and teach this new proof to classmates.

Planned Intervention

♦ Students or student groups will conduct a rehearsal/dry-run with the teacher. These dry-run lessons will be a source of student self-evaluation and teacher feedback. This process may include teacher modeling of teaching techniques and procedures.

Task Specifications for Developing the Student-Generated Product/Process

♦ Students or student groups will develop a 20-minute lesson on the alternative proof they learned.

♦ Students will teach this lesson to a group of their classmates.

Assessment of Performance Task

Dimensions of the student-taught lesson on an alternative proof prepared to demonstrate understanding of the Pythagorean theorem	Criteria for a score of 4	Criteria for a score of 3	Criteria for a score of 2	Criteria for a score of 1
Manipulates	The proof is taught thru students' use of manipulatives.	The proof is partially taught thru students' use of manipulatives.	The proof is taught thru instructor's use of manipulatives.	Manipulatives are not used.
Directions/ Procedures	The directions and/or procedures to be followed are clearly explained.	The directions and/or procedures to be followed are somewhat unclear.	The directions and/or procedures to be followed are unclear.	The directions and/or procedures to be followed are inappropriate.
Mathematical Equations	The proof is clearly explained thru the use of an appropriate equation.	The proof is partially explained thru the use of an appropriate equation.	The proof is inadequately explained thru the use of an appropriate equation.	The proof is not explained thru the use of an appropriate equation.
Lesson Adjustment	Learner feedback is effectively used to adjust the lesson.	Learner feedback is partially used to adjust the lesson.	Learner feedback is not effectively used to adjust the lesson.	Learner feedback is not requested.
Assessment	Student understanding is to be demonstrated thru use of manipulatives *and* the use of the formula.	Student understanding is to be demonstrated thru use of manipulatives *or* the use of the formula.	Students aren't given adequate opportunity to demonstrate understanding.	Student understanding is not assessed.

Resources to Be Made Available to Students

♦ Students will be assigned one of the alternative proofs to the Pythagorean theorem that appear on the *cut-the-knot* web pages and whatever other references the teacher decides will be of assistance to the student in preparing his lesson. See http://www.cut-the-knot.org/pythagoras/index.shtnl

Suggestions for the Teacher

Grade level

♦ This lesson could be adjusted to engage 8th grade students by an increased use of manipulatives and visuals.

Rubric scoring

♦ Class discussion regarding the dimensions and criteria found in the rubric will help students gain a clearer picture of what they are being asked to do.

♦ If the alternative proofs are taught by student-groups, individual students need to know that the dimensions of the rubric apply to each student not to the group as a whole.

♦ The assignment of students to small groups to develop a lesson on the alternative proof will require the teacher to be sure that each student is involved in the development and teaching of the lesson

Assigning an alternative proof

♦ Some of the alternative proofs are very abstract, while others can be demonstrated using manipulatives.
  • The teacher may wish to limit the selection of alternative proofs.
  • The teacher may wish to assign particular alternative proofs to specific students.
  • The teacher may wish to allow students who are mathematically proficient to select from some of the more complicated proofs.

References

The teacher may wish to check out the references at the end of the Web site to determine what additional assistance these sources may provide students in the preparation of their lesson.

Timing

The time allotted to each part of this exemplar is a major consideration, since each student or student group will need to have a rehearsal dry-run with the teacher and actually teach their proof. In addition, there will need to be follow-up reflections.

Seed Inquiry

Popular name:	Seed Inquiry
Grade level of lesson:	10th grade
Discipline:	Science

Standards and Performance Indicators Context

MST Standard 1

Students will use mathematical analysis, scientific inquiry, and engineering design, as appropriate, to pose questions, seek answers, and develop solutions.

- Formulate questions to explore everyday observations.
- Construct explanations of natural phenomena.
- Prepare and conduct research, record observations and measurements.
- Interpret organized data
- Modify their personal understanding of phenomena based on evaluation of their hypothesis.
- Engage in design process.
- Consider constraints and generate several ideas for alternative solutions.
- Plan and construct a model of the solution, exhibiting a degree of craftsmanship.
- Test their solution; describe how the solution meets design criteria.

MST Standard 3

Students will understand mathematics and become confident by communicating and reasoning mathematically.

- By applying mathematics to real-life settings, and
- By solving problems through the integrated study of numbers systems, geometry, algebra, data analysis, probability, and trigonometry.
- Represent numerical relationships in two-dimensional graphs.

Core Curriculum Outline Connection

- Core Curriculum Skills
- Use the appropriate units for measured and calculated values.
- Identify cause and effect relationships.
- Identify structure and function relationships in organisms.
- Dissect plant and/or animal specimens to expose and identify internal structures.
- Design and carry out a controlled, scientific experiment based on biological processes.
- Organize data through the use of data tables and graphs
- Analyze results from observations/expressed data.
- Formulate appropriate conclusions or generalizations from the results of an experiment.

Learning Objectives (which will become the dimensions of the assessment's rubric)

Students will increase their capacity to understand the nature of scientific inquiry.

EXPLORATORY PHASE
(Estimated time: 20 minutes)

Exploration of Prior Knowledge

1. Students are grouped into teams of three using some arbitrary process such as birthdays or by design using some other criteria to create teams composed of students possessing specific qualities.

2. Team members assume one of three roles:

 - Facilitator—to keep team members focused on the task
 - Materials coordinator—-to keep track of materials
 - Timekeeper—to help the team manage its time.

3. Each team member must keep inquiry notes—which are to include all observations, notes, data collection, conclusions, and reflections.

4. The teacher asks the teams to free associate and record their thoughts regarding the question, "What do you know about seeds that float in the air?"

5. Reporting out of the teams' thoughts, which are recorded and summarized on the board by the teacher.

6. Teacher facilitates a debriefing of the information provided by the teams with a focus on grouping like-thoughts.

Seed Characteristics Identification

1. Teacher distributes packets of local naturally-occurring wind-dispersed seeds. (These can be gathered by the teacher or purchased from horticultural society. Examples of such seeds are: dandelion, cottonwood, milkweed, maple tree, and grass seeds.)

2. The teams observe the seeds to create a listing of descriptive characteristics. (The characteristics that need to evolve through this process should include: general shape, length, width, depth, mass, surface area. If any of them don't, the teacher should point the class toward them.)

3. This is followed by a whole class reporting out. The purpose of this report–out is to come to a common understanding regarding the seed characteristics that need to be observed and recorded.

4. The student-teams create a data table to record their observations regarding the characteristics of the seeds in the packet that was previously distributed.

5. Students record the characteristics based on their observations.

DISCOVERY PHASE
(Estimated time: 2 to 3, 40-minute class periods)
Performance Task (including planned interventions and audience beyond the teacher)
Conduct a scientific inquiry into how seed-characteristics affect the distance traveled by wind-dispersed seeds.

The Initial Design of the Inquiry

The teacher directs teams to brainstorm focusing on the question, "What are the tests we should run on wind-dispersed seeds to reveal how they react in the air and the impact these reactions have on their wind-dispersal?"

1. The teacher conducts interventions as needed to move the individual teams to take into consideration the three tests that need to be run, which are: drop time in still air, distance traveled on a wind/fan-current, and time taken to travel to the furthest point on a wind/fan-current. (If the students come up with other tests these should be accepted but some form of the previously mentioned three need to be included.)

2. The student-teams develop recording devices to record the data from the tests they have determined need to be run. The teams send members to observe the tests and forms devised by other teams and adjust, as desire, their own tests and forms.

3. Once the teams have settled on the forms they will be using to record the data, the teacher asks the teams to come to some decisions regarding this question," What procedure should be followed to carry out the drop-test? (Things that need to be taken into account are: what will be the height from which the seed will be dropped; how will this distance be uniformly measured; how will the drop time be measured; how many times will the seed be dropped; will the number of times be averaged?)

4. While not expressly stating the above questions/considerations, the teacher intervenes as needed to move the individual teams to take these thoughts into consideration. Once the individual teams decide on their procedure, the teams conduct the drop test and record their findings.

5. Each team member must take his own inquiry notes, which will be the main evidence used by the teacher in judging the students' performance on the inquiry. (See the assessment rubric.)

Reflection based on Drop Test Results

6. After a team has conducted the drop-test, the teacher intervenes to ask the team to discuss what they have observed about the relationship between the characteristics of the seeds and the results of the drop-test. (Among the characteristics that need to be focused on are: mass and surface area. If these characteristics don't emerge from the discussion, the teacher needs to move the discussion in their direction.)

Wind Tests of Naturally-Occurring Seeds

7. After a team has completed the drop-test the team conducts the wind/fan test. (It is assumed that the team has concluded that there needs to be a wind test simulated through the use of fans. See step #1 above.)

8. If necessary, the teacher intervenes to focus the team on the need to develop a procedure to conduct the wind tests. (Considerations regarding these tests include: the distance from the ground the seed is released, the position and power setting of the fan(s), how to determine the distance the seed has traveled, the number of trials, if an average is to be calculated.)

9. Teams record the results of their tests.

Representing the Results

10. The teacher directs teams to create some mathematical representation summarizing the results of their three tests.

11. The teacher intervenes as necessary with the teams devising these representations. (Some representations include line and bar graphs.)

Debrief Results

12. The teacher facilitates a debrief/reflection based on the teams' results from its three tests. (Key questions focus on: the relationship between the results and the mass and the surface area of the seeds, the relationship between the time traveled and the distance traveled, other factors that have affected the results.)

13. During the debrief the teacher reminds the students to look to the rubric for guidance regarding what needs to be in their inquiry notes, drawing particular attention to the Reflection/Self assessment section of the rubric.

Task Specifications for Developing the Student-Generated Product/Process

The specifications regarding the task are enumerated in the assessment rubric.

Assessment of Performance Task

Dimensions of a student-conducted inquiry into how seed-characteristics affect the distance traveled by wind-dispersed seeds	Criteria for a score of 4	Criteria for a score of 3	Criteria for a score of 2	Criteria for a score of 1
The design of the inquiry	All the procedures, protocols, and means of displaying and analyzing data that the team designed and used were appropriate to the purpose of the inquiry.	Most of the procedures, protocols and means of displaying and analyzing data that the team designed and used were appropriate to the purpose of the inquiry.	Some of the procedures, protocols, and means of displaying and analyzing data that the team designed and used were appropriate to the purpose of the inquiry.	Few of the procedures, protocols, and means of displaying and analyzing data that the team designed and used were appropriate to the purpose of the inquiry.
Accuracy regarding gathering and displaying data	Recorded trial data on naturally occurring seeds is *accurate* regarding labels, measurements, etc. The mathematical representations *accurately* reflect the recorded data. Observations regarding the naturally occurring seeds *match* the individual seeds' characteristics.	Recorded trial data regarding naturally occurring seeds is *mostly accurate* regarding labels, measurements, etc. The mathematical representations accurately reflect the recorded data *most of the time* Observations regarding the naturally occurring seeds *mostly match* the individual seeds' characteristics.	Recorded trial data regarding naturally occurring seeds is *partially accurate* regarding labels, measurements, etc. The mathematical representations accurately reflect the recorded data *some of the time.* Observations regarding the naturally occurring seeds *sometimes match* the individual seeds' characteristics.	Recorded trial data naturally occurring sees is *somewhat in accurate* regarding labels, measurements, etc. The mathematical representations do not reflect the recorded data. Observations regarding the naturally occurring seeds *don't match* the individual seeds' characteristics.

Analysis	The inquiry notes *include* conclusions drawn from test data for naturally occurring seeds, including:	The inquiry notes *include most of* the following conclusions drawn from test data for naturally occurring seeds:	The inquiry notes *include some of* the following conclusions drawn from test data for naturally occurring seeds:	The inquiry notes *include few* of the following conclusions drawn from test data naturally occurring seeds:
	*The relationship between seed characteristics and distance traveled.	*The relationship between seed characteristics and distance traveled.	*The relationship between seed characteristics and distance traveled.	*The relationship between seed characteristics and distance traveled.
	*The relationship between seed drop time and distance traveled.	*The relationship between seed drop time and distance traveled.	*The relationship between seed drop time and distance traveled.	*The relationship between seed drop time and distance traveled.
	*The relationship between time in air and distance traveled.	*The relationship between time in air and distance traveled.	*The relationship between time in air and distance traveled.	*The relationship between time in air and distance traveled.
	All of the conclusions regarding the relationship between seed characteristics and seed distribution are supported or refuted by the data.	Most of the conclusions regarding the relationship between seed characteristics and see distribution are supported or refuted by the data.	Some of the conclusions regarding the relationship between seed characteristics and see distribution are supported or refuted by the data.	Few of the conclusions regarding the relationship between seed characteristics and see distribution are supported or refuted by the data.
Reflection / Self analysis	The inquiry notes contain reflections that *include*:	The inquiry notes contain reflections that include *most of* the following:	The inquiry notes contain reflections that include *some of* the following:	The inquiry notes contain reflections that include *few of* the following:
	*The purpose of the learning experience.	*The purpose of the learning experience	*The purpose of the learning experience	*The purpose of the learning experience
	*The new skills developed/ refined.	*The new skills developed/re-fined	*The new skills developed/ refined	*The new skills developed/ refined
	*New understandings.	*New understandings	*New understandings	*New understandings
	*Thoughts regarding the student's performance on the task.	*Thoughts regarding student performance on the task.	*Thoughts regarding student performance on the task.	*Thoughts regarding student performance. On the task.

Resources to Be Made Available to Students

- A packet of naturally occurring wind-dispersed seeds.
- Meter sticks
- A tape measure in meters
- Masking tape
- Graphing paper
- A stop watch
- A fan (teacher assistance required for safety. Safety considerations include: establishing safe distances from the fan, and the wearing of goggles while seeds are dispersed.)

Suggestions for the Teacher

Inquiries vs. Labs

This lesson focuses on the difference between science taught through a prescriptive lab experience vs. science taught through an inquiry-based learning experience. In this inquiry-based lesson the students are guided toward constructing inquiry procedures and protocols; they are not provided procedures and protocols to be followed. The students' work is not to fill out teacher-created forms but to decide what procedures and protocols they need to follow and then to develop their own forms, run the tests, record the data, analyze the data, come to conclusions, and reflect on what they have done. It is a good idea to develop forms and other scaffolding devices in advance to get a feel for what the students are being asked to do, have a detailed sense of how to guide students during interventions, and to have examples of such instruments if, after repeated attempts with your guidance, it is still necessary to provide additional assistance.

Inquiry Notes

The inquiry notes each student takes are at the heart of this lesson. It is suggested that the teacher collect these notes after each class. Reading the inquiry notes will allow the teacher to monitor student progress and to plan for additional interventions.

Grade-Level Considerations

This inquiry-based lesson can be profitably engaged in by 7th graders through students participating in Advance Placement Biology, with more and more sophisticated work being required of upper grade students.

This lesson incorporates ideas found in a learning experience titled, " Seed By Design," created by Joyce G. Valenti, which was peer reviewed by the New York State Academy for Teaching and Learning.

Explorer's Resume

Popular name:	Explorer's Resume
Grade level of lesson:	7th and 11th grade
Discipline:	Social Studies and English Language Arts

Standards and Performance Indicators Context

ELA Standard 3

Students will listen, speak, read, and write for critical analysis and evaluation.

♦ Make effective use of details, evidence, and arguments and presentation strategies to influence an audience to adopt their position.

Social Studies Standard 2

Students will use a variety of intellectual skills to demonstrate their understanding of major ideas, eras, themes, developments, and turning points in world history and examine the broad sweep of history form a variety of perspectives.

♦ Investigate the role and contributions of individuals and groups in relation to key social, political, cultural, and religious practices throughout world history.

♦ Present geographical information in a variety of formats including maps, tables, graphs, charts, diagrams, and computer-generated models.

Core Curriculum Outline Connection

Writing

♦ Understand the purposes for writing; e.g., explain, describe, narrate, persuade, and express feelings.

♦ Identify the intended audience.

♦ Use tone and language appropriate for audience ad purpose.

Speaking

♦ Speak to present opinions and judgements in, for example:
  • Small and large group discussions and presentations
  • Speeches
  • Debates
  • Interviews
  • Multimedia presentations.

♦ Present content, using strategies designed for the audience, purpose, and content.

♦ Adapt language and presentational features for the audience and purpose.

♦ Use volume, pitch, and rate appropriate to content and audience.

♦ Use visual aids and nonverbal communication to enhance the presentation

♦ Establish and maintain eye contact with audience.

Social Studies

♦ European knowledge was based on a variety of sources including accounts of early explorers and a variety of different maps.

♦ The technological improvements in navigation

♦ Desire to break into Eastern trade markets

♦ Geographical factors influenced European exploration and settlement in North and South America.

♦ Expansion of Portuguese spice trade to Southeast Asia and its impact on Asia and Europe

♦ Exploration and overseas expansion

♦ The extent of European expansionism

Learning Objectives (which will become the dimensions of the assessment's rubric)
The student will:

♦ Engage in historical research.

♦ Make a persuasive presentation based on historical research that includes:
  • The development of a resume, and a cover letter, and
  • A presentation through an interview.

Exploratory Phase
(Estimated time: 25 minutes)

♦ In groups of three, students are asked to identify an historic figure or a popular figure whose life interests them.

♦ The groups report and the teacher records their responses.

♦ The groups are then asked to pick their top three choices from the recorded individuals.

♦ The groups report and the teacher tallies the votes by putting marks next to the individuals voted for.

♦ The groups of students are then given an example of a resume as a model and asked to begin to develop a brief resume for one of the top three vote getters, remembering that the purpose of a resume is to get a particular job or type of job.

♦ After a few minutes, a group that has selected a particular individual writes what it has come up with on the board. (The idea is to have one example for each of the individuals selected by the groups.)

♦ The class then views the listed items from the resume and those who have selected the same individual add their listings etc.

♦ This process continues with the teacher using this activity as an opportunity to point out various aspects and issues regarding writing resumes. Again, particular focus should be put on the fact that resumes are written to get a job and that this should be reflected in the resume.

♦ (It is hoped that this process will be somewhat humorous, since the individuals selected will probably be from the students' popular culture.)

♦ The fact that there is the potential for three prototype-resumes, should give the teacher several opportunities to direct attention to the important aspects regarding the writing of resumes.

DISCOVERY PHASE
(Estimated time: 5 ½ hours)

♦ Research: One and a half 45 minute class periods and homework
♦ Resume preparation: One 45 minute class period and homework
♦ Cover page : One 45 minute class period and homework
♦ Interview preparation: One half 45 minute period and homework
♦ Conducting interviews: Two 45 minute periods
♦ Panel reports one 45 minute period and homework

Performance Task (including planned interventions and audience beyond the teacher)

Students will assume the identity of an explorer from the Age of Exploration who is attempting to secure a new exploration assignment. The explorer's efforts to secure the assignment will include a resume, cover letter, and interview before a panel.

♦ Student assumes the identity of an explorer from the Age of Exploration. (The way a student selects or is assigned an explorer needs to be taken into consideration. The process could be random (pulling one out of a hat) or by some form of selection. But whatever the process, the students should feel it was fair.)
♦ Students research the explorer they have chosen.
♦ Students prepare a resume and cover letter, which they submit to a panel of students who represent officials in charge of reviewing requests for financial and other official support for new voyages of exploration. This new voyage should be one that the explorer never took. It should be the one he "would have wanted" to take at the end of his career. If the explorer died on a voyage of exploration, the student should ignore this unfortunate fact and have him surviving to interview for a new expedition.
♦ Students interview before the panel of officials.
♦ The panel of officials writes a report to be submitted to the government or the company they represent.

Task Specifications for Developing the Student-Generated Product/Process

♦ The resume should be one or two typed pages long.
♦ The cover letter should be one typed page long containing at least three paragraphs.
♦ The interviewee should prepare for a 5 to 10 minute interview.
♦ The interview panel members should prepare questions for the same 5 to 10 minute interview.

Assessment of Performance Task

Dimensions for making a persuasive presentation as an explorer applying for a new exploration assignment	Criteria for a score of 4	Criteria for a score of 3	Criteria for a score of 2	Criteria for a score of 1
Research	Evidence cited and demonstrated by the interviewee/explorer includes most of the following regarding the explorer: • His previous accomplishments and contributions. • His knowledge of the science and technology of navigation. • His knowledge of geography and the impact of geography on the exploration assignment he is seeking. • The importance of the assignment he is seeking to the sponsoring country or backers. • His relationship with his crew/men. • His relationship with his previous sponsors/backers.	Evidence cited and demonstrated by the interviewee/explorer includes many of the following regarding the explorer: • His previous accomplishments and contributions. • His knowledge of the science and technology of navigation. • His knowledge of geography and the impact of geography on the exploration assignment he is seeking. • The importance of the assignment he is seeking to the sponsoring country or backers. • His relationship with his crew/men. • His relationship with his previous sponsors/backers.	Evidence cited and demonstrated by the interviewee/explorer includes some of the following regarding the explorer: • His previous accomplishments and contributions. • His knowledge of the science and technology of navigation. • His knowledge of geography and the impact of geography on the exploration assignment he is seeking. • The importance of the assignment he is seeking to the sponsoring country or backers. • His relationship with his crew/men. • His relationship with his previous sponsors/backers.	Evidence cited and demonstrated by the interviewee/explorer includes few of the following regarding the explorer: • His previous accomplishments and contributions. • His knowledge of the science and technology of navigation. • His knowledge of geography and the impact of geography on the exploration assignment he is seeking. • The importance of the assignment he is seeking to the sponsoring country or backers. • His relationship with his crew/men. • His relationship with his previous sponsors/backers.

Analysis and Synthesis	Both of the following make effective use of the student's research to make a persuasive presentation: • The resume • The cover letter	Both of the following make use of most of the student's research to make a persuasive presentation: • The resume • The cover letter	Both of the following make use of some of the student's research to make a persuasive presentation: • The resume • The cover letter	Both of the following make little use of the student's research to make a persuasive presentation: • The resume • The cover letter
Interview presentation skills	All of the following is used to make his interview persuasive: • The synthesized arguments are supported by the research. • The tone and language are appropriate. • The pitch is appropriate. • The rate of the presentation is effective. • The is an effective use of nonverbal communications. • There is an effective use of visual aids. • There is an effective use of eye contact. • The explorer displays a confidence. • The explorer is courteous and friendly.	Most of the following is used to make his interview persuasive: • The synthesized arguments are supported by the research. • The tone and language are appropriate. • The pitch is appropriate. • The rate of the presentation is effective. • The is an effective use of nonverbal communications. • There is an effective use of visual aids. • There is an effective use of eye contact. • The explorer displays a confidence. • The explorer is courteous and friendly.	Some of the following is used to make his interview persuasive: • The synthesized arguments are supported by the research. • The tone and language are appropriate. • The pitch is appropriate. • The rate of the presentation is effective. • The is an effective use of nonverbal communications. • There is an effective use of visual aids. • There is an effective use of eye contact. • The explorer displays a confidence. • The explorer is courteous and friendly.	Little of the following is used to make his interview persuasive: • The synthesized arguments are supported by the research. • The tone and language are appropriate. • The pitch is appropriate. • The rate of the presentation is effective. • The is an effective use of nonverbal communications. • There is an effective use of visual aids. • There is an effective use of eye contact. • The explorer displays a confidence. • The explorer is courteous and friendly.

Resources to Be Made Available to Students

• Sample resumes
• The rubric for assessing the performance task. (Class activities that require students to "score" student work using the rubric are recommended.)
• See also the scaffolding suggestions in section below, "Suggestion for the Teacher."

Suggestions for the Teacher

Resume , Cover Letter, and Interview

Scaffolding or interventions may include:
- Resume format and/or a cover letter format.
- Examples of actual resumes and cover pages.
- Student research into resume and cover letter formats online.
- Modeling through whole-class participation in all or part of the process.
- Exemplars from students' work-products from previous years.

Resources

- Scaffolding or Interventions may include:
- Providing a listing of resources.
- Bookmarking Internet web sites.
- Assistance of a librarian/media specialist.
- Preparing packets of research materials for special needs students to avoid overwhelming them with research. Or compiling a specific list of books and noting the pages that have appropriate information.

Panel of Officials

- Possible ways to assist panelists include:
- Turn the presentation-rubric into a reaction form or checklist that panelists can use to judge the cover letter, resume, and interview.
- Provide or have panels develop their own guidelines for judging the presentation.
- Have panels prepared questions for the interview portion of the presentation.
- Assist panelists in developing a way to harmonize their individual judgments into one panel report.
- Develop a process to turn a panel's judgment into a grade.
- Provide a way that explorer/interviewees can rehearse and get feedback from peers before their panel interview.

Writing Conventions

- Rough draft checkpoints may need to be established.
- Writing process interventions may be called for.
- Criteria regarding the mechanics/conventions of English may need to be introduced in some fashion.

Time and Scheduling Considerations

- Suggested time allotments, in particular for the Exploratory Phase, may need to be expanded for 7th graders.
- Suggested procedure regarding panel presentations/interviews.
  - Have 3 panels of 3 plus one "explorer" per panel (12 students) going at the same time in different parts of the room. The other students can continue to work on their resumes/cover letters/interviews. Or act as an additional audience for the interviews they select.
  - If each panel presentation takes 10 minutes, then 4 rotations can be accomplished in a 45-minute class period.
  - Two class periods would then provide enough time for 24 "explorers" to complete their interviews.
- Write-up time for panel reports would also have to be factored in.

This lesson incorporates ideas found in a learning experience entitled, "Exploration Resume Project," created by Constance A. Miller, which was peer reviewed by the New York State Academy for Teaching and Learning.

Museum Box Personal Profile

Popular name:	Museum Box Personal Profile
Grade level of lesson:	8th grade
Discipline:	English Language Arts

Standards and Performance Indicators Context

ELA Standard 1

Students will read, write, listen, and speak for information and understanding.

- Establish an authoritative stance on the subject and provide references to establish the validity and verification of the information presented.

ELA Standard 4

Students will read, write, listen, and speak for social interaction.

- Use a variety of print and electronic forms for social communication with peers and adults.
- Make effective use of language and style to connect the message with the audience and context.

Core Curriculum Outline Connection

-

Learning Objectives (which will become the dimensions/elements of the assessment's rubric)

- Write personal journals.
- Share the process of writing with peers and adults.
- Develop a personal voice that enables the reader to get to know the writer.
- Write personal reactions to experiences, events and observations using a form of social communication. Understand the purpose of writing: e.g., explain, describe, narrate, persuade, and express feelings.
- Identify the intended audience.
- Use tone and language appropriate for audience and purpose.
- Use pre-writing; for example brainstorming, freewriting, note taking, and outlining.
- Use the writing process (pre-writing, drafting, revising, proofreading, and editing.)
- Write for authentic purpose.

Learning Objectives (which will become the dimensions of the assessment's rubric)

Students will demonstrate the ability to write a focused, organized personal profile.

EXPLORATORY PHASE
(Estimated time:
- **Setting the stage for the museum boxes: One 40-minute class period**
- **Constructing the Museum Boxes: assign on a Friday, have the boxes brought in for a check on Monday: 20 minutes**
- **Give students until Wednesday to complete their Museum Box at home.)**

♦ Students are directed to write down one thing they might find in a museum.

♦ Students report out what they have written and the teacher records (and when items are repeated, tallies) what students report out.

♦ Teacher creates groups of three using the various categories created through using the report-out process as a guide.

♦ Teacher has the various groups draw an assignment out of a hat. The assignments all have to do with using a resource to creating a list of the types of museums that exist.

♦ The resources may include:

- Encyclopedia Britannia group
- Colliers Encyclopedia group
- World Book Encyclopedia group
- Internet search group #1
- Internet search group #2
- Internet search group #3
- Library search group #1
- Library search group #2

♦ The groups post their findings on newsprint.

♦ The teacher poses the following question, "Put a check mark next to those museums on your list that might contain a box of objects that were put in the box to tell you something about the person who made the box."

♦ The teacher, using the *carousel technique*, directs all groups to go around and look at the lists the other groups have developed, note the museums that have been checked, and put a check next to other museums that group members think qualify.

♦ The teacher conducts a debrief during which group members are asked to defend their position regarding why a museum box might be found in a particular museum and whose museum box might be found in which museum.

♦ Students are given the assignment to individually create their own museum box.

DISCOVERY PHASE:
(Estimated time: 30 minutes)
- Profile writing process: one to two 40-minute class periods
- Reaction piece writing process: one to two 40-minute class periods.)

Performance Task: (including planned interventions and audience beyond the teacher)

♦ Students will write a personal profile using the creation of a museum box as a way of focusing and organizing their written expression.

♦ See Task Specifications for details regarding the task.

♦ Students will view their classmates' museum boxes, read their classmates' personal profiles, and write a reaction piece on four of the students' boxes and profiles based upon a rubric developed through facilitation by the teacher (audience beyond the teacher).

Task Specification for Developing the Student-Generated Product/Process:

Exploration "Task" the Museum Box

♦ The museum box is a representation of the maker's interests presented in a graphic/three-dimensional format.

♦ The museum box is to have at least 8 items: pictures, artifacts, objects etc.

♦ The museum box is a shoe box displayed on end like a 3D picture

♦ The maker may wish to decorate the box itself.

♦ Do not include valuable items. (Instead make a photocopy).

Discovery Task the written Profile

The written profile is to:

♦ Be four paragraphs long.

♦ Use explanation, description, narration, persuasion, and expression of feelings to inform the reader

♦ why the items were chosen

♦ what the items represent.

♦ what they mean to the maker.

♦ Contain an introduction

♦ Contain a conclusion

Assessment of the Performance Task

Dimensions of a personal profile using a museum box as a way of focusing and organizing written expression	Criteria for a score of 4	Criteria for a score of 3	Criteria for a score of 2	Criteria for a score of 1
The Writing Process	Uses all of the following effectively • pre-writing, • drafting, • revising, • proofreading, • editing.	Uses most of the following effectively • pre-writing, • drafting, • revising, • proofreading, • editing.	Uses some of the following effectively • pre-writing, • drafting, • revising, • proofreading, • editing.	Uses few of the following effectively • pre-writing, • drafting, • revising, • proofreading, • editing.
Audience Awareness	The manner of expression and language are appropriate for the audience for which the profile was written. Adjustments are made based on peer and adult commentary.	The manner of expression and language are mostly appropriate for the audience for which the profile was written. Some adjustments are made based on peer and adult commentary.	The manner of expression and language are somewhat appropriate for the audience for which the profile was written. A few adjustments are made based on peer and adult commentary.	The manner of expression and language are infrequently appropriate for the audience for which the profile was written. No adjustments are made based on peer and adult commentary.
Expression of Purpose	It is clear that one or more of the following purposes for writing are being addressed: • Explanation Description • Narrative • Persuasion • Expression of feelings.	It is somewhat clear that one or more of the following purposes for writing are being addressed: • Explanation Description • Narrative • Persuasion • Expression of feelings.	It is not very clear that one or more of the following purposes for writing are being addressed: • Explanation Description • Narrative • Persuasion • Expression of feelings.	Makes it unclear that one or more of the following purposes for writing are being addressed: • Explanation Description • Narrative • Persuasion • Expression of feelings.

Personal Voice	Personal reactions to • experiences, • events, • observations, *are* in evidence.	Personal reactions to • experiences, • events, • observations, *are somewhat* in evidence.	Personal reactions to • experiences, • events, • observations, *are occasionally* in evidence.	Personal reactions to • experiences, • events, • observations, *are not* in evidence.
Conventions of English	The rules of • Punctuation, • Grammar, • Spelling, are *always* effectively and correctly employed.	The rules of • Punctuation, • Grammar, • Spelling, are *usually* effectively and correctly employed.	The rules of • Punctuation, • Grammar, • Spelling, are *sometimes* effectively and correctly employed.	The rules of • Punctuation, • Grammar, • Spelling, are *rarely* effectively and correctly employed.

Resources to Be Made Available to Students:
- Students are to provide their own items for the museum boxes.
- Art supplies should be made available as needed.
- Access to a copying machine should be arranged.
- Collecting shoe boxes from shoe stores can facilitate the process.

Suggestions for the Teacher

Exemplars

- The teacher may wish to create his own museum box and personal profile as an exemplar. There are pluses and minuses in doing this. The pluses are that it provides guidance. The minuses are that it may limit or curtail student engagement and problem solving.
- Photos of this year's museum boxes and copies of the accompanying profiles should be kept for use next year, either as exemplars or as interventions.

Additional aspects

- It is recommended that a peer review procedure be built into the writing process.
- It is recommended that the teacher facilitate the development of a peer reaction piece (outline or rubric form) by the students.
- The lesson could be expanded through oral presentations.

This lesson incorporates ideas found in a learning experience titled "Making a Museum Box," created by Elly Schleifer which was peer reviewed by the New York State Academy of Teaching and Learning.

Appendix B

The *Two-Step* and Other Models

Viewing the Two-Step with Other Models of Learning from Teaching

This appendix contains a brief discussion of the similarities and differences of the *Two-Step* model and five well-known models for lesson design. A more complete compare/contrast analysis is on the web site of the Institute for Learning Centered Education at www.learnercentereded.org.

There is conceptual compatibility between the Two-Step and many of the generally recognized, and professionally accepted, models for lesson design currently in use throughout the country. The author believes the Two-Step is consistent with theory supporting these other models, but it suggests aspects of understanding and ease of implementation beyond what other models have to offer. At the very least, the Two-Step offers an alternative for practitioners whose own styles of learning may not align well with other models.

Much has been written over the past few years about models of teaching, structures, and theories that help teachers decide how to approach and engage their students. The two most widely used instructional paradigms, the behaviorist/transmission and the constructivist/interactive, are home for most of these models. Ours, the Two-Step model described in this text, is constructivist in nature and simple in structure, yet complex in all of its possibilities. In the next sections, the Two-Step model is compared and contrasted with other models that teachers might use or be familiar with.

Madeline Hunter's Mastery Teaching Model

Hunter's contribution is a practice model. Although it has contributed mightily to the field of education in many ways, as a training model it has done little to promote understanding of the type needed in a modern economy and polity.

For several decades, Madeline Hunter was education's most well-known name. From her position at UCLA's campus school, she pulled together many accepted findings and practices from various sources and produced her TIP (theory into practice) model. Taking many forms, depending on which version was being disseminated, Hunter's plan had seven steps and a closure activity. It was easy to follow, seemed to give good advice, and kept things under control in a classroom. It also gave us a vocabulary that many teachers still use today:

- Set
- Objective
- Input
- Model
- Understanding
- Guided (practice)
- Independent (practice)
- Closure

Hunter's thinking can be described as following this logic: The teacher has to hook the students to get started, then the teacher can explain the objective and teach the new content. The students must see the teacher "do" the new content correctly, and then they get to practice it themselves—first, with help; second, working alone. At that point, the lesson can be concluded in a way that makes the students aware of what the teacher had taught them. In a nutshell, it is a nice, tight, self-contained lesson that follows behaviorist traditions and makes learning an issue of effective practice.

Trowbridge, Bybee, and Powell's 5E Model

The 5E is a powerful and attractive instructional model, and its steps help teachers make decisions as the learning moves forward. We think that the Two-Step does this at least as well, and the Two-Step calls for more professional decision making and allows more freedom.

Designed primarily by science educators for secondary science teaching, the 5E model has a classic constructivist structure. Trowbridge, Bybee, and Powell (2000) envision a five-phase model in which learners begin to investigate phenomena and eventually complete the learning cycle by creating conceptions, theories, and generalizations based on their work. The five phases, whose titles capture the essence of the students' actions, are listed as follows:

1. Engagement
2. Exploration
3. Explanation
4. Elaboration
5. Evaluation

Marzano's Dimensions of Thinking/Learning

Over several iterations, David Marzano and his associates developed a framework to help educators think more effectively about the impact of their pedagogical decisions on the thinking experiences and the cognitive demands being put on students. Although the direct comparisons being made here are drawn from a text that he (alone) wrote for ASCD (Marzano, 1992), other works on Dimensions (from the McRel group) do exist, are noteworthy, and are very similar to this one.

We see the Two-Step model as including the best of Marzano's work, streamlined and simplified for teachers use.

Differentiated Instruction

At the time of this writing, Differentiated Instruction seems to be everybody's favorite new approach to talking about teaching. As originally designed by Tomlinson (1999) and adapted for classroom instruction by Heacox (2002), this systematic approach to instruction holds out the hope that full-inclusion and heterogeneous classrooms can see teachers modify and adapt practices that allow learners (and groups of learners) to complete meaningful tasks that are tiered (differentiated by difficulty, complexity, and interest) and yet stand as valid and standards based.

There is no advice at all as to how to get students moving to the point where the challenging task has been internalized and students are excited, have shared ideas, and are ready to embrace their challenges. In other words, there is no *exploratory* phase at all.

Understanding by Design

The last of our samples of instructional models is perhaps the most famous and the one that has been recognized by many educators as of the highest quality. Internationally known scholars Grant Wiggins and Jay McTighe created Understanding by Design (Wiggins & McTighe, 1998) to revolutionize assessment and therefore to change the way we go about teaching students. To them, assessment drives instruction: Teachers teach in the way that they feel is consistent with the way students are to be tested, a system some have derided as "teaching to the test," a seriously deficient, defensive approach (McNeil, 1996). By expanding assessment to be a much more creative and authentic reality, and one that is more thoughtful and more student centered, the author has produced a system that encourages students to engage in a great deal of meaningful learning activities that always strive for deeper understanding of important content.

This whole book may be interpreted as a crashing attack on standardized tests while being amazingly supportive of high standards. It is popular because it is provocative and profound, but it needs tremendous translation to put into daily use in K–12 classrooms.

Summary of Conclusions

Each of the models described in this section has aspects that are potentially powerful as learning approaches in student-centered and thinking-centered classrooms. Hunter's notion of anticipatory set was the first experience many current teachers had in putting the work of thinking and learning on the student: All of the other models expanded and modified that act, and today the Two-Step stands as the most useable approach in that genre. We think it answers the limitations in other models while maintaining an elegantly simple design.

It must also be said that the evolution of schooling practices reflects demands by society and are consistent with research. In some ways, the reform movement in education has been itself driven by forces in the society, marketplace, workforce, and research community. But all reforms recognize that teachers are the ones who have to implement any significant change: They are at the point at which real change and real impact occurs. Thompson and Zeuli (in Sykes & Darling-Hammond, 1999) make it obvious that all the new standards and assessments are moving toward a *thinking*-centered pedagogy. They say it succinctly and powerfully this way:

> The essential point—the inner intent—that seems so seldom grasped even by teachers eager to embrace the current reforms is that to learn the sorts of things envisioned by reformers, students must think. In fact, such learning is almost exclusively a product or by product of thinking. By "think" we mean that students must actively try to solve problems, resolve dissonances between the way they initially understand a phenomenon and new evidence that challenges understanding, put collections of facts or observations together into patterns, make and test conjectures, and build lines of reasoning about why claims may be true or not. Such thinking is generative. It literally creates understanding in the mind of the learner. . . . Students do not get knowledge from teachers or from books. They make it by thinking, using information and experience. (p. 346)

It is pretty clear that our strategies, contained in the Two-Step model, are designed to accomplish what we all want from education and today are expected to deliver: competent, analytical, knowledgeable, and willing, thinking people who become good decision-making citizens, are democratic and empathetic in orientation, and are effective and productive workers in a technological, data-driven pluralist society.

We hope that the readers who use this model realize these potentialities.

References

Airasian, P. & Walsh, M. (1997). Constructivist cautions. *Phi Delta Kappan*, *78*(6), 751–756.

Alleman, J. & Brophy, J. (1998). Assessment in a social constructivist classroom. *Social Education*, *62*(1), 32–34.

Applefield, J. M., Huber, R., & Moallem, M. (2001, January). Constructivism in theory and practice: Toward a better understanding. *High School Journal*, *84*(2), 35–54.

Beck, I. L. & McKeown, M.G. Learning words well—A program to enhance vocabulary and comprehension. *The Reading Teacher, 36*(7), 622–625.

Bennett, T. (1998). *The good life.* New York: Pocket Books/Simon & Schuster.

Blumenfeld, P., Soloway, E., Marx, R., and Krajcik, J. (1991). Motivating project based learning: Sustaining the doing, supporting the learning. *Educational Psychologist, 26*(3/4), 369–398.

Bransford, J. (1999). *How people learn: Brain, mind, experience, and school.* Washington, D.C.: National Academy Press.

Brooks, J. & Brooks, M. (1993). In search of understanding: The case for constructivist classrooms, Alexandria: VA: Association for Supervision and Curriculum Development.

Brophy, J. & Alleman, J. (1998). Classroom management in a social studies learning community. *Social Education, 62*(1), 56–58.

Bruer, J. T. (1993). *Schools for thought: A science of learning in the classroom.* Cambridge, Mass: MIT Press

Bruner, J. (1968) *Toward a theory of instruction.* New York: W. W. Norton.

Chase, W. G., & Simon, H. A. (1973). Perception in chess. *Cognitive Psychology*, *4*(1), 55–81.

Clements, D. (1997). (Mis?) Constructing constructivism. Teaching children mathematics, *4*(4), 198–200.

Cobb, P. P., Yackel, E. & Wood, T. (1992). A constructivist alternative to the representational view of mind in mathematics education. *Journal for Research in Mathematics Education*, *23*(1), 2–33.

Covey, S. R. (1990). *The seven habits of highly effective people.* New York: Fireside

Danielson, C. (1996). *Enhancing professional practice: A framework for teaching.* Alexandria, VA: Association for Supervision and Curriculum Development.

Darling-Hammond, L. (1999). Educating teachers: The academy's greatest failure or its most important future? *Academe, 85*, 26–33.

Dewey, J. (1910). *How we think.* Boston: DC Heath & Co.

Dewey, J. (1938). *Experience and education.* New York: MacMillan

Dryden, K. (1995). *In school: Our kids, our teachers, our classrooms.* Toronto, Ontario, Canada: McClelland & Stewart.

Duffy, T. M. & Jonassen, D. H. (Eds.). (1992). *Constructivism and the technology of instruction: A conversation.* New Jersey: Lawrence Erlbaum.

Ellis, A. K. (2001). *Research on educational innovations* (3rd ed.). Larchmont, New York: Eye On Education.

Eppink, J. A. (2002). Student-created rubrics. *Teaching Music, 9*(4), 28–32.

Foote, C. J., Vermette, P. J., & Battaglia, C. F. (2001). *Constructivist strategies: Meeting standards and engaging adolescent minds*. Larchmont, New York: Eye On Education.

Fosnot, C. T. (1996). *Constructivism: Theory, perspective and practice*, New York: Teachers College Press.

Gardner, H. (1999). *The disciplined mind: What all students should understand*. New York: Simon and Schuster.

Grennon Brooks, J. (1990). Teachers and students: Constructivists forging new connections. *Education Leadership, 45*(5), 68–72.

Heacox, D. (2002). *Differentiating instruction in the regular classroom: How to reach and teach all learners, grades 3–12*. Minneapolis, MN: Free Spirit Publishing.

Herman, J. L., Aschbacher, P. R., & Winters, L. (1992). *A practical guide to alternative assessment*. Alexandria, VA: Association for Supervision and Curriculum Development.

Howe, R. (2003). *The quotable teacher*. Connecticut: Lyons Press.

Hunter, M. (1982). *Mastery teaching*. El Segundo, CA: TIP Publications.

Konkoski-Bates, B. & Vermette, P. J. (2003). Working the room: Teacher decision-making in constructivist settings. Manuscript submitted for publication.

Knapp, M. S. (1995). *Teaching for meaning in high-poverty classrooms*. New York: Teachers College Press.

Ladson-Billings, G. (1994). *The dreamkeepers: Successful teachers of African-American children*. San Francisco, CA: Josey-Bass.

Lagemann, E. C. (2000). *An elusive science: The troubling history of educational research*. Chicago: University of Chicago Press.

Lambert, L. (1995). *The constructivist leader*. New York: Teachers College Press.

Marlowe, B. & Page, M. (1998). *Creating and sustaining the constructivist classroom*. Thousand Oaks, CA: Corwin Press.

Marzano, R. J., Pickering, D. J. & Pollock, J. E. (2001). *Classroom instruction that works: Research-based strategies for increasing student achievement*, Alexandria, VA: Association for Supervision and Curriculum Development.

McNeil, J. D. (1996). *Curriculum: A comprehensive introduction* (5th ed.). New York: Harper Collins.

Moshman, D. (1982). Exogenous, endogenous, and dialectical constructivism. *Developmental Review, 2*(4), 371–384.

Newmann, F. M. (1990). Qualities of thoughtful social studies classes: An empirical profile. *Journal of Curriculum Studies, 22*(3), 253–275.

Newton, D. P. (2000). *Teaching for understanding: What it is and how to do it*. New York: Routlege/Falmer.

Piaget, J. (1973). *To understand is to invent: The future of education*. New York: Grossman.

Perkins, D. (1999). The many faces of constructivism. *Educational Leadership, 57*(3), 6–11.

Perkins, D. (1992). *Smart schools: From training memories to educating minds*. New York: Free Press.

Perrone, V. (1994). How to engage students in learning. *Educational Leadership, 51*(5), 11–13.

Phillips, D. C. (1995). The good, the bad and the ugly: The many faces of constructivism. *Educational Researcher, 24*(7), 5–12, 178.

Prawat, R. (1992). Teachers' beliefs about teaching and learning: A constructivist perspective. *American Journal of Education, 100*(3), 354–395.

Reed, A. J., & Bergemann, V. E. (2001). *A guide to observation, participation, and reflection in the classroom.* Boston: McGraw Hill.

Reinsmith, W. A. (1993). Ten fundamental truths about learning. *The National Teaching and Learning Forum, 2*(4), 7–8.

Richardson, V. (1997). *Constructivist teacher education: Building new understandings.* London: Falmer Press.

Scheurman, G. (1998). From behaviorist to constructivist teaching. *Social Education, 6*(1), 6–9.

Sousa, D. A. (2002). *How the brain learns.* (2nd ed.). Thousand Oak, CA: Corwin Press.

Sykes, G., & Darling-Hammond, L. (Eds.). (1999). *Teaching as the learning profession: Handbook of policy and practice.* San Francisco, CA: Jossey-Bass.

Tomlinson, C. A. (1999). *The differentiated classroom: Responding to the needs of all learners.* Alexandria, VA: Association for Supervision and Curriculum Development.

Trowbridge, L. W., Bybee, R. W. & Powell, J. C. (2000). *Teaching secondary school science: Strategies for developing scientific literacy.* Upper Saddle River, New Jersey: Merrill.

Vermette, P. J. (1998). *Making cooperative learning work: Student teaching in K–12 classrooms.* Upper Saddle River, New Jersey: Merrill.

Vygotskii L. S. (1978). *Mind and society: The development of higher psychological processes.* Cambridge, MA: Harvard University Press.

Wenzlaff, T. L., Fager, J. J., & Coleman, M. J. (1999). What is a rubric? Do practitioners and the literature agree? *Contemporary Education, 70*(4), 41–46.

Wiggins, G. & McTighe, J. (1998). *Understanding by design.* Alexandria, VA: Association for Supervision and Curriculum Development.

Windschitl, M. (1999). The challenges of sustaining a constructivist classroom culture. *Phi Delta Kappan, 80*(10), 751–755.

Windschitl, M. (2002). Framing constructivism in practice as the negotiation of dilemmas: An analysis of the conceptual, pedagogical, cultural and political challenges facing teachers. *Review of Educational Research, 72*(2), 131–175.

Wlodkowski, R. (1986). *Motivation and teaching: A practical guide.* Washington, D.C: National Education Association.

Wolfgang, C. (2001). *Solving discipline and classroom management problems: Methods and models for today's teachers* (5th ed.). New York: John Wiley & Sons.

Zahorik, J. (1995). *Constructivist teaching.* Bloomington, Indiana: Phi Delta Kappa Educational Foundation.